ADVANCE PRAISE FOR
THE WRITING WORKSHOP

"There are many guides to scientific writing out there, and I read most of them in preparation for teaching a writing workshop at MIT. Barbara's was the one I referred students to most often. It's down-to-earth, funny, and packed with advice that extends well beyond the fundamentals of good scientific writing to topics ranging from reproducibility and open science to time management and work/life balance. The resources for instructors are also excellent: She has templates to help students set both short- and long-term goals and in-class exercises to help novice writers hear the difference between clunky writing and writing that sings. What is perhaps most distinctive about Barbara's book is that she conveys the sense that writing should be a kind of meditation practice: a way to stay grounded in a supportive community while engaging deeply with ideas from a place of focus and clarity. I can't think of a better book to support new and emerging writers."

—**Laura Shulz**, professor of cognitive science,
Massachusetts Institute of Technology

"This book is a gem. Funny, thoughtful, and humane; packed with wise advice and deep insights. This is essential reading for any academic who wants to be more prolific and write better. (Which means that it's essential reading for all of us.)"

—**Paul Bloom**, Brooks and Suzanne Regan Professor of
Psychology at Yale University and author of *Against Empathy*.

"This book is practical, funny, easy to use, and effective. Reading this book is like sitting down with a close friend who also happens to be a writing expert. The book provides writing advice, exercises, and motivation to get those pages written. And I speak from personal experience—I used this book's guidance to carve out time from what seemed like an unworkably busy schedule to write, and the result was an article that will be published later this year."

—**SARAH LAWSKY**, Benjamin Mazur Summer Research Professor of Law, Associate Dean of Academic Programs, Associate Dean of Finance, Pritzker School of Law, Northwestern University

THE WRITING WORKSHOP

Write More,

Write Better,

Be Happier
in Academia

BARBARA W. SARNECKA

HOW TO CITE THIS BOOK

This book was printed on demand and published by the author. The reference in APA (6th ed.) style is:

Sarnecka, B. W. (2019). *The writing workshop: Write more, write better, be happier in academia.* (n.p.): Author.

Library of Congress Control Number: 2019912575

Cover and interior design by Lindsey Cleworth
Penguin illustrations by Julia Majdali Facer

CONTENTS

Preface to the Print Edition. xi

Acknowledgments. .xiii

Introduction. 1
    *   Community   5
    *   Practice   7
    *   Instruction   8

1. The Workshop 11
    *   Structure your meetings   14
    *   Create social accountability with
        a shared writing log   21
    *   Reframe rejection   31
    *   Adapt and grow   39

2. Planning Your Time. 45
    *   Think like a founder   46
    *   Build your individual development
        plan   56
    *   Build your term plan   62
    *   Build your weekly plan   68

3. The Practice of Writing **77**
* Question your beliefs about writing 78
* Draft with kindness 87
* Revise to continue your thinking 96
* Revise for the reader 103

4. Literature Reviews **111**
* Understand literature reviews 111
* Build your reading list 115
* Read strategically 121
* Write the literature review 130

5. Scientific Articles **139**
* Understand the IMRaD structure 140
* Start by making great figures 146
* Draft an article from meta-
  material to methods 156
* Present and discuss your results 164

6. Proposals **175**
* Asking for money 177
* Understand the funding game 180
* Write the proposal 185

7. Presentations **197**
* The elevator pitch 197
* The poster 202
* The talk 204
* Practice your presentation 230

8. Paragraphs........................**235**

    * Understand "hamburger"
      paragraphs   236

    * Manage information flow within
      the paragraph   245

    * Make it clear what you're
      referring to   250

    * Use signposting as needed   258

9. Sentences **265**

    * Understand readability   266
    * Write readable sentences   272
    * Understand imageability   283
    * Write imageable sentences   284

10. Words............................. **291**

    * Choose simple and specific words 292
    * Be kind to your readers   298
    * Omit needless words   309

Epilogue **325**
References...........................**327**
Credits **339**
Index................................ **341**
About the Author **353**

PREFACE TO THE PRINT EDITION

There are so many reasons to love a printed book. Just as a handwritten letter feels like a gift in this age of email, so does a book that you can actually hold in your hands. You can read it for hours without eye fatigue. It never needs charging. You can squeeze it hard during the suspenseful scenes and it will not shatter. (Spoiler: There are no suspenseful scenes in this book.) You can take it hiking and drop it on the ground, or read it in the bath and get it wet, or lose it under the seat of your car for months at a time, and it will still be just fine! You can give it to a friend when you're finished, which is a nice thing to do. You can put sticky notes in it, and then even after it is closed, the edges of the sticky notes will poke out like little flags saying, "Here was something you liked! Remember?"

A printed book has one drawback, though—it contains no hyperlinks. You can find all of the online supplementary materials by going to the Open Science Framework project for this book at https://osf.io/n8pc3/.

ACKNOWLEDGMENTS

This book came out of the graduate writing workshop that I teach in the Department of Cognitive Sciences at the University of California, Irvine. The insights here are not mine alone, but those of our ever-changing community of writers. It was Megan Goldman who suggested creating the writing workshop class in the first place; Ashley Thomas and Emily Sumner came up with the idea of a shared rejection collection; Galia Bar-Sever came up with the brilliant, hive-mind method of giving writing feedback and her brother Dan Bar-Sever coined the term "feedback forum." Readers in the humanities can thank philosophers Darby Vickers and Rena Goldstein for insisting that the book be written for a wider audience than just STEM researchers.

Other participants shaped the workshop by sticking around for multiple terms (in some cases up to five years) and creating a culture of kindness and respect that persists to this day—particularly Karen Arcos, Sierra Broussard, Christian Herrera, Carolyn McClaskey, James Negen, Teya Rutherford, K. J. Savinelli, and Kyle Stephens. The students in the workshop while the book was being written served as beta readers: Alandi Bates, Colleen Chen, Jeff Coon, Priyam Das, Alex Etz, Hannah Forsythe, Jessica Gonzalez, Joseph

Nunn, Yao Pei, Paulina Silva, Bobby Thomas, Tim Trammel, and Sirui Wan.

Thanks to Sarah Lawsky and Lisa Pearl, two of the smartest professors and kindest people I know, for their detailed, thoughtful feedback on early drafts. Thanks to Sonya Rasminsky for bringing her psychiatric expertise to the discussion of mental health issues in the book. Thanks to my colleagues in Cognitive Sciences, particularly Barbara Dosher and Emily Grossman, and to my department chair Ramesh Srinivasan, for supporting my choice to work on a new topic and write about what interested me instead of staying in my lane.

Thanks to my editor, Michael Dylan Rogers. I've been asking around, and plenty of my colleagues have authored books, but none has received the kind of editorial support that you've given me. I realized it during one of our teleconference meetings when I said, "Which outline are we working from now?" and you said, "Oh, I can just tell you the outline . . ." and then you listed each chapter and its content from memory, without even looking at your notes. I thought, *This guy knows my book better than I do.* When I describe that moment to colleagues, the mixture of disbelief and longing on their faces confirms that I made the right decision in working with you.

Thanks also to Lindsey Cleworth for bringing your beautiful design sense and wisdom to the production of the book. You're the only person I know who consistently finishes things early, and the book looks just the way I pictured it, except somehow better. If I ever write another book, I want you to design it.

Finally, thanks to my family—Greg, Ted, and James—for your constant love and support. You guys are my very favorite people in the whole world.

INTRODUCTION

Research is writing. No one gets a fellowship, a PhD, a postdoc, a job, a grant, or a promotion except by writing, which means that professional researchers are by definition professional writers.

Writing is required at every step of the research process. When researchers review literature, they take notes. These notes are not photocopies of the literature—they summarize key ideas and pull out quotations that are relevant to the researcher's own project. Researchers take notes in meetings with their advisors and collaborators; they jot down ideas for new projects; they outline plans for data collection and analysis; they sketch figures. At some point the lead researchers on a project become its authors, drafting the report that will communicate their findings to the wider community. The early drafts of this report help the authors work out their argument. The later drafts make the argument understandable to readers. At every step in the process, researchers are writing, because writing is thinking.

Writing is thinking

Given the centrality of writing to all aspects of research, and the fact that researchers are evaluated by their written output, one would expect academics to be preoccupied with the writing process. Most faculty members would like to produce more and better writing than they do (in particular, they would like to get more research published and more proposals funded), and most PhD students would like to write more, too. But academics don't talk nearly as much about writing as they talk about other research skills, such as experimental design or statistical analysis. Doctoral programs typically offer little or no explicit instruction in academic writing, and little or no help in developing and maintaining the kind of regular writing practice on which long-term productivity depends.

Writing is explicitly discussed only when researchers are evaluated. When I tell other professors that I'm interested in academic writing, the most common response I get is "Ugh, I have a graduate student who could use your class." When PhD students fail to progress, it's usually because they aren't writing. In other words, we evaluate students on their writing, but we make no attempt to help them write. This is bad pedagogy.

Of course not everyone is badly supervised. My own advisor (Susan Gelman of the University of Michigan) was, and is, a delight. But the doctoral program itself was typical in that it offered very little in the way of training or support for academic writing. In that kind of system, students who are lucky enough to work with a great advisor might do OK, but most students aren't so lucky. Many advisors struggle with writing themselves and don't know how to help their students. Even for advisors who write a lot and write well, the process may be completely intuitive. These advisors tell me that they can identify good writing, but they don't know how to explain what makes it good and don't know how to help their students produce it.

This mismatch between what we teach students and what we expect from them reinforces the worst aspects of academic culture. When we don't acknowledge that writing is difficult, students assume it should be easy. When we don't teach students how to do it, they assume they should already know. Then when they inevitably struggle, they imagine themselves to be the exception rather than the rule, and they feel like impostors. It doesn't occur to them that many faculty have an uneasy relationship with writing themselves.

The problem of impostor syndrome around writing connects this conversation to a much broader one. Academia is in the midst of a mental health crisis, and graduate students and postdocs are suffering the most. As Harvard PhD student Dwayne Evans (@RunDME) tweeted:

> When people said "grad school is hard" I thought they meant the "pushed outside your comfort zone" kind of hard, not the "sobbing uncontrollably for 20 minutes in a stairwell for the 5th time this semester" hard. I guess I missed the memo . . .

Evans's bravery in expressing his feelings is rare; the feelings themselves are anything but. In a 2014 survey of 2,561 academics by Britain's *Guardian* newspaper (Thomas, 2014), a whopping 87% of PhD students reported symptoms of anxiety, and 78% reported symptoms of depression. When asked whether they had told anyone at work about these problems, more than half (56%) said no. A survey of 790 PhD students at the University of California, Berkeley (UC-Berkeley Graduate Assembly, 2014) used a validated clinical measure—the Center for Epidemiologic Studies Depression Scale (Radloff, 1977)—and found that by that stricter definition, about

47% of students met the clinical criteria for depression. Similar rates of mental distress and depression have been found in recent studies of PhD students in Belgium (Levecque et al., 2017) and across the globe (Evans et al., 2018). In fact, rates of anxiety and depression in PhD students are more than six times higher than in the general population, measured with the same scale.

Correlation is not causation, of course, and it's possible that anxious and depressed people are just six times more likely than other people to pursue PhDs. But that seems implausible. As a report by the University of California's Office of the President (Dimsdale & Young, 2006) put it:

> Graduate students as a group have been identified as a population at higher risk for mental health concerns. The level of stress for graduate students is magnified by their relative isolation from the broader components of campus life, the intense academic pressures of their advanced studies, and the increased presence of family and financial obligations. (p. 4)

Authors of the UC Berkeley report point out that the intensity of graduate study itself sets students up for mental and physical stress, leading to exhaustion and worse.

> Success in graduate school is dependent on the ability to perform at a high level repeatedly over multiple years, which entails some costs. Effortful mental work is resource-intensive for the body and cognitive strain is often associated with decreases in mood which, absent adequate support, could lead

to depression over time. (UC-Berkeley Graduate Assembly, 2014, p. 9)

In the words of Frederik Anseel (quoted by Pain, 2018), "There is probably a serious problem with mental health in academia," and it "probably has something to do with how academia is organized as an industry, how we train people, how we manage people, and how careers develop."

By treating academic anxiety and depression as an individual health issue rather than a public health issue, we (faculty) avoid asking the uncomfortable question of how our own institutions contribute to the problem. It's time to ask that question. When one person has asthma, that person should see a doctor. But when 40% of people have asthma, and 80-90% of people have breathing problems, something is wrong with the air.

So what can we do about it? How can we make the environment of academia fit for human habitation? For lab-based research, principal investigators have a big role to play in promoting healthy work environments (Maestre, 2019). But to support academic writing, for researchers both inside and outside of labs, we must focus on creating *communities of practice and instruction*.

Community

The writing help that students get—such as it is—typically happens without much social interaction. The student writes a draft of something and submits it to a faculty member, who returns it after some period of time with comments. Many researchers have no regular time set aside to write with others, share successes and setbacks related to writing, or get real-time, face-to-face feedback on drafts and outlines.

This is a shame, because academic writing is the kind of thing that people seem to learn best through what are called "Communities of Practice" (Wenger, 1999, 2011). These are groups of people who share an interest in doing something and who learn how to do it better as they regularly interact. Academic writers already belong to communities—departments, cohorts, seminars, labs, and informal groups of friends. These communities can become communities of practice, and sometimes instruction, for academic writing.

All of the material presented in this book has been developed in the context of a graduate seminar in academic writing that I teach at the University of California, Irvine. We meet weekly to write together, to discuss our writing goals and practices, and to offer each other encouragement and feedback. Because our group is an official course, it also includes an instructional component— explicit teaching about the craft of academic writing.

Writing is a creative act. In order to be maximally productive over the long term, people must take care of themselves. So in addition to talking about writing, we also talk about ways to balance the demands of academic work with the other things that we need as human beings. I've come to believe that belonging to a group like this is essential not only to doctoral training but also to well-being throughout one's academic career. Chapter 1 of this book is about writing groups—what the different kinds of writing groups are, how we run our writing group, and how you can set up your own.

Practice

Communities of practice require a practice. Academic writing is like most skills, in that the best way to get better at it is just to do it a lot. In particular, there are advantages to writing little and often. Not only is distributed practice more effective than massed practice (which is why studying a little each day works better than cramming before a final), but short sessions of writing are simply easier to fit into a busy work schedule than long ones. If you can learn to write in 15-minute chunks, you will be able to write (at least a little) through the periods when heavy teaching loads, small children, administrative tasks, chronic illness, and other realities make long blocks of uninterrupted writing time a rare luxury. In our workshop, we call writing in short chunks of time *ninja writing*, which makes us feel both superpowered and pleasantly sneaky.

In addition to regular writing, our workshop aims to help people establish and maintain practices for well-being. Academic work can be relentless, especially in the early years of a career. It requires intense effort, which must be sustained for months or years, and much of the work is done in isolation. Many of us respond to these pressures by berating, blaming, and punishing ourselves for not achieving more. But those strategies don't work very well or for very long. The way to maintain productivity over a lifetime is to first take care of your physical and mental health. So in our writing workshop, we help each other find healthy, sustainable ways of living and working.

Our workshop also teaches people how to plan their research and writing. For most students, graduate school is the first time in their lives when they are fully responsible for their own progress. With no teacher or boss to tell them what to do, many students languish for years in doctoral programs, achieving little or nothing.

In our workshop, we walk together through the process of making long-term, medium-term and short-term writing and research plans. We set aside time during workshop meetings to make these plans, and we update them regularly. Chapter 2 lays out the system of planning that we use; Chapter 3 explains the writing practice in depth.

Instruction

The last key ingredient in doctoral writing education—and this might take place as part of a writing group or separately, in the form of books or seminars—is explicit instruction about the craft of research in a particular discipline. The genres of academic writing (literature reviews, research articles, fellowship proposals, conference presentations, and so forth) are new to doctoral students, as are the norms and customs related to peer review and publishing. Students benefit from an introduction to these genres and norms. Chapters 4-7 of this book present information on the craft of research in experimental and quantitative behavioral science. If that's not the kind of research you do, some of the information in those chapters may not apply to you, and you should feel free to ignore it.

Chapters 8-10 discuss writing style at the level of the paragraph, the sentence, and the word, with the goal of making writing as clear and easy to understand as possible. The central challenge of academic communication is to convey complicated, often highly technical, and abstract information in a way that readers can follow and learn from. There is also an ethical argument to be made for clear and accessible writing: It is inclusive. When readers can't understand what the author is saying, they are shut out of the conversation.

Of course, in a larger sense this whole book is instruction. It teaches readers how to create a writing workshop to write more, write better, and live happier professional lives. Many instructions are phrased as action steps such as "Streamline your teaching" and "Write like a ninja." These action steps should be treated like recipes in a cookbook. When a recipe says, "First melt the chocolate over low heat; then add three drops of peppermint oil," it doesn't mean that people who dislike chocolate or peppermint should force themselves to make the dish or that adding four drops of peppermint oil instead of three is an affront to good taste. Recipes are written as a series of action steps because that's the clearest way for a cookbook author to tell readers how to make the same dish that the author made. Some people follow recipes to the letter; others use them as suggestions. This book can be used the same way. If you read something in this book and feel skeptical, I hope you'll give it a try anyway. But if you give something a real chance and you hate it, then stop doing it.

The worst thing in academic writing is not that people write in binges, or fail to plan their writing, or put too much text on their slides, or make misleading figures, or use too much jargon. The worst thing in academic writing is the way we set standards for ourselves and then beat ourselves up when we fail to meet them. This book is meant to make your life easier, not harder. So as you read it, please just take whatever appeals to you or applies to you, and leave the rest.

Happy writing.

1

THE WORKSHOP

Emperor penguins breed during the cold Antarctic winter, where temperatures can reach -30C and below. To conserve energy and protect themselves from the cold, they adopt a behavioral strategy of huddling close together in large groups. Huddling is considered key to their ability to live in such a cold place. They have different huddling patterns across different breeding stages, with the largest number of penguins huddling during the egg incubation period, when the males must survive fasting while also trying to keep their eggs warm. (Lynne, 2018)

The academic environment can feel as harsh and unforgiving as the South Pole in winter. The ceaseless workload, the sense of always being compared to others, the fear of falling short or missing out, the uncertain future—these things can suck the happiness and well-being out of a person as surely as Antarctic winds can suck the warmth out of a lone penguin. That's why the dominant metaphor of this chapter — the metaphor that best describes the writing workshop itself as a living, breathing community of practice—is that of the penguin huddle. To join a writing workshop is to use "social huddling" (the official term for what penguins do) to keep ourselves and each other warm and thriving.

A community of practice is any group of people who have a common interest in doing something (in our case, academic writing) and who get better at it by meeting and talking about it together (Wenger, 1998, 2011). Humans naturally and happily form communities of practice for just about everything we want to do well.

Online gamers, for example, are a huge community of practice. They interact regularly online; they exchange information about hacks and glitches in games; they watch videos of expert players. Knitters are another community of practice. Friends spend time together knitting; experts teach novices to knit; there are countless knitting books, magazines, blogs, and festivals where knitters gather in large numbers.

Just by reading this book, you are participating in a community of practice. The people in this community are trying to figure out how to be productive, successful academic writers without sacrificing their physical and mental health.

———

I was not a very happy graduate student. In retrospect I was suffering from pretty serious anxiety, but I didn't recognize it at the time. I was aware of being worried all the time, feeling like I had to work constantly, like I could not afford time to sleep or relax. But I didn't know enough about anxiety or depression to recognize that there might have been help available, or that it might have been possible to feel better. I just assumed that being miserable was the price I had to pay for getting a PhD. It was a reasonable assumption, given that my peers seemed as unhappy as I was.

During my first year of graduate school, I remember someone saying that 50% of the students who started our PhD program wouldn't finish it. At the time, we took that to mean that only the toughest, smartest people would make it through. Now, as a faculty member myself, I think that any PhD program with 50% attrition is an indictment of the faculty who run it. If half the students who enter your program change their minds and walk away, you're doing something very wrong. But at the time, I saw my own and my fellow students' suffering as morally virtuous, as if sacrificing our happiness and well-being proved that we were serious scholars.

I completed the PhD and a postdoc and took a job as an assistant professor at the University of California-Irvine in the Department of Cognitive Sciences, where I still am today. I had two kids by then—one born while I was in graduate school and the other born nine days after I started the faculty job. For the next seven years I was working my butt off, both at the office and at home. But I was also starting to figure out a better balance between work and the rest of my life. Before I had children, I was willing to bury myself in work to get a PhD. It seemed like there would be plenty of time to relax later. But by the time I started the faculty job, I had a five-year old and a new baby. If I buried myself in work until I got tenure, I would miss my kids' childhoods.

So I became very interested in issues of work/life balance. I very much wanted tenure, but I didn't want to sacrifice my health and well-being, or that of my children. I soon realized that academic success is all about writing. It's not about being smart or hardworking, because everybody in academia is smart and hardworking. It's about writing a lot and writing well.

My senior colleagues implicitly understood this. I remember one faculty meeting early on, where we were discussing the personnel case of another assistant professor in the department. Our senior colleagues were evaluating her case, and I was secretly afraid that they might criticize her for not having an extramural grant. "Has she been applying for grants?" someone asked. The department manager confirmed that she had indeed submitted multiple grant proposals during that review cycle, but none of them had been funded. "Oh, well. That's OK then," said another colleague, and everyone nodded in agreement. No one seemed bothered that the grants hadn't been funded—they were experienced enough to regard funding decisions like weather: It's nice when it's favorable, but the important thing is to get up and go to work every day, rain or shine.

My preoccupation with writing, productivity, and wellness led me to read and talk about them incessantly. Eventually, my grad students asked me to teach a graduate seminar. The department agreed, and the writing workshop was born. I've taught it continuously, every quarter of every year since then.

Structure your meetings

The simple fact of meeting up is a huge step toward building community. It works best if the meeting has some kind of structure, so that it becomes a real community of practice. Traditionally, different types of writing groups serve different functions: Write-on-site groups provide quiet support and companionship during writing; writing accountability groups provide social support for setting and working toward goals; writing classes provide direct instruction in the craft of writing; writing workshops provide feedback on drafts. Your writing group can include any or all of these elements, depending on what you need and what appeals to you.

Our workshop meetings follow a predictable structure, developed through trial and error over many years. Like other graduate seminars at our university, our seminar meets once a week for 10 weeks, and each meeting lasts 2 hours and 50 minutes. Our meetings include the standard seminar fare of assigned readings and in-class discussions—we read one chapter of this book per week—but our meetings also incorporate writing on site, social support, and feedback. Each of these elements is useful, and we've found that when we combine them a synergy occurs: The whole is greater than the sum of its parts.

WRITE QUIETLY TOGETHER

Write-on-site groups are those where people meet at a designated time and place to sit quietly and write. That's the only defining feature of these groups; everything else is flexible. Some groups include two people ("writing buddies"); others include dozens or hundreds. They might write for 30 minutes or several hours; they might meet daily, weekly, or monthly; they might meet only for quiet writing, or people might arrive early or stay late to socialize. They might meet in a cafe, a library, a classroom, a group member's home, or anywhere else that is relatively quiet and has room enough for all the members to sit and write. These groups can be very helpful for people who feel isolated or stuck in their writing practice—there is something both comforting and energizing about writing in the quiet company of others.

In our workshop, we start each meeting with 30 minutes of writing in silence. Those who arrive early to the class might greet each other and chat, but when the meeting time starts, everyone begins to work quietly. This continues for 30 minutes. There are always people who arrive late to class, and that's fine. They just enter the room quietly, take a seat, and start writing alongside everyone else.

If you haven't tried quiet writing in a group, you might wonder why we bother. When a colleague of mine recently heard about the practice, she said, "I don't get it. Isn't that what we all do in our offices every day?" It's true that in principle quiet writing is something any of us could be doing at any time. But many of us find it difficult to write during a work day. When we are in our offices, people stop by. Or we find ourselves catching up with email or rushing off to a meeting. For many of us, the write-on-site time at the beginning of the workshop is an oasis of calm in the middle of a busy work day. I always feel a little sad when it ends.

CHECK IN

Writing accountability groups can be especially useful for writers who feel isolated in some way. The group helps members stick to their weekly writing goals by giving them someone to answer to. Group members don't need to have overlapping research expertise, just the willingness to show up every week, in person or by phone or video conference, to be accountable to the group and help hold others accountable. These groups help people stay focused on writing goals and finish writing projects.

Checking in with other group members at an in-person, face-to-face meeting can be a wonderful source of social support. But people can also provide accountability for each other online or via text or email. For example, our shared daily writing log and rejection collection both evolved as natural extensions of this aspect of the workshop. Each of these is described in its own section below.

As the leader of the group, I keep track of the time during our quiet write-on-site period. After the initial 30 minutes, I ring a little bell (it's actually a Tibetan singing bowl) to let everyone know it's time to stop writing. Then I start the class by saying something like, "Welcome to Week 8, Everyone. How did your writing go last week?" I often ask whether anyone got any rejections, and if someone did, we all cheer for them and thank them for contributing to our next rejection party. If someone got an acceptance, of course we cheer for that too, although I usually make a joke like, "Well, it won't get us any closer to a party, but I guess it's better than nothing."

I often look at the shared daily writing log for the previous week and invite people to comment about their entries (e.g., "Oh no, Jeff, it says you felt burned out and unproductive this week. Do you think it was all the traveling on top of the concentration exam you just took?" or "Paulina, you wrote here that it was your best week of the quarter. That's great! Did you do something different or just get lucky?") Often someone will raise a problem they've been grappling with (e.g., "I'm working on this literature review, but the reading list is growing out of control. How do I know what to read and what to skip?") and the group will spend some time discussing the problem and suggesting solutions.

One of the great benefits of having everyone from first-year graduate students to postdocs in the same workshop is that for every person who raises a problem, there's usually a more senior person who has recently solved the same problem in their own work and a more junior person who learns something just from listening to the exchange. This is known in education research as "near-peer mentoring."

If you have only a handful of people in your workshop (say, two to four people) and you want to create a more formal accountability structure, you can. Dedicated "accountability groups" typically meet once per week. At each meeting, each person gets a set amount of time (usually 15 minutes) to answer four questions: (1) What were your goals for the previous week? (2) Did you achieve those goals? (3) If you didn't achieve the goals, what prevented you? (4) What are your goals for next week? If your group has more than four people, there may not be enough time to devote 15 minutes to each person at each meeting. In that case, the checking-in period may have to be more loosely structured.

DISCUSS AN ASSIGNED READING

After the check-in period, we discuss whatever reading was assigned for the meeting. This is the part of the workshop that most resembles a traditional graduate seminar. In the early years of the workshop, we read a variety of books on scientific communication and nonfiction writing style. Over time, I developed more and more of my own opinions about the topics we were discussing, and I eventually wrote the book that you are reading now.

You may choose to have assigned readings and discussions as part of your writing group. (Although you should be aware that people are likely to skip the readings unless the group is led by a faculty member and has the official status of a course.) After you finish this book, there are many others that work well for academic writing groups. Two classics to start with are *The Craft of Research* by Booth et al. (2016) and *Style: Toward Clarity and Grace* by J. M. Williams (1990). Schimel's (2012) *Writing Science* gives practical tips on structuring scientific articles and grant proposals; *They Say, I Say: The Moves that Matter in Persuasive Writing* by Graff and Birkenstein (2018) is a guide to arguments in philosophy and the humanities. People who like structure may enjoy the step-by-step worksheets in Belcher's (2019) *Writing Your Journal Article in Twelve Weeks*, and Becker's (2007) *Writing for Social Scientists* is insightful about what makes academic writing difficult. A book about how to tell stories that engage people—particularly useful for grant writing, but also fun to read—is *Made to Stick: Why Some Ideas Survive and Others Die* by Heath and Heath (2007). To make good-looking posters and slides, study *The Non-Designer's Design Book* by R. Williams (2014). The clearest explanations of graphing principles are in *Creating More Effective Graphs* by Robbins (2013).

HOLD A FEEDBACK FORUM

The last thing we do at every meeting is give feedback to group members on brief (one single-spaced page or two double-spaced pages) writing samples. At the first meeting of each term, each member signs up for a day to get feedback. We allot 30 minutes per person and schedule one or two people per meeting. When the appointed time arrives, the author uploads their writing sample to a shared Google Drive folder that we can all access. We use the "suggesting" function in Google Docs (we call this "setting phasers to stun"), and all of us read and comment silently on the document at the same time. We do this for about 20 minutes, followed by 10 minutes of verbal discussion. Figure 1.1 is a screenshot taken during one of our feedback forum sessions. You can watch a video of the process on the Open Science Framework project for this book.

In a traditional writing workshop, members meet once a month, or perhaps as often as once a week. Each meeting is devoted to

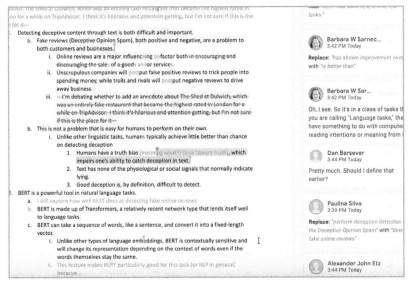

Figure 1.1

giving feedback to one person. Several days before each meeting, the person who is scheduled to get feedback sends whatever they've written to the group, and everyone is supposed to read it. Then during the meeting itself, the group discusses the work. Reading and commenting on a full-length article before each meeting is a lot of work, so this kind of setup requires real commitment from the members—not just to attend the meetings but also to prepare for them.

The members must also have the necessary expertise to give each other useful feedback, so if they are from completely unrelated fields, it won't work as well. Nor will this kind of group work for people who need more help than casual readers can provide. If a person needs extensive one-on-one tutoring, the campus writing center may have more resources than a group of friends. If a person needs many hours of help (e.g., to restructure a whole book), a professional editor is a better choice.

We tried to do something like a traditional feedback group in the early years of our writing workshop. One person would email a draft of a whole paper to the group, and everyone was supposed to read it before the meeting. The problem was that most people didn't read it. In a group of 10 to 15 busy people, many of whom didn't know each other well and felt overwhelmed by their own workloads, few were willing to spend the hours needed to read and comment on a classmate's article before each meeting.

The modified feedback forum works much better for us. Now, no one has to read anything before the meeting. Two pages may not sound like much of a writing sample, but it is. The specific aims page of a grant proposal to the National Institutes of Health is only one page. A topic-sentence outline of a whole article can fit into two pages. Two pages is enough for a conference abstract accompanied by a figure or for a brief research statement of the kind required with many job applications. Two pages is plenty. Most importantly, the quality of feedback that people get is much higher now than it was before. Reducing the burden on readers and shifting the emphasis to short pieces of writing such as outlines and abstracts has resulted in a much better feedback forum for us.

Create social accountability with a shared writing log

Imagine that you are a gardener. If you work really hard in your garden, can you make the sun shine today? No. Can you make tomatoes appear on the vine today? No. Sometimes there is sunshine and sometimes there is rain. You simply work in the garden most days and trust that, eventually, tomatoes will appear.

The same is true for your academic career. The only thing you can control is how you spend your time. You can't control what gets done, you can't control how good it is, and you certainly can't control what other people think of it. Those things are like the weather. All you can do is sit down to write every day—or at least most days—just as you would work in a garden.

The only thing you can control is how you spend your time.

In practice, working in the garden means writing every day. Freewriting or journaling is a fine place to start. This and other principles of good writing practice will be explored further in Chapter 3, but for now the most important thing for you to know is this: Over the long term, people who alternate between long, draining binges of writing and periods of not writing at all produce much less than people who cultivate the habit of writing little and often.

Unfortunately, cultivating a regular writing habit is easier said than done. Most people agree that regular writing sounds like a good idea, but without the support of a community, they find it difficult to establish and nurture that practice. Support for your writing practice need not be confined to meeting times. Consider keeping in touch with other workshop members and creating accountability through a shared writing log—an online spreadsheet for tracking your weekly and daily writing goals and progress.

Last year a colleague at another university heard that I teach a graduate writing course, and she called to ask me about it. She had agreed to teach a writing course in her department, and she was delighted to learn that I had already prepped one. I was happy to share my teaching materials, but when I started explaining what we actually do in our workshop—quiet writing time, checking in, feedback forum, and so forth—she was taken aback. This was not what she had in mind.

Talking with her, I realized how much our workshop has changed over the years. My friend was envisioning the workshop I started out with—the one where we asked what makes good writing good. She wanted to talk about sentence structure and word choice. I view those problems the same way I view sudoku puzzles: They are small, self-contained, fun, and easy to solve once you know how. I still have fun fixing bad sentences, and the last few chapters of this book are devoted to nuts-and-bolts fixes for common writing problems. But I no longer see those mechanical problems as the place where academic writers need the most help.

Today I think the real value of the writing workshop is in helping people manage bigger writing problems: how to find time to write, how to overcome

writing anxiety, and, above all, how to work hard enough to be successful with-
out destroying your own mental and physical health in the process.

I know that for faculty members, the idea of talking with graduate students
about well-being can sound horribly awkward. "That's just not the culture of
my institution," was how a friend of mine, a professor at another university, put
it. Well it wasn't always the culture of my institution, either.

BUILD A WRITING LOG FOR YOUR WORKSHOP

Many writing coaches suggest that writers keep a log to track the amount of time they spend writing, the number of words they write, their mood on a given day, or other variables. This is a way of bringing conscious attention to one's writing practice, following the famous principle that "what gets measured, gets managed" (Drucker, 1954). In other words, when people start tracking their writing practice, they generally pay more attention to it.

Members of a writing group can support each other's writing practice by tracking writing together. One easy way to do this is to make an "accountabilibuddies" (from "accountability buddies") arrangement with one or more friends. For example, let's say that you all have the goal of writing at least a little bit each day. Simply agree that you will text or email each other each day after you've written something. No response is necessary; just knowing that someone out there is aware of whether you wrote or not today is motivating for many writers.

If you want even more social support and accountability online, you can make a shared daily writing log. Create a new online spreadsheet in a place where everyone can access it. Make a column for each day, and invite writing group members to grab a row and log their writing. If you want to get fancy, you can have more than one column per day. Figure 1.2 shows an example of our spreadsheet, which has three columns per day: The first column is for daily writing goals; the middle one is for logging whether we wrote or not (this one starts out white, with conditional formatting to turn yellow when someone types "yes" or orange when they type "no"); and the third column is for positivity. More on that later. There's also a column at the beginning of each week for weekly writing goals and a column at the end (not visible in the figure) for reflecting on the week. More examples and templates can be found on the Open Science Framework project for this book.

USE THE LOG TO SUPPORT WRITING PRACTICE

Setting weekly and daily goals for your writing can go a long way toward reducing anxiety because it allows you to separate navigation (i.e., deciding what you will write) from driving (i.e., the actual writing). The practice of systematically planning your writing and setting long-term, medium-term, and short-term goals will be covered in depth in the next chapter. But right now, let's use your initial burst of enthusiasm to get you started with a shared daily writing log.

If you are using a log like the one shown in Figure 1.2, begin the week by deciding what writing goal you want to achieve and put it in the column at the beginning of the sheet. Next, break your weekly goals into daily goals and put those in the first column for each day. You can fill all these columns at the beginning of the week, or you can fill in goals for just the first few days and leave the rest open, knowing that you will use those days to mop up work that didn't get done earlier.

The middle column for each day gets filled in on the day itself. Most people underestimate the value of a regular, daily writing

NAME	Weekly goals (fill in at start of week)	Goals for the day (fill in at start of week)	Did you write? (Even 1 min counts)	Grateful for
		MONDAY		
		September 30, 2019		
Barbara	- 10 pages of MC manuscript - Comment on poster for ESS	√2 pages of MC √Send ESS feedback on poster	yes!	Earl Gray tea
Ji-Young	Submit TLW at current bio, and get data collection sorted out.	incoorperate CK feedback. Format manuscript in current bio format set up meetings digest notes from CDS and email interested people my poster	yes	The conference effect. I am feeling 20x more motivated thanks to my recent conference. Ready to get stuff done!
Khalil	(1) Finish specific aims page, (2) start introduction sections	lab work	yes, but very little	Breaks during writing workshop class =P
Hector	Working memory intro/lit review Hein statements	read novelty review, ICL, meet emre	Yes	Cheerful gardener, grateful grad students, and helpful profs
Yasmin	Tone scramble paper edits, NRSA emotional prosody justification, collect data	speech scramble stim, study for midterm	No	health care

Figure 1.2

practice. Writing little and often tends to dissolve the psychological and emotional barriers to starting and teaches people the crucial skill of writing in short chunks of time. A writing log can encourage writing little and often by having people just record whether or not they wrote that day, rather than asking them to record how long they wrote or how much they produced. Creating a supportive environment in which people can establish and nurture a daily(ish) writing practice is one of the most important functions of a writing workshop.

Here's how current workshop member Jessica, a PhD student in logic and philosophy of science, describes her relationship with writing:

> *I used to love writing. But since starting grad school, I've developed a lot of anxiety in general, and especially about writing. There are very high expectations, and it seems to be assumed that grad students will just "get it" after reading so many examples of professional papers. I had this vision of the day that the clouds would part and the sun would shine down on me, and I would be endowed with brilliance and crystal-like clarity. The writing workshop has helped me break these types of misconceptions and realize how much they were inhibiting my writing. Now I see writing as a skill to be learned through practice. When I feel stuck, there are very specific writing techniques I can use in order to keep my footing and get "unstuck." Most importantly, I have learned to shift my perspective, be patient with myself, be OK with rejection and critical feedback, and enjoy writing again.*

USE THE LOG TO SUPPORT POSITIVITY PRACTICE

Human beings have a negativity bias. If, from a class of 100 students, you receive 99 positive evaluations and one negative, you will probably pay as much attention to that one negative opinion as you pay to all the 99 positive opinions together. But if the reverse is true—if you receive 99 negative and one positive evaluation— you will probably disregard the positive evaluation completely and remember the course as an unmitigated disaster. Psychologists like to say that our brains are like Velcro for negative experiences and Teflon for positive ones.

This makes sense from an evolutionary standpoint. Proto-humans who spent their time scanning the environment for threats and obsessing over real and imagined problems presumably survived at higher rates than their happy-go-lucky contemporaries, so the negativity bias isn't something to criticize ourselves for. But even if it gave our ancestors an edge in survival, the effects on our every-day mental and physical health are not good. Most of us find it too easy to focus *only* on negative experiences, and over the long term, this contributes to anxiety and depression.

The good news is that just as we can lift weights to make our bodies stronger, we can also cultivate pleasant thoughts and positive emotions to strengthen the neural pathways that subserve these experiences. Do not misunderstand—the goal is not to ignore negative experiences or deny painful emotions. Suffering is part of being human. But being human also means having the ability to step back a bit and reflect on our experiences and emotions so that we don't suffer needlessly.

A basic principle of neuroscience is Hebbian learning, sometimes summarized as "if it fires, it wires." This is another way of saying that humans develop habits of thinking just as we develop habits of speech and behavior. Each time a person suffers a depressive episode, for example, their chances of being depressed again in the future increase, as the neural pathways underlying their depressed mental state are strengthened. Conversely, intentionally cultivating positive states of mind for as little as 15-30 seconds at a time is enough to start changing the brain in a positive direction. (For a nontechnical overview of the neuroscience behind these practices, see Hanson, 2009)

Consider adopting some form of positivity practice as a group, along with your writing practice. On the shared daily writing log shown in Figure 1.2, the third column for each day is devoted to positivity. Here are some suggestions for tried-and-true positivity practices, but feel free to experiment and discover your own.

Gratitude

This is one of the best-studied positivity practices (for review, see Wood, Froh & Geraghty, 2010). Spend 15-30 seconds a day thinking about something you feel grateful for and list it on the log. Some examples:

> "My dog, for loving me regardless of what I publish."

> "American sports, with lots of productivity-enabling commercial breaks."

> "A weekday that felt like a weekend day."

An excellent time to practice gratitude is before going to sleep at night. The 1954 movie *White Christmas* features the song "Count Your Blessings (Instead of Sheep)." The songwriter, Irving Berlin, said that he got the idea for the song from his doctor, who advised him to count his blessings as a treatment for his insomnia.

Savoring

Spend 15-30 seconds really enjoying a sensory experience. Instead of gulping your morning coffee while you rush off to your first meeting, take a minute to savor the smell, the taste, and the warmth of the cup in your hands. A few more examples:

> "I listened to ocean waves yesterday. Such a lovely sound."

> "Watching bees on the lavender bush outside the lab building."

> "Stepping into a hot shower."

Kindness

One of the great pleasures of human life is doing something to help someone else, even if it's a very small act. Of course it feels good to receive kindness, but it also feels good to be kind. Examples:

> "Helped a woman with her bag on the airplane."

> "Took care of lots of chores in the house since my partner sprained her ankle and isn't very mobile."

> "Helped an undergrad understand Nuer marriage practices (and didn't get mad when she showed up 45 minutes late)."

Age Quod Agis (Do what you are doing)

This Latin phrase comes from the Jesuit tradition; it is very similar to the Buddhist practice of mindfulness. To practice *Age Quod Agis*, pick a simple, boring task such as making a cup of coffee, washing dishes, or walking from your office to the bathroom—something that you would ordinarily do mindlessly. But this time, try to slow down and bring all of your attention to the task while you're doing it. For just 15-30 seconds, take a break from thinking about all the other stuff you have going on today, and just let yourself be completely absorbed in the task at hand. This is a gentle way to dip your toe into the practice of meditation.

Empathy

Look around you today for a person who has had very different life experiences from you, and spend 15-30 seconds thinking about something you have in common with that person. For example, everyone wants to be safe, everyone wants to be heard, everyone gets sick and injured, everyone is afraid of dying.

I gave a talk recently on positivity practice at a weekend yoga festival here at UC-Irvine. As I was getting ready to leave the house, my 19-year-old son, who was home from university for the weekend, asked what I was going to talk about. I told him the talk was about practicing positivity, which meant deliberately cultivating pleasant emotions for just 15-30 seconds at a time. He was skeptical, but I assured him that it is based on extensive research evidence. Then his tone changed, and he told me this story:

> *When I was 12 or 13 years old, I was at soccer camp, and I was bored. The camp counselors had said that there was*

going to be a prize for the kid who was the nicest, so I decided to try to get the prize for being the nicest kid. I decided to compliment other kids on anything that they did well—any compliment I could think of that wasn't insincere, I would say it. And the weird thing was, at the end of the day, I felt great! Even after I stopped trying to notice good things, I just kept noticing them. And I felt really good.

I asked him whether he won the prize in the end. He said he didn't remember, but he didn't think so. I thought it was lovely that what stuck in his memory was the intrinsic reward of the positivity practice—the way it made him feel—rather than the extrinsic prize or lack of it.

Reframe rejection

As a researcher, you can plan and carry out research, and you can submit written reports of that research to journals and conferences. But you have no control over how reviewers will react to it. If you make your sense of achievement contingent on reviewers liking or accepting your work, you allow your happiness to depend on the whims of strangers.

Worse yet, you will be unhappy most of the time, because most submissions are rejected. Even papers that ultimately get accepted and grants that ultimately get funded are usually rejected one or more times first. The problem is that people tend to advertise their successes and keep quiet about their failures, which gives each individual the impression that everyone but them is succeeding.

Imagine that your department has 100 people. Each person submits 10 papers per year, receiving nine rejections and one acceptance. No one talks about their rejections, but they mention the one acceptance to everyone they know. So what each person personally experiences is 90% rejections, but what they hear about from others is 100% acceptances.

The impostor phenomenon (Clance & Imes, 1978) is the internal sense of being an intellectual phony. This phenomenon is usually discussed as a misperception—as though the person who feels like an impostor is interpreting evidence incorrectly. But if what you experience is 90% failure, and what you hear about from other people is 100% success, then of course you will feel like everyone else is more successful than you. The problem is not that people misinterpret evidence. The problem is a culture where people feel ashamed and secretive about failure.

Our shared rejection collection is our way of replacing shame and secrecy with openness and mutual support. The collection is simple—it's just an online spreadsheet to which we all contribute our rejections. Each time we amass 100 rejections, we have a party. Figure 1.3 shows an example.

A party after every 100 rejections works well for cognitive scientists. If you are in another field, you may decide on a different number. For example, my friend Sarah, a law professor, tells me that law articles regularly rack up 100 rejections in a single submission cycle. If that's true in your field, you might consider having a party at each multiple of 1,000 rejections instead of 100.

The rejection parties themselves are just ordinary parties. We choose a date and time for the party, and I send invitations by email to everyone who contributed a rejection to that group of 100. I host the party at my house, although we've also had it outdoors, at a park near campus with barbeque grills and picnic tables. Everyone brings food and drinks to share. I bring champagne and a cake that says "Rejected!" When it's at my house, we have a fire in the fireplace where people can burn their printed rejections if they want to.

We have only a little bit of ceremony, which is that we make three toasts.

	Date	Your Name	Rejected for/by	Quotations from reviewers, or other notes or comments	The Bright Side (Optional)
1	7-Dec-2017	Barbara	University Internal Funding Mechanism	I was talking to this office in university administration, telling them about this project I'm working on, and asking if they had any ideas about where I could look for seed funding. They said it sounded like a great project and they suggested that I apply for this award through their office. So I did. And they rejected my application. On my birthday.	Well, at least I tried. I applied for an award that I didn't know about before. Now that I know about it, maybe I'll apply again in the future and get something. Drafting the application wasn't difficult, and now I have some text about the project that I can use in future grant applications. Also, it will be easier for me to say no without guilt next time that office asks for faculty to help with something.
2	10-Dec-2017	Haruto	University Job	none	They sent me a rejection letter at least
3	10-Dec-2017	Haruto	University Job	none	the people who were interviewed were with one except postdocs, and they all do great work
4	10-Dec-2017	Amelia	University Job	none	Location is smoggy
5	10-Dec-2017	Khalil	Research School	none	I have learned alot about my ego. :)
6	10-Dec-2017	Amelia	College Job	none	i have so many to add to the rejection collection!
7	10-Dec-2017	John	University Job	none	Location would be too cold for the dogs (obviously)
8	10-Dec-2017	John	University Job	none	too cold for the dogs again
9	11-Dec-2017	Yasmin	Creative Writing Contest	none	I can refine my submission and submit to an even BETTER award cycle.
10	12-Dec-2017	Mindy	Grant	They said it was too ambitious -- didn't believe I could collect the data.	I'll collect some pilot data and then try again, with some proof of concept!
Fall down seven times, get up eight. (Japanese proverb)					
11	December 15th, 2017	Ava	Grad School Application	none	Too far away from family
12	20-Dec-2017	Maria	Internship	Company is getting rid of this lab group!	Nobody will get it, so it's the opposite of personal! And the researcher was super nice and emailed me back with some other suggesions.
13	21-Dec-2017	Isaac	Summer Science Program	The program was cancelled	Well, at least I wasn't the only one since they rejected everyone
14	21-Dec-2017	Isaac	Internship	They said I didn't "meet minimum qualifications" which is odd since I definitely did according to their application	If they said I didn't meet minimum qualifications because they assumed psychologists don't do quantitative things, then I don't want to work there anyway :p
15	21-Dec-2017	Yasmin	PhD Internship	none	really competitive company and I wasn't sure I could do this anyway since it was a 6 month-long internship
16	21-Dec-2017	Brad	Business Intelligence/Data Analyst Job	Got pretty positive comments about how they'd love to interview me again in the future. The position was just "way" more business-oriented than expected and I lack business knowledge on making	I know now that I at least need to learn some business jargon but if I gain some knowledge on that, I can reapply in the future. Also at least I got past the first interview, which

Figure 1.3

CELEBRATE YOURSELF

The first toast is to ourselves. It takes courage to submit things, knowing that most things are rejected. And it's an act of generosity to share a rejection with the group. So we first drink to ourselves and each other, for having the courage to get all these rejections and the generosity to talk about them.

For several decades, psychologists have known that good mental health is associated with high self-efficacy and an internal locus of control. In plain language, that means people who are focused on things they can do—on aspects of their lives that are within their control—are happier than people who are focused on things they can't control. If you design a research study, carry it out, write a report of it, and submit it for publication, you've done everything you could, and you should feel good about that. What happens after it leaves your desk is out of your control. Reviewers will like it or they won't; the editor will accept it or reject it; people will read and cite it, or they won't. But you've done the part that was yours to do, so celebration is in order.

For many years—while I was a graduate student, postdoc, and assistant pro-fessor—one of my favorite daydreams was of flunking out. I would imagine a future in which I kept showing up and doing my work, but it just wasn't enough. So, through no fault of my own, I would flunk out of the PhD program. Or I would not get a job. Or I would not get tenure. In this daydream, I would leave academia entirely. I know these sound like negative daydreams, but I found them comforting. I would imagine my alternative career, perhaps as a yoga teacher. I guess it was a way of fantasizing about quitting without being a quitter. But it was also comforting because it clearly distinguished between things that were in my control and things that were not. When I felt discouraged or overwhelmed, I would decide to just keep collecting and analyzing data, keep writing papers and grant proposals, keep showing up to teach. Maybe that would be enough; maybe it wouldn't. Some days I kind of hoped it wouldn't, because I liked imagining my life as a yoga teacher. Once I got tenure and flunking out was no longer a realistic possibility, I missed the daydream. On days when I didn't love my job, it was nice to imagine that circumstances beyond my control might one day propel me into a different life.

CELEBRATE THOSE WHO REJECTED YOU

The second toast is to the people who rejected us. The reviewers, editors, hiring committees, etc. who gave us the big thumbs-down. Judging other people's work is no fun. Reviewers agree to review as a service to the profession. They put aside their own work to help improve someone else's, knowing that the authors will be angry rather than grateful for their criticism. Sometimes the reviewers themselves feel defensive, imagining the anger of the authors, and the reviews come out sounding harsh. Judging other people's work is an unpleasant and unrewarding job, but our disciplines couldn't function without it. So we drink to the people who do it.

Academia functions because scholars volunteer their time and expertise to review each other's work. Reviewing pays nothing and counts for nothing toward promotion and tenure; it is truly a service to the community. No author likes receiving criticism, but in most cases peer reviews do improve the work. Reviewers sometimes write cranky and tactless comments because they feel slighted (e.g., they feel they should be cited in the work and they aren't), or because they resent the time spent on the thankless work of reviewing, or because they imagine the authors resenting them and they feel defensive. But ultimately, reviewers are providing a service. Similarly, the people who serve on hiring committees and fellowship committees are doing a service. They could be spending their time on their own work, raising their own academic profiles, making themselves more successful and more famous. Instead, they agree to serve on committees because universities can't function unless someone does that work.

Take comments from the first round of review seriously. Ignoring them is an excellent way to alienate reviewers and get your paper rejected the second time around. I once reviewed a manuscript presenting two rather poorly designed experiments on children's counting behavior. Instead of a lit review in the introduction, the authors had written, "There is not really any literature on children's counting behavior to review." That's an absurd statement, but I figured the authors must be very new to the field (hence their ignorance), so I wrote a paragraph or two explaining that there is actually a big literature in this area, and I provided a list of about 25 articles and books that were directly relevant to their study, which I thought would help them get a good start on a lit review. The editor gave them a decision of revise and resubmit.

When the revised manuscript was sent to me for a second round of evaluation, there was still no lit review. The authors had merely replaced the sentence saying that there was no literature with a sentence saying, "There is such a huge literature on children's counting behavior that we can't possibly review it all here."

It completely changed my attitude toward the authors. My first response had been sympathy. I assumed that they were very new researchers—probably students—whose advisors didn't know anything about research in children's counting and couldn't point them in the right direction. But when I saw the revised manuscript, I realized that the authors hadn't reviewed the literature because they didn't want to make the effort. Given that I was contributing my time and expertise to review their work, their attitude made me angry. I wrote a letter recommending a flat rejection with no option to resubmit, and the editor agreed.

CELEBRATE THOSE WHO GOT IT INSTEAD

The third toast is to the people who got what we wanted instead of us. The ones who got the grants we applied for, the jobs we wanted, the publications in the journals that rejected us. All of us who are sincerely trying to understand the world and teach others are on the same team, including the people who got the jobs and grants that we applied for over the past few months. So we raise a glass to them and wish them good luck.

A line in the poem *Desiderata* by Max Ehrmann (1948) goes, "If you compare yourself with others, you may become vain or bitter, for always there will be greater and lesser persons than yourself." It's true that everyone engages in social comparison, and it makes no one happy. Whatever you can do to minimize this tendency in yourself will add to your quality of life. Consider that your real opponents are not the other researchers in your field; your real opponents are ignorance and confusion. It is ignorance that leads policy makers to defund research and education and confusion that leads people to reject scientific consensus about important issues and to spread false and misleading information that causes harm.

My college roommate, Laura, loved politics. We were undergraduates together at the University of Iowa. Laura grew up in the Chicago suburbs and went to the University of Iowa in part so that she could organize students for Illinois Senator Paul Simon's 1988 presidential campaign. We shared a room when we were 19, and we've been close friends ever since.

About 15 years ago, we were talking on the phone one day, me in California and Laura in Washington, DC, where she has enjoyed a successful career working in international health organizations. She seemed bothered about something, and when I asked her what was wrong, she said that she felt like a loser. Many years before, after we had graduated from college and before either of us went to graduate school, I had moved to Japan to teach English, and Laura had returned home to Chicago. One of her first jobs was to organize volunteers for the campaign of Illinois senator Carol Moseley Braun, and one of the volunteers who had worked for her on that campaign was now going to run for the Illinois Senate himself.

"I was his boss," Laura said. "He worked for me. And now he might be a senator. He's going to be more successful than me, and it makes me feel like a loser. What did I do wrong? How did this happen?" I reminded Laura of how successful she was and how many people would love to have her life, but I understood her feelings. Teddy Roosevelt said that comparison is the thief of joy. Comparing ourselves to other people only ever makes us feel bad, but it's so hard not to do it. "Look at it this way," I said to Laura. "Say this guy who worked for you gets elected to the senate. Is that so bad? You say that he was a nice guy, that he was smart, and that he worked hard. So we should be happy for him to succeed." On a practical note, I said, if she was going to feel bad every time she heard this guy's name, she might be signing up for a lot of unhappiness because he seemed pretty impressive. And his name was quite unique too: Barack Obama.

Adapt and grow

Writing groups are infinitely variable and should be varied to suit the needs of their members. If your top priority is accountability, you might want to try the classic, four-person accountability group that meets for one hour per week and spends 15 minutes talking about each person's goals and progress. Write-on-site groups, on the other hand, can be much bigger. In fact, a write-on-site group of five or more people often works better than a group of just two or three, because there is less temptation to chat. Even groups of forty people or more can practice quiet writing very effectively together. For feedback, groups of anywhere from three to fifteen people work well.

You might choose to meet for one, two, or three hours, in a class-room, conference room, cafe, or library. Or group members could take turns hosting at their homes and allot time at the beginning or end of the meeting for eating, drinking, and socializing. A few tips to keep in mind are: (1) Very small groups require very dedicated members. If your group includes only two or three people and they cancel or miss meetings when life gets busy, the group won't last very long. (2) If you don't have a faculty member involved, people probably won't do assigned readings. Again, everyone is busy and no one is looking for more work. So if you want your group to have the structure of a seminar, it's probably best to set it up as a real seminar, with a faculty member teaching it. Conversely, if you don't have a faculty member who wants to participate, consider limiting your group to peer-based practices such as quiet writing together, making term plans, and exchanging feedback.

Ultimately, your writing group should be as big or as small as you want it to be and should serve whatever needs you have today. Try things out, keep what you like and ditch the rest—a successful huddle is any huddle that shelters you and your fellow penguins from the cold.

When the workshop first began, we had only four or five members—just my own graduate students, plus a couple of others from cognitive sciences. But soon other people started to hear about the workshop, and now we typically have between 10 and 15 members, mostly from social sciences and education, but a few from other parts of the university. All of the writing workshop practices described in this book are the ones we've arrived at through trial and error, over the dozens of iterations of the workshop that I've taught over the years. Two or three years ago, I realized that I had become bored with the research topic I had been working on for the past 15 years (the development of number concepts in early childhood.) What I was really interested in now was the writing workshop, and the positive effects it seemed to have on the members, including me.

This wasn't as different from my previous work as it sounds. My work in cognitive development focused on how acquiring the counting system of a language—which people in numerate societies do in childhood—makes it much easier to mentally represent numerical information. Many times, I've stood in front of audiences and explained how the kinds of numerical information humans can represent without a counting system are limited and how learning to count and use numbers transforms our thinking in profound ways, allowing us to overcome the natural limitations on our working memory and the coarseness of our innate numerical perception.

Literacy is not so different from numeracy. Learning a writing system transforms our ability to represent and manipulate linguistic information, much as learning a number system transforms our ability to represent and manipulate quantitative information. And the process doesn't stop when we learn to read in childhood. I continue to be amazed by writing as a form of enhanced thinking, by the way it compensates for the limits on our memory and attention, allowing us to focus for much longer on a single idea and consider much more information than we could keep track of with spoken language alone.

I'm also interested in the meditative qualities of writing. When we put a thought on paper, we can observe and reflect on it. Writing, like meditation, is difficult because looking at one's own thoughts is a profoundly uncomfortable experience. We feel self-conscious and self-judging. It's hard to look at what's there, because we're so distracted by what we think ought to be there. The key to both meditation and writing is learning to observe our own thoughts with a little less judgment and a little more kindness.

CREATE THE CULTURE YOU WANT

A kind and supportive community is the ground from which a strong writing practice can grow. The culture of your writing workshop reflects many small choices that you make, and sometimes it is reflected back in surprising ways.

I met Darby at a rejection party at my house. There was a fire in the fireplace. I had invited guests to bring hard copies of their rejections to burn, and some people were doing that. Others were playing board games. (Get a lot of nerds together in the same room and it's helpful to have board games.) I saw that Joseph, a mathematical behavioral scientist, was playing a board game with my 12-year-old son James, and I felt grateful to Joseph for including him. But most people were standing around the food and drinks table talking, which is why it was noticeable that Darby was sitting down.

She was sitting sort of hunched over and looking miserable—quiet and pale. My student Emily, then in her third year, said to me, "This is my friend Darby. She's in Philosophy. She's been having a hard time, and I invited her to the party. I hope that's OK." I said that of course it was fine.

As the evening wore on and people started to leave the party, Darby was still sitting in that chair by the table. I tried to talk with her a little, gently, because she looked so fragile. "This is so nice," she said. "You guys are so nice." She looked like she was on the verge of tears. She later told me that the party happened at a time when she felt desperately in need of writing support. During her first two years of graduate school, she had been told that she needed to improve her writing. But it wasn't clear how to do that, other than to read well-written philosophy papers and hope that her own writing would get better with practice. At the time of the party, she had eight weeks left to complete a major piece of writing for her candidacy exam, and she felt increasingly anxious that she wouldn't finish in time, or that the quality would not be good enough to pass.

ERR ON THE SIDE OF INCLUSIVENESS

A writing workshop is a place where students and faculty from across the academy can learn from and support one another. So when forming and developing your workshop, try to err on the side of inclusiveness. Make the choice to keep your door open to all the different types of scholars who can benefit from, and contribute to, your community of practice.

—————

By the end of the evening almost everyone was gone, and Darby was one of just three or four people left. I told her that I hoped she would join us in the writing workshop the next term. She asked several times if I was serious, and I said that of course I was. Her doubts had to do with the fact that philosophy is so different from cognitive science. What if there was no common ground? How could she give anyone useful feedback? Would our methods work for the kind of writing she had to do? I said I didn't know, but she would be welcome to join us.

Because she was a third-year grad student, Darby was actually more experienced and knowledgeable than many of the students in the workshop, and it turned out that she had a lot to offer. She read people's writing samples closely and gave deep and insightful feedback. Her analytical skills were just amazing. (That's a philosopher for you.)

During Darby's first quarter in the workshop, she decided to apply for a grant to run a small conference. This was a grant for humanities faculty, and although Darby was not faculty, her advisor said that he would submit the proposal if she did the work of writing it. She was really nervous, having never written a conference proposal before, but I gave her a draft of the "Proposals" chapter for this book to help her get started. She worked on the conference proposal, brought it into the workshop for feedback, and the conference was funded.

Darby became an outspoken advocate of the writing workshop, even making a presentation about it at a meeting of the American Philosophical Association. Darby advocated for graduate students to form writing workshops and for philosophy departments to add them to the curriculum. She argued that writing workshops are a way to offer writing support and social support to everyone, including early-career philosophers from historically underrepresented groups.

THRIVE TOGETHER

If you make an effort to create a real community of practice with other dedicated, curious, creative people, you are bound to be blown away from time to time by someone's success. This doesn't mean that everyone will succeed at everything they do, but on the whole you will find plenty of reasons to be optimistic. It's much easier to practice positivity together than alone.

Soon, Darby became like a different person: much happier and a real leader of the group. One incident in particular stands out in my mind. I live in a neighborhood that is owned by the university, and all the houses belong to university faculty and staff. My next-door neighbor is a philosophy professor, and he and his family had just moved from Scotland a couple of years prior. My family had invited theirs over for Thanksgiving dinner, and we got to talking about the writing workshop. I told my neighbor that we had a philosopher in the workshop: Darby.

He said, "What? Darby doesn't need a writing workshop. She could do all this with one hand tied behind her back. She's one of the strongest students in the department—a real star. She's the last one who needs your help." This illustrates a core misconception people have about the workshop—that it is somehow remedial, and that "good" students don't need it. At the next workshop meeting I told everyone (including Darby) what my neighbor had said. She was laughing and a bit embarrassed and said she didn't feel like a star. But she is one.

———————

For all the reasons discussed in this chapter, a writing workshop is an ideal way to create the community necessary for your writing practice to thrive. But in order to sustain that practice, you will need to manage your time wisely outside of the workshop meetings. The next chapter is about how to do this.

2

PLANNING YOUR TIME

One of the best things about an academic job is that, outside of a few fixed commitments such as classes and regular meetings, you can pretty much decide your own schedule. If you want to work at night and sleep late in the morning, you can. If you need to take your car to the mechanic or go to an event at your child's school in the middle of a workday, it's no problem. This day-to-day schedule flexibility gives outsiders the impression that academic jobs are easy; what they don't realize is that academics are still expected to produce a lot of work. The old joke is that you can work any 80 hours of the week you want.

Despite the flexibility, academics often feel that they don't have time to write. Even without writing, you probably have enough other tasks to keep you busy all day. The problem is that if you are evaluated based on your research output (which means writing), then all of the nonwriting, nonresearch work that you are doing every day counts for little. So you must carve out and protect time for writing. And because your writing practice depends on your overall health and well-being, you must also carve out and protect time to sleep, play, interact, exercise, and reflect.

When you don't make plans, you have to make decisions on the fly. This makes the work harder than it needs to be. By stopping from time to time to reflect on where you're going and how you will get there, you free up your mind to focus on day-to-day tasks the rest of the time. This makes for a calmer, happier, and more productive work life.

Think like a founder

All of us were undergraduates before we were PhD students, so we approach the PhD program with the implicit model of an undergraduate degree program in mind. Getting an undergraduate degree is all about taking classes, so new PhD students focus too much on their classes and worry too much about their grades, not realizing that their grades hardly matter anymore. (If you are in the UK or Europe, your experience may be different, but North American programs typically start out with two years of classes, followed by three or four years of full-time research.) Ask someone with a PhD how often they've been asked for their graduate-school transcript.

After a year or two, PhD students figure out that their success really depends on producing research. So they shift to a different (but still incorrect) model, which is to think of themselves as employees and their advisors as bosses. *My advisor knows how to produce research*, they think. *I shall await further instructions.*

It is understandable that students have this model. In most work environments, someone tells us what to do. We succeed by following instructions, first from teachers and later from bosses.

But as a PhD student, you are your own boss. Some advisors give their students projects to work on at first, but the ultimate goal of a PhD program is to train students to do original research. (That's why many faculty members, when they recruit PhD students, don't necessarily prefer students who earned perfect grades as undergraduates. Perfect grades just show that a student can follow directions perfectly.) After the first year or two, most advisors stop assigning tasks. The idea is that the students will come up with their own research projects and pursue them independently. But most students have never had to design and plan their own work. So the advisors wait for the students to do something, and the students wait for the advisors to tell them what to do. This can go on for years.

This misunderstanding about who will make something happen is a very common problem among graduate students. They start the PhD program full of enthusiasm and good intentions. They work hard at their classes for the first two years. In the third year, they no longer take classes. The days stretch out before them, empty and directionless. They'd be happy to do some work, but their advisor isn't assigning them anything to do. This would be irritating, but at the same time the advisor doesn't seem upset with them, so they figure that everything must be OK. The third and fourth years go by without much happening. The meetings with the advisor start to grow tense. The advisor appears to be waiting for them to do something, but maddeningly, won't say what. The student thinks, *Stop playing games already and just tell me what to do!* The advisor thinks, *Stop sitting around and do something already!* Each feels increasingly frustrated and disappointed with the other.

If you are a PhD student, instead of thinking of yourself as an employee, think of yourself as the founder of a new startup company. Just as a startup founder has a good idea for a new business, you have a good idea for a new research program. Your university is your incubator: It provides what you need to get your research up and running. This includes help with housing and living expenses for a few years, access to a university library, and a network of experts in your field who can advise you. Depending on your research, you may also need other things: people to participate in your experiments, permission to stay at the Antarctic research station, an fMRI machine, a scanning electron microscope, or whatever. Your advisor is a consultant and collaborator, but ultimately it's your research program and you have to keep it moving forward. Nothing will happen unless you make it happen.

FOCUS ON WHAT'S IMPORTANT (NOT WHAT'S URGENT)

In a 1954 speech, Dwight D. Eisenhower famously said, "I have two kinds of problems: the urgent and the important. The urgent are not important, and the important are never urgent." (garson, 2014). Eisenhower attributed this insight to a former college president, which seems fitting because the problem of how to balance urgent against important tasks is one that academics always have to manage.

In most academic jobs, particularly during the early years, the most important work we do is our own original research, and especially writing. (Your teaching may or may not also count for something, depending on the kind of job you have.) The important projects on your individual development plan and term plan compete for your time with an endless parade of urgent, but ultimately less important tasks: student emails to answer, papers to grade, manuscripts to review, committee meetings to attend, administrative paperwork to fill out, etc.

To make matters worse, at least three powerful forces push you to do the urgent tasks instead of the important ones. These are (1) social accountability; (2) the pleasure of doing something easy; and (3) the mere urgency effect.

First, urgent tasks often have built-in social accountability: Other people want you to do them, and those people will be inconvenienced or annoyed if you don't. Research and writing tasks, by contrast, have little or no short-term social accountability. If you spend six weeks working on a paper and then get bored and abandon the project, no one else will even know (much less object). But if you fail to prepare for a lecture, you will spend a very uncomfortable hour with a room full of bored and resentful students. So it's natural to have a strong urge to work on the lecture instead of the manuscript. This is how social accountability pushes you to do urgent things before important ones.

But social accountability can be used to your advantage as well. One of the most important reasons to join a writing workshop is to harness the power of social accountability to help you do the writing that's most important for your career.

The second reason it can be tempting to do urgent tasks instead of important ones is because usually, urgent tasks are easier than important ones. Writing is difficult. It requires thought and concentration. But many urgent tasks require very little thought. Forms must be filled out, images must be added to lecture slides, emails must be answered, and so on. None of us feels like doing something hard (such as writing) when we could do something easy. So in the writing workshop, we are always looking for ways to make writing easier.

The third reason that urgent tasks get prioritized is called the mere urgency effect. Mere urgency—the feeling that time is running out—makes us want to do a task even if it's not really worth doing. If you are a parent, you've probably discovered the trick of counting to get compliance from young children. Saying, "Get down off that coffee table right now!" gets you nowhere. But saying, "Get down off that coffee table by the time I count to three: one, two . . . ," gets much better results.

The same principle seems to work for adults. In their article "The Mere Urgency Effect," Zhu et al. (2018) found that people tend to do urgent tasks rather than important ones even when there's no rational reason to:

> Results from five experiments demonstrate that people are more likely to perform unimportant tasks (i.e., tasks with objectively lower payoffs) over important tasks (i.e., tasks with objectively better payoffs), when the unimportant tasks are characterized merely by spurious urgency (e.g., an illusion of expiration). The mere urgency effect documented in this research violates the basic normative principle of dominance—choosing objectively worse options over objectively better options. People behave as if pursuing an urgent task has its own appeal, independent of its objective consequence (p. 1).

How do we counteract the mere urgency effect? By giving ourselves schedules and accountability for writing and by protecting our appointed writing time as seriously as we protect our time for teaching and other appointments.

In most academic jobs, nonresearch tasks fall into two major categories: teaching and service. To protect your time for important practices of writing and well-being, you will need to learn to say no.

I still remember the first meeting I ever had with a senior colleague who was, at the time, chair of my department. It was in the summer, just after I was hired.

The chair asked how long ago I'd arrived in town (I had moved from a postdoc in Boston), and I said six weeks.

"Six weeks?" He exclaimed, "You must be really anxious to get to work! Is your lab space set up? Do you have everything you need?"

I thanked him and explained that since my younger child was only 10 weeks old, I couldn't work very long hours anyway. (I was actually on maternity leave for the fall quarter.) I said, "He goes to daycare for a couple of hours every afternoon, but I don't really feel comfortable having him go longer than that yet. He's only two and a half months old."

The chair nodded and looked thoughtful. "Two and a half months . . . that's . . . yes, that's . . ." He frowned, suddenly alarmed. "That's very young to be in daycare!"

What?! I thought. A minute ago I wasn't setting up my lab fast enough, and now he's judging me for not being home with the baby? "Well," I explained slowly, as if to a small child, "If he wasn't there, I couldn't be here."

"My children didn't go to daycare until they were much older," he said firmly. "They were home."

"Mm-hmm," I said, trying not to throw my coffee at him. "And did you work full-time?"

"Yes, I worked!" He said. "I worked, and my wife stayed home with the kids." I searched his face for some trace of understanding, but there was nothing. He didn't see a problem. He believed that new assistant professors should work 60 hours a week, and he also believed that babies should be at home with their mommies. What's the problem? It had never been a problem for him.

"Well, my husband is not going to stay home with the kids," I said, "So we use daycare." I thanked him and left his office.

I had many experiences like this, with different people, at work and outside of it. I share the story not to make my colleague look bad (he's actually a lovely man) but to illustrate that I know what it's like to put on a game face at your academic job. To feel that you can't show weakness, even when you're suffering, because people don't understand what your life is like and if they knew what you were dealing with, they would judge you or lose respect for you.

STREAMLINE YOUR TEACHING

Over the course of your career, you will almost certainly make a bigger impact on people's lives through your teaching than through your research, so you want to do a good job. But between the time actually spent in class and the time spent on preparation, grading, office hours, answering student emails, etc., teaching can suck up all of your time. So you need to be smart about it. Here are a few time-saving tips to get you started.

A new prep (i.e., a class you are teaching for the first time) takes far, far more time than a class you've taught before. So if you have a choice, try to teach the same classes year after year.

In general, teaching prep will fill the amount of time available for it. So decide how much time you will spend, and stop when that time is up. That means you'll often go to class with lectures, assignments, and activities that are *good enough for now*, even if they're not as good as you'd like them to be. (You can always make improvements next time you teach the class.)

Instead of running your office hours on a drop-in basis, convert at least some of them to an appointment system using a free service such as YouCanBook.me, Square Appointments, or SimplyBook .me. This both discourages undergraduates from lingering pointlessly in your office and prevents them from showing up all at once, in an anxious horde, on the day before the paper is due.

Don't waste time writing line-by-line comments on student papers. When you have a lot of grading to do, create a rubric (Schuman, 2014). When you grade each paper, check boxes on the rubric and let the rubric determine a grade. (You can nudge it up or down as you see fit.) Give the rubric back to the student with the grade and a note saying, "If you would like more detailed feedback on the paper, I would be happy to provide it. Just make an appointment during my office hours."

ONLY TAKE ON SERVICE THAT SERVES YOUR PURPOSE

Service is work that helps your department, your campus, your community, or your profession but doesn't contribute to getting your own research done. This includes serving on committees, organizing department colloquia, reviewing for journals or funding agencies, etc. If time is money, service is charitable giving. And just as you can't give money to every worthy cause, you can't give your time to everyone who asks for it either. So only agree to service that is meaningful to you or that you will learn something useful from.

Be especially careful about taking on service commitments if you are a member of a group that's historically been underrepresented in the academy. Studies of large, nationally representative samples of faculty show that women perform significantly more service than men (Guarino & Borden, 2017) and that faculty of color, queer faculty, and faculty from working-class backgrounds spend a disproportionate amount of their time on service work, leaving less time for the work that matters for tenure and promotion (Social Sciences Feminist Network Research Interest Group, 2017).

Of course, avoiding unwanted service is easier said than done. If you are a pretenure faculty member, saying no to a service request typically means saying no to a senior colleague, which can be frightening. You might worry that if you say no, your colleagues will vote against your tenure case down the road. But you can get a reality check by asking around: Has anyone ever been denied tenure at your school for doing too little service? At most schools, the answer is no. The hard truth is that for academics, research productivity (and sometimes teaching, depending on the job) is valued above all else. If you can learn to tolerate a little social awkwardness by politely saying no to extra service, your career will benefit in the long run.

When we were assistant professors, my colleague Emily and I made a pact that neither of us would agree to do any service without first talking it over with the other person. I learned to say, "Let me think about it and get back to you," instead of just saying yes when someone asked me to serve on a committee or a grant panel. Then I'd forward the email to Emily and say, "Do you think I should do this?" Emily and I would talk about it: How much time would it take? Would I learn anything useful from it? For example, reviewing for federal funding agencies can take a lot of time, but it can also help you understand what those agencies are looking for, which is useful when you write your own grants. Often our conversations would go like this:

ME: *So, they're asking me to sit on this budget committee . . . I'm probably going to say yes, but we promised we'd check with each other, so . . .*

EMILY: *Do you want to do it?*

ME: *Do I . . . want to? . . . I mean . . . well no, of course I don't want to . . .*

EMILY: *How much time will it take?*

ME: *Well, they meet once a month for three years. Plus I'd probably have to read stuff before the meetings.*

EMILY: *Once a month for three years? Why are you saying yes to this?*

ME: *Umm . . . (considering for a moment) . . . because the budget committee is important? And . . . I guess . . . I'm flattered that they asked me?*

EMILY: *OK well, you can be flattered and still say no. They're not going to give you tenure for doing service. Look at [name of our colleague]. He's an obnoxious jerk, and he just got tenure. You think he did any service?*

ME: *Well . . . no. But only because no one wants to serve on a committee with him.*

EMILY: *Right!*

ME: *OK, but why do I have to be a jerk to get tenure? I can't stand [obnoxious colleague]. I don't want to be like him!*

EMILY: *You don't have to be a jerk, but you don't have to say yes to everything, either. You can say, "I'm sorry, I can't. I have too much on my plate right now. But thanks for thinking of me!"*

Looking back, I see how helpful those conversations were. More often than not, I was prepared to say yes to a request and Emily talked me out of it. And I did the same for her. I'm so grateful that we had each other during that early, stressful period of our careers. It's good to have a buddy.

ACCEPT THAT NOT ALL THE URGENT STUFF WILL GET DONE

This fact is, the list of urgent tasks never ends. If you try to get everything done, not only will you fail (because the list is infinite) but worse, you will not write. So you must decide how much time you will give to the urgent tasks and try not to give them any more time than that.

I've had the same schedule for years. I wake up in the morning and write in bed. Recently, I've been starting my day with "morning pages"—three pages of longhand freewriting—as a sort of writing-based meditation (Cameron, 2019). After the morning pages, I switch to work-related writing. I try to write for one hour on the project closest to publication. Then I get up, do a little yoga, and take my dogs for a walk, which is another chance for quiet reflection.

When I get back from the dog walk (typically around 10 or 11 a.m.), I eat breakfast and start on the urgent work. I check email, go over my schedule of teaching and meetings for the afternoon, and consult the to-do list. I start with the low-hanging fruit (high-priority tasks that can be finished quickly) and move on to high-priority tasks that take longer. I don't go in to campus until noon or later. (If I have no meetings or teaching, I don't go in at all.) Evenings are for family: I walk the dogs again, supervise homework, drive kids to activities, and make sure everybody eats.

Now you may be thinking, "That all sounds very sane and balanced, but I couldn't do all the urgent tasks on my list in that amount of time." My answer is, neither can I. Not all the urgent tasks get done. They get delegated to someone else, or put off until tomorrow, or to next week, or to never. The most important tasks always get done. But some tasks just aren't important enough to be worth my time, so they never get done. I can live with that.

I have to live with it. What's the alternative? There are only so many hours in a day, and if I wasn't willing to let any of the urgent stuff slide, I'd have to give up something else. I'd have to give up some of the time I'm spending on writing, or exercise, or sleep, or being with my family. But those tradeoffs wouldn't reflect my values.

Build your individual development plan

The term "individual development plan" (IDP) comes to academia from industry, where there is evidence that people who make deliberate career plans with specific, step-by-step goals go on to earn higher salaries, more promotions, and more responsibility in their jobs (Ng, Eby, Sorensen & Feldman, 2005). They also report feeling more satisfied and more successful in their careers than people who don't make such plans (Abele & Wiese, 2008). This is probably why the National Institutes of Health (NIH) strongly recommends that all graduate students and postdocs working on NIH-funded grants have IDPs and that the principal investigators describe the progress on those IDPs when they submit their annual Research Performance Progress Report (Rockey, 2013).

IDPs are especially important during periods of high uncertainty, such as when you are a postdoc. A study of 7,600 postdocs found that those who worked with their advisors to develop a plan for their own postdoctoral training were more productive, more satisfied with their jobs, and less likely to experience conflict with their advisors than those who didn't make a plan (Davis, 2005). Plans provide structure; the less structured your job is, the more you need a plan.

––––––

In our Graduate Writing Workshop, we set aside time during our first meeting each term to make our IDPs and term plans together. We set a timer for 45 minutes per plan and just do it. It may seem like an odd use of class time, but we've found that if we don't make these plans together, most people won't make them at all. There is something anxiety-provoking about making an IDP and a term plan if you've never done it before—people tend to get overwhelmed with details and give up. When we do it together, we emphasize that the point is just to sketch things out. Put down whatever you can put down in 45 minutes, and fill in the details later. When we do it this way, everyone seems to get through it just fine, and everyone leaves the meeting with an IDP and a term plan.

KEEP YOUR LONG-TERM GOALS IN SIGHT

An IDP is useful for anyone who has to plan their work, but especially for people in tenure-track jobs. If you will be facing a tenure decision down the road, you want to spend most of your work time on activities that count toward tenure at your institution and on those projects that will pay off (in the form of publications or grants) in time to be counted for your tenure case. You don't just need to work hard; you need to allocate your time and energy efficiently. An IDP that covers the period from now until you submit your tenure case can help you do that.

I update my IDP when we cover this lesson in the writing workshop and throughout the year as needed. Making an IDP helps me stop and reflect on my priorities. As I mentioned earlier, I started my first faculty job (the job I still have) just one week before my second child was born. For the next seven years, between trying to get tenure and raising two kids, I was so busy that time passed in a blur, and now I hardly remember those years. I'm very glad to have tenure and my kids, but life is short and I don't want any more years to pass in a blur. I want to be thoughtful about how I spend my time.

Your IDP is a rough plan—just a sketch, really—of the work you'd like to do over the next few years. It's not specific or detailed; it's just a list of the most important projects you plan to work on, and when. The IDP in Figure 2.1 shows three research projects in various stages of completion. (If you are a new PhD student, you might have only one project, and that's just fine.)

The columns on the IDP show academic terms. Feel free to use semesters, quarters, or whatever your university uses. IDPs typically cover at least one year, and no more than five. Yours can cover whatever number of years makes sense for you. For example, you might want your IDP to show the period from now until you finish your PhD program, or until you get tenure. If you will be applying for jobs soon, your IDP might only cover the next year or two, because it's hard to plan when you don't know yet where you will be.

Figure 2.1 shows the IDP of a PhD student who does experimental science and has three projects in the pipeline. The project called "Reusable Hairy Bottom-Dwellers" is well underway: The data have been collected and the next step is to analyze those data, write the paper and submit it for publication. The second project, "Randomized Snail Deception," is still in the piloting stage. The third project, "Folk Dancing Intervention," is a new study that the student has been thinking about but hasn't started working on yet. These three studies are represented on the IDP as three rows, with the project closest to publication at the top. This student also plans

		2019			
		Winter	**Spring**	**Summer**	**Fall**
PROJECTS	**Reusable Hairy Bottom-Dwellers**	Data analyses, start writing	Finish writing & submit	Revise & resubmit	
	Randomized snail deception	Finalize design for Experiment 1, get IRB approval	Collect data for Exp 1, design Exps 2 & 3	Collect data for Exps 2 & 3, analyze data from Exp 1, start drafting paper	Analyze data from Exps 2 & 3, add to paper, submit.
	Folk dancing intervention			Design study & submit IRB paperwork	Start writing phase I of registered report after Randomized Snail Deception is submitted
OTHER	**PhD program requirements**	Advance to candidacy			
	Career		Apply for summer internships in industry	Internship?	

Figure 2.1

to advance to candidacy (a milestone that happens around the third year in most North American PhD programs) in the upcoming term and to apply for internships for the upcoming summer.

Keep in mind that the IDP doesn't *commit* you to anything. You can always change it later. You can change it tomorrow, and again the day after that, and again every day for the next five years if you want to. The only purpose of the IDP is to help you think through what your major work projects are, roughly what steps will be required for each of them, and which of them you will work on first.

DIFFERENTIATE PLANS FROM WISHES

The most important rule of planning is that your plan can only include things that are within your control. If you lose sight of this rule, you are likely to make yourself miserable trying to control things you can't.

Research is creative, which means there is built-in uncertainty. No one can predict when discoveries or insights will occur. You can spend 10 hours working on a paper and feel that you are no closer to finishing it than when you started. Of course that's not true—you are actually 10 hours closer. But because you don't know how long the whole thing will take, it's hard to see progress.

Your plan can only include things that are within your control.

You also can't control what other people think or do. Even if I'm in a big hurry to get a project done, I can't make the Institutional Review Board of my university approve my research design any faster. I can't make my collaborators do their part any sooner or any better. I certainly can't make reviewers like the work.

All this uncertainty and lack of control is stressful. One can't help but wonder: *Will I think of any good ideas? Will I be able to produce good research? Will I get a PhD? Will I get a job?* The uncertainty makes us afraid, and often we cope by pushing ourselves harder. Or we might cope by avoiding thinking about work altogether. The problem is that no matter how hard we work or avoid work, the uncertainty doesn't go away. So we must find a way to make peace with the possibility that we might flunk out, or produce only bad ideas, or never publish a word, or be unemployed for the rest of our lives, or whatever it is that we are afraid of.

In the writing workshop we deal with these possibilities by acknowledging them. When we make our IDPs and term plans, we distinguish between plans (things that are within our control) and wishes (things that are not in our control). Only things that are within our control can go on the IDP and term plan. All we can do is use the time we have, as best we can.

On any given day, the only thing you can control is how you spend your time. You can't control how long things take to get finished, you can't control how good they are, and you certainly can't control what other people think of them.

FIND OUT WHAT IS EXPECTED OF YOU

If you are a student or postdoc, make an appointment with your advisor to discuss your IDP and make sure they agree that your plan is a good one. Particularly if you are a PhD student, your advisor and your grad program have implicit expectations about the amount of work you will produce before you graduate. These expectations vary widely from one field to the next, and you need to know what they are.

If you are in a field where researchers publish empirical journal articles, ask how many articles you should be aiming to complete during graduate school. In my field, three articles is a good target number. Most people don't have three articles actually accepted for publication by the time they graduate, and occasionally someone has more than three accepted, but three is a reasonable number of projects to have underway.

In many areas of the biological and natural sciences and engineering, publications are shorter and may have many more authors, and people publish much more frequently than we do in psychology. In the humanities, the opposite is true: Publications are long (often books, rather than articles) and almost always single-authored.

Of course these generalities are subject to a thousand exceptions, so don't take my word for it. Talk to your advisor. If you are an advisor, talk to your students and postdocs. Help them get a general sense of how much time you think it should take to do the kind of work you do and how much work you expect them to complete during their time with you.

Build your term plan

After making your IDP, you are ready to build your term plan. Term plans have the same general structure as IDPs, except that they take the goals for this term (from the IDP) and break them down into weekly goals. Figure 2.2 shows an example of a term plan. Only a few columns are shown so that the figure will fit on the

ABCD: Always Be Collecting Data!		Goals for Fall 2019	UCI Week 1	UCI Week 2	UCI Week 3
			30-Sep	7-Oct	14-Oct
PROJECTS	Reusable Hairy Bottom-Dwellers	Data analyses, start writing	Preliminary analyses	Meet with advisor to go over preliminary analyses; do additional analyses	Draft method section
	Randomized snail deception	Finalize design for Experiment 1, get IRB approval		Meet with advisor about Exp 1 design; submit IRB paperwork	(Allow 2 weeks for IRB)
OTHER	PhD program requirements	Advance to candidacy	Meet with advisor to discuss requirements for advancement and who should be on committee. Email faculty to invite to committee	Create doodle poll to collect faculty availability for meeting	Schedule advancement meeting for late Nov. / early Dec.

Figure 2.2

page. A real term plan should have a column for each week of the semester or quarter.

List your term goals in order of priority. Writing and research goals come first, but if you also want to list other kinds of work, that's fine. As in the IDP, the highest priority is the project closest to publication (or submission, in the case of funding proposals).

Note that the term plan doesn't include every project on the IDP, only the ones that have goals for the current term. For example, the project "Folk Dancing Intervention" from the IDP in Figure 2.1 is not on this term plan. The term plan can also include things that are not on the IDP but that you want to keep in mind when setting your goals for each week. Perhaps you know that there are weeks when you will be traveling, or your children will be out of school, or you will have a million papers to grade. You can note those things on the term plan to help you estimate how much research and writing you will be able to do.

USE YOUR DEADLINES

A few years ago, the Geosciences arm of the National Science Foundation (NSF) was struggling to cope with all the grant proposals it had to process. Submissions always spiked before a deadline, so the folks at NSF decided to try eliminating deadlines and let people submit proposals whenever they wanted. The result? Submissions dropped by 59%! Without a deadline, more than half of would-be applicants never turned in a grant proposal at all (Hand, 2016).

It makes perfect sense that many of us in academia rely on external deadlines to structure our time. Deadlines have, it is said, a wonderfully concentrating effect on the mind. The problem with relying too much on external deadlines is that most research projects don't have them. If you are writing a grant, the funding agency may have deadlines. If you are writing a book, you may be able to negotiate a series of writing deadlines with the publisher. But the regular research and writing that you do probably doesn't have any deadlines. So if you don't know how to *set deadlines for yourself,* you'll struggle to produce enough work. That's why you need a term plan.

The most important things to put on your term plan are your own research and writing projects. But you may have other work you want to plan as well. The examples above include a goal of advancing to candidacy in a PhD program; the term plan helps you think through the steps required to do that. You may need to ask faculty members to serve on your advancement committee, schedule a time and place for the advancement meeting, make sure you have met all of your department's requirements for advancement, and so on. You may have to write an advancement proposal of some kind that will be sent to your committee members at least two weeks before the meeting so they have time to read it. Or perhaps you will need to write a talk to give at the advancement meeting. Whatever you have to do, you can use the term plan to think through it in a calm, organized way.

If you are applying for jobs this term, there's plenty of work to do: asking for letters of recommendation, revising and getting feedback on your application materials, keeping track of application deadlines, and so on. You can use your term plan to list all of these things and think about when (in which week of the term) you want to do them.

BE GENTLE WITH YOURSELF

Most of us greatly underestimate how long tasks will take. A good rule of thumb is to take your first guess and multiply it by a factor of 2.5. In other words, if you think it will take you one week to draft a conference abstract, try to give yourself two and a half weeks. Over time, as you see what actually gets done in a day, a week, or a summer, you can adjust your plans accordingly.

You should also revisit your term plan every month or so, because they do tend to go off the rails. In our writing workshop, we make a new term plan at the beginning of each 10-week quarter. We update the plans in the middle of the quarter (about five weeks later), and we reflect on them at the end. We are well aware that things never go as planned. We often mention the Prussian military strategist Helmuth von Moltke the Elder, who said that no plan survives contact with the enemy (Hughes & Bell, 1993). In this case the enemy is real life, always messing up our plans.

You may wonder: If plans always change, why do we bother making them at all? The answer is that the process of planning itself is very valuable. It's where we take time to think about what our priorities are and what steps we need to reach our goals. As another adage made famous by Dwight D. Eisenhower goes: "Plans are worthless, but planning is everything" (garson, 2017).

SET GOALS THAT ARE SPECIFIC AND MEASURABLE

Planning works in a feedback loop: You make a plan, try to carry it out, reflect on what did and didn't work, and use this information to make your next plan. This feedback process can't happen if you don't know whether you achieved your goal or not.

That's why it's important to set goals that are specific and measurable (Locke, Shaw, Saari & Latham, 1981). For example, perhaps one of your goals for this term is to review the literature on changes in French rural life after World War II. But there's always more literature out there to review, so you'll never really be done. The solution is to put specific, measurable weekly goals on your term plan. For example,

| Week 1 | Make a reading list of papers and books on mid-20th century French life; schedule meeting with advisor to go over the list. |
| Weeks 2-10 | Review 10 papers or book chapters per week (two papers per day, Monday through Friday), write one paragraph of |

Plans are worthless, but planning is everything.

> notes about each paper or chapter, just summarizing the main ideas; keep the notes and reading list in Zotero library.

Planning involves a lot of guessing, which does get easier after a while. For each goal, think about the steps that it will require and how long those steps will take. Then assign the steps to weeks of the term.

For example, let's say that your IDP includes the goal "Submit Paper X" for this term. Let's further assume that you are a scientist, and Paper X has an IMRaD format (introduction, method, results, and discussion). You've already completed data collection and analysis, and you have a draft of the introduction and method sections. So the work you have left is to draft the results and discussion and then revise the whole paper. For your term plan, you make those steps explicit and assign them a timeline.

How much you can write in a week depends on all sorts of things, so just take your best guess until you get used to planning. Some people aim for 20 lines per day; others for one or two pages per day; still others for 5,000 words per week. Please set whatever goals seem reasonable to you, and then adjust them up or down based on how much you actually get done. After a few weeks, if you're usually meeting or exceeding your goals, you can update your plan to be more ambitious. If you are usually falling short (which is far more common) you can update your plan with more modest goals.

DISCUSS YOUR TERM PLAN WITH A MENTOR

If you are a graduate student or a postdoc, it's a very good idea to schedule an appointment with your advisor to go over your term plan. Make sure that you are in agreement about the work you are going to do this term. Many bad experiences with advisors stem from confusion about what is expected.

Your advisor may also have some insight into whether your plan is realistic. For example, if you have given yourself two weeks to collect data and your advisor knows that it will take at least two months, they can tell you that. Plus, walking into your advisor's office with a term plan makes you seem organized and independent.

Even if you are no longer a student, discussing your term plan with a trusted colleague can be helpful—particularly if you are in a job where your colleagues will vote on your personnel case. If you discuss your research plans with a senior colleague, that person will learn about your research and can become your ally. Later, when your personnel case is discussed at a faculty meeting and you aren't in the room, that person can advocate for you.

Build your weekly plan

In our writing workshop, we begin each meeting with a period of quiet writing time. People use this time to make their calendar for the week, or just to write. When you first start making a weekly calendar, you may want to allocate as much as half an hour to work on it. But once you get in the habit of doing it, the whole process takes only a couple of minutes. To start, you just need a blank calendar and your to-do list, which may be in your head, on scraps of paper, in an app on your phone, or wherever you keep it. Planning your week is necessary not only for work productivity, but also for health and well-being. This is the time to prioritize things that really matter to you.

BLOCK OUT TIME FOR SLEEP

Sleep is essential. Most adults ages 18-64 need around seven to nine hours per night, and ideally you should go to bed and get up around the same time every day (Hirshkowitz et al., 2015). Of course there is some individual variation, but if you always need an alarm to wake up, you're probably not getting enough sleep. And if you're sleeping for a lot more than nine hours a day, you may be depressed or physically ill.

When you have a lot to do, it's tempting to use some of your nighttime hours to get caught up on work. Resist that temptation. The effects of sleep debt on cognitive function are well documented: When you get less sleep than you need, your thinking is measurably impaired. People whose sleep has been restricted show slower reaction times and poorer performance on measures of attention, working memory, long-term memory, decision making, motivation, visuomotor performance, response inhibition and a host of other cognitive measures (Alhola & Polo-Kantola, 2007; Killgore, 2010). One study summarized the effects of sleep restriction by comparing them to the effects of alcohol:

> After 17–19 hours without sleep . . . performance on some tests was equivalent or worse than that at a BAC [blood alcohol concentration] of 0.05%. Response speeds were up to 50% slower for some tests and accuracy measures were significantly poorer than at this level of alcohol. After longer periods without sleep, performance reached levels equivalent to the maximum alcohol dose given to subjects (BAC of 0.1%). (Williamson & Feyer, 2000, p. 649)

If you ask graduate students (or any professionals in high-stress careers) about their sleep schedules, you will find many who insist that they don't need much sleep. They'll say, "I function just fine on four hours a night." Individuals differ, of course, but keep in mind that your ability to gauge your own functioning is impaired by lack of sleep—so if your performance is impaired, you probably don't know it. The only way to really know how much sleep you need is to go to bed without setting an alarm and see what time you wake up naturally. (If you are sleep deprived, you may have to do this for a few days to get caught up on your sleep before you can get an accurate measure.) If you're having trouble sleeping, a good place to start is by keeping a sleep log, which can give you a sense of what's really going on at night. The National Sleep Foundation has a good free one available on their website, along with a list of healthy sleep tips.

The bottom line is this: Humans need sleep. When we don't get enough, the first thing to suffer is our high-level cognitive functioning. So if you are a human with a job that depends on thinking, don't shortchange yourself on sleep.

SET ASIDE TIME FOR PLAY

Play is anything you do purely for the pleasure of doing it. If you are obliged to do something, it's not play. If you are doing it as a means to an end, as a way of achieving or accomplishing something else, it's not play. Children suffer greatly when they are deprived of play, but even for adults, play is necessary for health and well-being.

The difference between work and play is more about the circumstances of what you're doing than the activity itself. Take cooking, for example. Cooking can be enjoyable and relaxing if you are free to cook when and what you want. But when you come home exhausted at the end of a long workday and have to get dinner on the table for tired and cranky children, it definitely feels like work.

Creative intellectual work is extremely demanding. It requires sustained mental effort over a period of years. People know that they can't drive across the country without stopping for gas; they know that they can't use their phones for a week without recharging them. So why do people imagine that they can work all the time without resting? They can't. If they try to, their mental and physical health will suffer. In particular, two forms of play that are very worthwhile are exercise and social interaction.

DECIDE WHEN YOU WILL EXERCISE

The brain is part of the body, and exercise makes the brain work better—particularly the parts of the brain that are responsible for sustained concentration and abstract thought. People who get moderate exercise score higher on tests of executive function (Yaffe et al., 2001), learning and memory (Berchtold et al., 2010) and attention (Budde et al, 2008) than people who don't exercise. As we age, exercise seems to protect our brains from cognitive decline (Barnes, et al., 2003; Kramer et al., 1999; Van Boxtel et al., 1997). If you are a scholar, saying that you don't have time to exercise because you're too busy working is like saying you don't have time to put gas in your car because you're too busy driving.

In addition to its cognitive benefits, exercise helps combat anxiety and depression. Both aerobic and anaerobic exercise are helpful, and you don't even have to exercise a lot (Blumenthal et al., 2007; Jayakody, Gunadasa & Hosker, 2014; Penedo & Dahn, 2005). Go for a walk around campus with a friend at lunchtime; do a couple of push-ups as soon as you get out of bed; take the stairs instead of the elevator. Exercise is cheap, effective, and free of side effects.

Just to be clear: If you are grappling with acute anxiety or depression, you should seek help from a therapist or doctor. Exercise by itself is not a substitute for psychotherapy or medication. But it can be a useful add-on to those things, and it can help all of us stay healthier and happier over the long term.

ENSURE THAT YOU INTERACT

The academic life is isolating. Many people move to a new place for graduate school, move again to take a postdoc position, and move a third time to start a job. Each time, they leave behind the friends they made in their previous location. But humans are deeply social animals, and friendly social interactions are essential (not desirable, *essential*) for our health and well-being (Lin, Ye & Ensel, 1999).

A big reason to join a writing workshop is to give and receive social support around the challenges of academic writing. But you also need social interaction in your life generally. If you live with a friend or romantic partner, you may have social connection built into your day, which is wonderful. But note that being a caregiver to children or others does not count as social interaction. It does not support your mental health in the way that friendships do (Kawachi & Berkman, 2001).

If you don't live with friends, make it a point to cultivate friendly interactions during the day. These don't have to be deep friendships—even casual social interactions contribute to well-being (Epley & Schroeder, 2104; Sandstrom & Dunn, 2014). If you're walking out of the building to get a cup of coffee and you walk past a colleague in their office, pause in the doorway and say hello. Ask if they want to walk with you to get coffee. You don't have to talk about anything deep or personal. Just walk to the cafe, stand in line together, get your coffee, and walk back to the office. You did it—social interaction!

Yes, this can be awkward. The culture of many academic departments is so grim, serious, and judgmental that you may feel self-conscious even inviting someone for coffee. If you're a graduate student, chances are that a lot of your peers are at least mildly depressed, which can make socializing difficult even if they're lonely. And particularly among new graduate students, insecurity often leads to posturing, where people try to present themselves as more competent or successful than they actually feel. But despite all that, your university is probably full of decent, thoughtful, smart people. Make an effort to get to know a few of them.

COMBINE YOUR TO-DO LIST AND FIXED COMMITMENTS

If you feel overwhelmed by the number of items on your to-do list, try assigning each task a priority (A, B, or C) and also an estimate of how much time the task will take to complete. Priority A tasks that won't take long are low-hanging fruit; do them right away. Then move on to Priority A tasks that will take longer. When all the Priority A tasks are done, move on to Priority B, again starting with the tasks that can be finished soonest. Keep going until you run out of time.

Quick to-do items may not need to be written on the calendar. But if a task will take half an hour or more, you'll probably need to designate a specific time to do it, or it will never get done.

A fixed commitment is anything that requires you to be in a specific place at a specific time. This includes classes, meetings, office hours, times when you must drop off or pick up children, and so on. These structure your time, so they need to be on your weekly calendar too.

Putting your to-do list on the same calendar as your structured time allows you to find synergies between the two, such as when you can knock off an item on your to-do list on the way to a fixed commitment.

DECIDE WHEN YOU WILL WRITE

If you don't consciously make time for writing, you probably won't write. Urgent tasks will expand to fill all the time you have available. You can start to reclaim your days by setting aside time—as little as five or ten minutes a day—to do even a little bit of writing. It may seem like you can't write much in five or ten minutes a day. But every time you sit down and open a document and start writing, you overcome the barrier to starting, and you change your relationship to writing by a tiny bit. If you only have the energy to make one change, focus on writing every day, even if it's only for a couple of minutes. For many years, the slogan I repeated to myself to help me stay focused on this goal was, "Either you wrote today, or you didn't." If I wrote, it was a good day, even if I only wrote one sentence.

As mentioned in the previous chapter, writing little and often is better than binge writing. To be clear, there's nothing wrong with writing for many hours in a row if you have time for it, and if you are writing regularly. But for many people, binge writing means hours or days of writing, interspersed with weeks, months, or years of not writing. Writing little and often helps you overcome the resistance that leads to the long dry spells. In practical terms, it's also much easier to find ten 15-minute time slots in a busy week than one 150-minute time slot. So if possible, resolve to write every day and block out time for it on your calendar.

The easiest way to make sure you write every day is just to write before you do anything else. Many people write before they even get out of bed in the morning, but not everyone is a morning person. Some people wake up feeling antsy and have too much nervous energy to write, but if they go for a run or a bike ride, they can write afterward. Other people feel groggy in the morning and prefer to do less-demanding tasks for the first hour or two after they wake up. Some people swear they work best late at night. Please experiment to find what works best for you.

Whenever you decide it will be, once you've scheduled your writing time, protect it as seriously as you protect the other appointments on your calendar. If you were scheduled to give a lecture at 10 a.m. and a colleague asked you to meet at that time, you would say no. Try to do the same with your writing time. It's just as important and deserves the same respect.

3

THE PRACTICE OF WRITING

Consider two metaphors for writing. In the first, writing is mining. Ideas and written products are resources to be extracted, destroying the earth in the process. If you think this way about writing, you will interpret your own exhaustion and depletion as evidence that you are working effectively. When your rate of production is slow, it will seem that you should dig deeper, work harder, punish yourself more. The mine metaphor can pervade a whole discipline. If ideas are a nonrenewable resource, everyone will try to hoard them. Researchers will see each other as competitors and suspect each other of stealing. In the back of everyone's mind will be the fear that eventually, all the resources (all the ideas, all the insights, all the knowledge) in a given area will be depleted.

Now consider an alternative metaphor: Writing is gardening. Just as a gardener works regularly to water and weed and prune the garden, a writer works regularly on projects. Knowledge, and written products such as articles and proposals, are the fruit of this garden. Knowledge is a renewable resource, generated in the process of writing itself. Opportunities to discuss the work with others are welcome, because creativity is enhanced by the exchange of ideas. Early drafts are not expected to be perfect; ideas take time to ripen and some projects take years to bear fruit. When production slows, the solution is not punishment but nurturing. When a tomato plant isn't growing well, a gardner doesn't say, "Shame on you for being unproductive! No more water for you until you produce a tomato!" Instead, the gardner looks for ways to enrich the soil and take care of the plant better. This is the most important implication of deciding to treat writing as gardening rather than mining. This chapter is about how to cultivate a regular writing practice. It connects the long-term and weekly planning processes introduced in the last chapter with principles you can apply daily.

Question your beliefs about writing

Let's start by examining some beliefs that make it difficult to establish and nurture a regular writing practice. When people join the writing workshop and are persuaded to try writing *little and often*, these wrong perceptions gradually dissipate.

WRITE LIKE A NINJA

"I can't do anything in less than two hours," people say. "I spend the first hour just looking over what I wrote before and trying to remember what I was doing." When people don't have a regular writing practice, they often avoid working on a given project for weeks or months. Then, when they finally return to it, it takes them a while to remember what they were doing. But that doesn't happen when you write more often. When you work on a project regularly, it takes no time at all to remember where you were and pick up your train of thought again.

Similarly, many people put off writing until they face a deadline. Then, because they underestimate how long the writing will take, they end up working for hours on end, or through the night. For some reason, the lesson they take from this is not *If I had worked on this for 30 minutes a day starting last month, the results would be better and I wouldn't have missed a night's sleep.* Instead they think, *I write in all-night binges because that's just the kind of intense, creative genius I am.*

This illustrates the way that people stop using their common sense when they think about writing. If you were told on June 1 that you had to walk 90 miles by June 30, would you choose to walk three miles a day for 30 days, or would you wait until the evening of June 30 and try to walk the whole 90 miles at once? If you wanted to buy something for $10,000, would you start putting aside a little bit of money every week, or would you hope to one day find $10,000 just lying around?

It's not that writing for long periods of time *per se* is bad. There are famous writers who claim to lock themselves in a room and work solidly for 18 months before emerging with a finished manuscript. If that's possible for you—if you are retired or independently wealthy, for example—then by all means, write that way. But most academic writers simply don't have the luxury of writing in long, uninterrupted chunks of time. We have classes; we have meetings; we have family responsibilities. If we can't write in short chunks of time, we won't get many chances to write.

The most prolific writers do what we in the workshop call **ninja writing**—writing in sneaky little sessions of 10 or 15 minutes throughout the day. It's a good idea to set aside some time for writing in your calendar and supplement it with ninja writing whenever you have a few minutes free. Many people find that once they've done some writing on a given day, it's relatively easy to go back later in the day and do more.

WRITE WITHOUT INSPIRATION

Some stories that people tell about writing feature a mysterious force called *inspiration*. To be inspired literally means to be "breathed into," as in the story of Genesis, where God breathes life into Adam. The thing about inspiration is that it's completely outside our control. Who are we to resist the will of the gods? "I can't schedule my writing—I have to be inspired," people sometimes tell me, shrugging helplessly.

The fact is, writing is sometimes easy and sometimes hard. Sometimes it's fun and sometimes it's a slog. Everyone loves to write when it feels easy, when they are excited about what they're writing, when they like the results—in other words, when they feel inspired. At other times, writing is less fun. But professional writers, including academics, do it anyway.

Yesterday at 2 p.m. I had to give an undergraduate lecture about how Freud and Erikson influenced modern developmental psychology. Did I feel like giving that lecture? Did I look forward to uttering the phrases "oral fixation" and "penis envy" in front of 130 nineteen-year-olds? No, I did not. In fact, I felt downright uninspired. But at 1:45, I got up from my desk, walked across campus to the lecture hall and gave the damn lecture—because it's my job.

It really is the same with writing. If writing is a hobby for you, feel free to wait for inspiration. But if writing is your job, you can't afford to do it only when it's easy and pleasant. You can write without feeling inspired, just like you can teach, grade papers, attend meetings, and answer email without feeling inspired. Inspiration is lovely, but it's not a requirement.

———

Thirty years ago, the psychologist Robert Boice (1983; summarized in 1990, pp. 82-84) conducted a small but influential study on academic writing and inspiration. He recruited college professors who were having trouble writing and finishing projects and randomly assigned them to one of three conditions. Professors in Condition 1 agreed told to avoid "all but emergency writing" for the 10 weeks of the study. Those in Condition 2 scheduled 50 writing sessions, but were told that they should only write during those times if they were in the mood. Those in Condition 3 also scheduled 50 sessions of writing and were told that they should write during those times no matter what kind of mood they were in. (To motivate them, Boice had them make out checks for $15 and told them that if they didn't write, he would send the checks to organizations they hated.) Each participant met with Boice weekly to report how many pages they had written, and they also kept track of the number of new creative ideas they had.

Boice found that participants who were assigned to write on schedule *even when not in the mood* produced both more writing and more ideas. Those in Condition 1 (abstaining from all but emergency writing) wrote an average of 0.2 pages per day and had a new idea only every five days. Those in Condition 2 (writing on schedule, but only if they felt like it) wrote 0.9 pages per day and had a new idea every two days. Those in Condition 3 (writing on schedule whether they felt like it or not) produced 3.2 pages per day and had *a new idea every day*. Inspiration is simply not as necessary as people think.

WRITE TO FIND OUT WHAT YOU WANT TO SAY

The incorrect assumption here is that writing and thinking are separate. In reality, writing is a form of thinking. And it's often better than the kind of thinking that happens only in your head. When you think without writing, the amount of information you can manipulate is strictly limited by your working memory. When you write, you can work with much more information because you can trap it on the page and it won't disappear in a couple of seconds, the way information in your working memory does. In this way, writing adds to your cognitive capacity. It's like digging with a shovel instead of with your hands. If you don't know what your argument is, start writing and find out.

To illustrate this point, consider the work of Dean Simonton, who studies intelligence, creativity, talent, and genius. He has spent decades analyzing patterns of productivity by scientists and artists. One of the most robust findings in his work is the "equal-odds rule" (or "equal-odds principle"), described by cognitive psychologist Michael Martinez as follows:

> Among the more surprising of Simonton's findings is that high levels of professional recognition, or eminence, are strongly a function of overall productivity. This contrasts with a more intuitive belief that highly acclaimed scholars receive recognition for every work that they produce. That is not the overall pattern. Instead, Simonton found that the probability of producing a highly recognized work product, such as an influential research article, is roughly the same for all contributors, whether eminent or not. This is what Simonton called the equal-odds principle. What distinguishes highly

eminent scholars is the overall volume of works they produce. By sheer dint of productivity, those who reach professional eminence stack the odds in their favor of producing another masterpiece. (p. 224)

Simonton's equal-odds rule says that mathematically, no one seems to have better ideas than anyone else—it's just that some people produce *more* ideas than others: more great ideas, more terrible ideas, more average ideas. Imagine that all the ideas yet to be born are in a normal distribution from terrible to brilliant, and every new idea by every person is drawn randomly from that distribution. No matter who you are, every one of your ideas has an equal chance of being the greatest or the worst one in history, and of course most ideas fall somewhere in between.

If having ideas is like rolling dice, then the way to produce as many high rolls as possible is just to roll the dice as many times as you can. Similarly, the way to produce brilliant ideas is just to produce as many ideas as you can and pursue the ones that seem best. If another researcher has had three times as many deep insights as you, they've also had three times as many mediocre observations and three times as many foolish notions. (You never saw those, because they weren't published.) So don't just generate one idea; generate a dozen. Pick the best ones to develop further and forget the rest. What's the best way to generate ideas? By writing.

DECIDE WHAT COUNTS AS WRITING FOR YOU

At this point in the discussion, someone usually asks what counts as writing. You are the boss of you, so you can decide what you will count as writing. But as a starting point, here are the criteria that many in our workshop use.

Definitely writing

An activity is definitely writing if it involves generating words and sentences that will lead (however indirectly) to publications and funding proposals with your name on them. This includes free-writing; taking notes on literature; drafting; outlining; revising; preparing conference posters and talks; making figures; proofreading; responding to reviewer comments; and writing up results that probably won't make it into the paper just to think them through.

Activities that count as writing if you're tempted to avoid them

There are also activities that you may decide to count as writing or not, depending on how you feel about them. If you find these things easy to do, and you are tempted to do them instead of the tasks on the first list, then you probably shouldn't count them as writing. But if you find them difficult or you tend to avoid them, then go ahead and count them as writing to help motivate yourself. Some examples: designing and programming experiments; writing and debugging code; collecting and analyzing data.

Definitely not writing

Activities that don't get you any closer to submitting a publication or proposal definitely should not count as writing. Some examples: teaching preparation; grading; email; writing letters of recommendation; committee work (reviewing job applicants, writing up personnel cases, etc.); reviewing (manuscripts for journals, grant proposals for funding agencies, etc.).

CONSIDER HOW MUCH WRITING TIME IS ENOUGH

The minimal goal of just writing every day is the most important one for building your writing practice. Still, it's likely that some readers will want a guideline for how much writing is enough. If you feel that way, aim to work for one hour a day on the project closest to publication. Except for crunch times, such as when you have a grant proposal due, one hour of actual writing a day is plenty to keep you on track throughout an academic career.

Before I ever started the writing workshop, I spent years trying to figure out how much writing was enough. Twenty years ago, my goal was to do 10 hours of writing per week—two hours a day, Monday through Friday. I almost never met that goal. Day after day, I would fail to write for two hours. At the end of the day, I'd vow to make up the missed time on the following day, only to fall short again. I felt constantly disappointed, ashamed, and angry with myself.

Instead of having compassion for myself and asking what was really preventing me from writing as much as I wanted, I blamed myself. Periodically I panicked, sure that I wasn't getting enough work done and was going to fail. (When I was a grad student, I'd think I was not going to get a PhD. When I was a postdoc, I'd think I was not going to get a job. When I was an assistant professor, I'd think I was not going to get tenure.) I would direct these anxieties into some new resolution to write more (Three hours a day! Four hours a day!) and the whole cycle would start over again. I was like a person who goes on a strict diet and then eats something prohibited and is filled with self-loathing and self-punishment. It was a miserable, unhealthy way to live.

I don't know exactly when things started to change for me. Maybe it was after I got tenure and my fears subsided, allowing me to see things more clearly; maybe it's because of the practices we tried out over the years in the writing workshop. I actually think that I started the writing workshop in part because I wanted to figure out a better, healthier way to do things. But whatever the causes, I'm in a completely different place with my writing practice now.

Over the past few years, as I've learned to prioritize and protect my writing time, to write little and often, to practice self-compassion and follow the other practices described in this book, I've spent more and more time writing. I routinely log 20 or 30 hours a week of writing now, which would have been unthinkable 10 years ago. A big reason, it must be said, is that my kids have gotten older. (Little kids suck up unbelievable amounts of time and energy.) But I think another reason is that I've stopped wasting so much time and energy beating myself up. When I stopped blaming and punishing myself, I actually became far more productive.

I write a lot now because I genuinely enjoy it and look forward to it. I find myself writing throughout the day—first thing in the morning, last thing in the evening, while the quiche is in the oven, while I wait to pick up my kids, ~~during faculty meetings and department colloquia~~, whenever I have a few minutes. Writing now feels like the easiest and most enjoyable part of my job. On days when I can't write very much (e.g., when I'm at a conference) I miss it. I'm telling you this in the hope that you won't have to spend 20 years punishing yourself like I did. Judgment and blame don't make anything grow better—not your garden, not your child, and not your writing practice.

Draft with kindness

There is an old joke in the U.S. Navy that goes, "The beatings will continue until morale improves." When we imagine that having less compassion for ourselves will make us more creative, we are following the same reasoning. When we encounter resistance in our efforts to write, instead of taking better care of ourselves, our impulse is to berate ourselves for being lazy, disorganized, undisciplined, or untalented. But beating ourselves up in this way just makes it even harder to write.

The beatings will continue until morale improves.

When it's time to write, you may be seized by a strong impulse to do something else. Please think of your resistance as a friendly monster, who loves you and is trying to protect you. It knows that writing makes you vulnerable. Whatever you write is sure to be judged and criticized, and that's scary. Your friendly resistance monster knows that if you don't write, you can't be judged.

Your resistance monster wants to protect you, above all, from the pain of not being good enough. So the key to getting started is to redefine what is "good enough" for today. I'm not saying that you should care less about your career or about the quality of your work in the long run. I'm saying that if you're having trouble writing *today*, the answer is to lower your expectations for *today's* writing.

LOWER THE QUANTITY: WRITE JUST A LITTLE

A good way to get started is to pick one very small, easy thing to do. Remember that *any* writing is enough to let you put a "yes" on the shared daily writing log. For example, edit the caption for one figure; add one in-text citation; change one word in the abstract.

———

My favorite thing to do when I'm really struggling is to set a timer for five minutes and commit to writing for just that long. A curious thing often happens: Although I have frequent impulses to quit writing (especially at the beginning), they don't happen to coincide with the end of the timer, so I keep going. My thought process goes something like this:

> *9:05 p.m.. Ugh, look at the time! The whole day has gone by and I haven't done any writing. Why didn't I write first thing in the morning? I'm way too tired to write now . . . I will just have to put a "no" on the writing log. And I'm always preaching about a daily writing practice . . . I'm supposed to set an example! I'm such a hypocrite! OK, I'll write for five minutes, just so I can put a "yes" on the log. But that's all. (I set the timer for five minutes).*

> *9:06 p.m.. There, I fixed a typo. How much time left? Four minutes. (Sigh.) OK, I'll look at one more sentence . . .*

> *9:09 p.m.. Nice, I revised a whole paragraph. What does the timer say? Still one minute left. OK, I can keep going for one more minute . . .*

9:10 p.m. (Timer goes off). Shut up you stupid timer, I'm in the middle of a sentence . . . (I set timer for another five minutes).

9:13 p.m. There, another paragraph done. Can I stop now? Hmm, two minutes left on the timer. OK, I can do just another two minutes . . .

Often, I end up resetting the timer again and again. After a while, I get annoyed by the frequent interruptions and I start setting it for longer increments—10 minutes, or 15. I almost always end up writing longer than the five minutes I set out to write.

ALTERNATE LITTLE CHUNKS OF WORK WITH LITTLE REWARDS

There may be days when you can't limit your writing to just five minutes, because you have a pile of work to do and a deadline. In situations like that, consider alternating little chunks of work with little rewards as a way to keep yourself motivated and prevent burnout.

Once I was complaining to my friend and colleague Lisa Pearl. I said, "This journal review is a month overdue and I promised the editor I'd finish it today, but all I want to do is lie on the couch and read a novel."

Lisa said, "How about alternating? You could do one section of the review, and then read one chapter of the novel." What a good idea! Now I use Lisa's system whenever I have trouble getting started on a pile of work. (The tough thing, of course, is going back to the work after each reward period. But I still find it easier than trying to work with no rewards at all.)

LOWER THE QUALITY: WRITE SOMETHING BAD

Allowing yourself to write things that are bad is one of the most useful skills you can develop. Creativity is possible only when judgment is suspended. Practice the skill of lowering your expectations and just writing something, no matter how bad it is.

Let's say that my writing goal for today was to work on a manuscript, and I'm feeling a lot of resistance. Instead of writing in bed as soon as I wake up, I get up and walk the dogs. When I come back, instead of writing, I make breakfast. Eventually, I realize, I'm avoiding writing. Then I have a conversation with myself that goes something like this:

RATIONAL ME: *I have to write. I have to do an hour on the manuscript today.*

ANXIOUS ME: *Noooooooooooooo! I regard this manuscript with fear and loathing!*

RATIONAL ME: *Why?*

ANXIOUS ME: *This manuscript has to be a work of genius. It must be trenchant and incisive and profound and change the way everyone thinks about this topic forever.*

RATIONAL ME: *Oh, get over yourself. This paper is not going to change anyone's life. "Friends, loved ones, thank you all for being here to celebrate with Ashley and Rob on their special day. Now, the bride's sister will read to us from 'Number-Concept Development in Preschoolers from*

	Diverse Linguistic and Socioeconomic Backgrounds' by Sarnecka et al, 2019."
ANXIOUS ME:	*OK, well that's silly. Of course no one will care THAT much about it. But this work is important. It has to perfectly encapsulate all the research that's ever been done in this field, in a way that everyone agrees with—including the people who did the original work and also the ones who criticized it—and it has to frame the key issues in a way that even beginners can understand but that experts will also be hugely impressed by. And it has to describe the study we did, and the contribution it makes, which . . . OH GOD WHAT IF OUR STUDY DOESN'T MAKE ANY CONTRIBUTION?!*
RATIONAL ME:	*Oh for goodness sake, calm down. It's not going to be the best or the worst paper anyone's ever seen. It's just going to be a paper.*
ANXIOUS ME:	*But it has to be REALLY GOOD!*
RATIONAL ME:	*Well you can't write anything really good. All you can do is write something terrible and then revise it a million times. It will get a tiny bit better each time, and eventually it won't be terrible anymore. Can you write something terrible?*
ANXIOUS ME:	*Oh, I can definitely write something terrible.*
RATIONAL ME:	*Great! Do that.*

TELL YOURSELF THAT IT'S NOT REAL WRITING

In order to help free yourself to write something bad, experiment with ways to signal that the text you're generating is not "real" writing.

I often put drafts in green font. Other people type in a notepad app or on sticky notes or they write by hand on paper. Last week in our workshop, one person said that she types her drafts in all caps because, "I know it will have to be rewritten because there's no way to just hit a single key and change it to regular case." I gently informed her that actually, the capitalization of large blocks of text can be changed with a single command. "Don't tell me that! I can't know that!" she cried. We all laughed and reassured her that I had been mistaken, and sadly the technology to do such a thing does not yet exist.

SPEAK INSTEAD OF WRITING

If you can't get started writing, consider speaking instead. Ask a friend to sit down with you and listen while you explain what you want to say. Record this conversation, either as an audio file or as a transcript using voice recognition. It may feel awkward at first, but as you get comfortable talking with your friend, you may be able to relax and focus on explaining your ideas. Afterward, you can go back and use the audio file or the transcript as the basis for a draft.

DELAY THE URGENT TASK 20 MINUTES

Many of us avoid the important task of writing by doing other, urgent tasks instead. We call this "work-crastinating." Instead of writing we do teaching preparation, answer emails, grade papers, etc. *You have to do these tasks sooner or later anyway,* says the resistance monster, in a reasonable voice. *Why not get them out of the way now?*

And before you know it, the day has gone by and you haven't done any writing.

In those situations, try asking yourself whether the urgent task can wait 20 minutes. In other words, when you sit down to write and suddenly think that you should really prepare a lecture or respond to student emails instead, ask yourself: *Does that really have to be done right this second, or can it wait 20 minutes?* Resolve to do just 20 minutes of writing, and then work on the lecture, respond to the emails, or do whatever it is that seems so urgent. Often people find that after they've been writing for 20 minutes, their resistance (which was really a form of anxiety) has subsided to the point where the other task no longer seems so urgent, and they may even choose to keep writing for a bit longer.

———

I can sit down at my computer at 9 a.m. to write but get distracted by the fact that the computer screen is covered with smudges.

> *9:00 a.m. This screen is filthy! I can't work like this. Now let me see . . . I know you're not supposed to use paper towels to clean a computer screen because they can scratch it . . . You're supposed to use cotton, right? . . . Is this T-shirt made of cotton? Hmm, I don't know. I really need one of those special microfiber screen-cleaning cloths. I'm sure I have one around here somewhere . . .*

> *9:04 a.m. Oh good, here it is. Now let me just clean the screen . . . that's better . . . oh wow, look at this keyboard! How did it get so dirty? Look all these grubby fingerprints on the keys—what am I, a coal miner? Well, I'm just going to take a cloth with some grease-cutting stuff on it and wipe off*

the keys . . . That's better. Hmm, there's still a lot of crud in-between the keys . . . I need some compressed air. Or better yet, a wooden toothpick. Yes. I need a wooden toothpick. Because I am a person who takes care of my equipment. Now where were the wooden toothpicks? I'm pretty sure I had some in the kitchen somewhere . . .

9:14 a.m. Here they are—wooden toothpicks. Waaaay at the back of this cabinet. Hmm. Now that I've taken most of the stuff out of this cabinet, I might as well take out the last few items and wipe down the shelf underneath . . .

At these moments, it doesn't feel like I'm avoiding writing. It's more like I suddenly discover some miraculous initiative to do some other task—maybe even one I've been avoiding for a long time.

Joseph, a member of our writing workshop, had a manuscript that he had not worked on for a year. At one meeting he said that his goal for the upcoming week was to work on the paper. But at the next meeting, he still had not worked on it. He explained that when his scheduled writing time had arrived, he suddenly felt motivated to recaulk the shower, which his wife had been asking him to do for months. He spent the rest of his writing time that week on the shower project. When he came to class, he was disappointed about not working on the manuscript, but happy that his shower was finally fixed.

SCHEDULE QUIET WRITING TIME WITH FRIENDS

Another helpful practice is to schedule quiet writing time with colleagues or friends. Many people find writing in the presence of others easier than writing alone. Scheduling quiet writing time creates social accountability for writing. If you privately decide to write at

9 a.m., it's easy to ignore your plan when the time comes. But if you've agreed to meet a friend somewhere at 9 to write together, it's harder to change the plan. Even if you're part of a workshop that meets regularly, forming an additional smaller group that meets just for quiet writing can be a good way to get additional support for your daily writing practice.

Another chronic impediment to writing is what we call in the workshop "Negative Self-Talk TV." These are the intrusive thoughts and images that make you feel bad and make it hard for you to work. It's like a TV tuned to a channel you don't want to watch—perhaps the TV in a waiting room. You didn't pick the show and you don't enjoy the show, but the TV is way up high on the wall, and no one seems to have the remote, so you're stuck with it.

Like real-life TV shows, Negative Self-Talk TV shows depend on ratings. The more attention you give them, the longer they stay on the air. It doesn't matter whether the attention is positive or negative—whether you watch the shows religiously or make angry calls to the network demanding that they be cancelled, you are still giving them your attention, and that's what keeps them going.

In our workshop, we've developed a method for grappling with Negative Self-Talk TV. When one of us notices a new "show" running on repeat in our mind, we mention it during a workshop meeting and ask our friends to help us think of a name for it. This highlights the absurdity of the shows and robs them of some of their power. Here are some of our long-running hits.

"The Biggest Loser." The show in which I compare myself to other people and come up short.

"Jackass." The show that plays endless clips of me in the past—making a fool of myself, hurting people in some way, or just generally saying and doing things I now regret.

"So You Think You Can Science?" This was a show described by a member of our workshop who was pursuing a PhD in psychology after getting an

undergraduate degree in architecture. She felt like a fraud because she wasn't a "real" psychologist. It was a classic case of imposter syndrome: In fact she finished her PhD and was awarded postdocs by both the National Science Foundation (NSF) and the National Institutes for Health (NIH).

"Are You Smarter than a Fancy U Undergrad?" One workshopper was applying for postdoc positions at a prestigious university and couldn't shake the fear that the faculty there would deride her proposal and compare her intellectual merits unfavorably with that of their own undergraduates.

New shows appear all the time. Recently I was having lunch with a former workshop member who said that she and a colleague at her new job had discovered that they both had this recurrent thought: "My work is probably no good, but at least I'm a really nice person."

"Oh wow," I said, "That's so funny, and so sad! It should be a new Negative Self-Talk TV show—we should think of a name for it."

"We did." she said. "We call it 'Miss Congeniality.'"

Revise to continue your thinking

Expertise in writing is different from expertise in other domains. When we think about any skill, we imagine that experts do things faster and more easily than novices. We imagine novices struggling for a long time with a task and experts breezing through it quickly. But that's not the case with writing.

> Expert writers generally are found to work harder at the same assigned tasks than nonexperts, engaging in more planning and problem solving, more revision of goals and methods, and in general more agonizing over the task. (Scardamalia & Bereiter, 1991).

That's right—experts spend *longer* than novices doing the same writing task, but they get much better results. Experts produce more drafts, because they understand that writing is a form of thinking. The act of writing allows us to see our own thoughts more clearly and reflect on them, which allows the thinking to evolve. Experienced writers know this, and they don't consider it a waste of time to generate a draft, and then a topic sentence outline, a revised topic sentence outline, and two more drafts.

Novices think of writing as a way to communicate ideas; experts use it as a way to *develop* ideas. In the words of Scardamalia and Bereiter (1987), novices see writing as *knowledge telling*, whereas experts see it as *knowledge transforming*.

CREATE A TOPIC-SENTENCE OUTLINE (ALSO CALLED A "REVERSE" OUTLINE)

A draft is an earlier, rougher version of the final thing (for example, an article) that you are trying to write. A draft is approximately the same length as the article, it has paragraphs like the article does, and so on. But there's another thing you can work on, particularly in the early stages of writing process, and that's a topic-sentence outline.

A topic-sentence outline is composed of nothing but topic sentences, each one representing a paragraph in the article. That's the ideal, anyway. In real life, every draft has quite a few paragraphs that lack topic sentences, and in those cases you can just write a sentence that sums up the main point of the paragraph. You end up with an outline of just sentences, and it functions as an X-ray of the skeleton of your argument.

You can make a topic-sentence outline before you draft, but it's often even more useful to make one after you have already generated a full-length draft. To do that, cut and paste just the topic sentence of each paragraph into a new document, writing topic sentences for the paragraphs that don't have them, and arrange them into an outline. This is sometimes called "reverse outlining" (Cayley, 2011), because it goes from draft to outline, with is the reverse of the traditional order.

Early in the writing process, when you are working out big, structural problems, there are many advantages to working with a topic-sentence outline rather than a whole draft. You can revise the outline—rearranging some points, deleting others, expanding some, combining others—until you are happy with it, and you don't have to deal with the whole clumsy, full-length draft.

Of course you can't do everything with outlines. Drafts are where you actually attempt to write out the argument, present the evidence, draw the connections, and so on. So, expect to go back and forth between drafting and outlining. Use outlines to work out the general structure of what you're writing; use drafts to work out the specifics. Another advantage of a topic-sentence outline is that you can ask your writing buddies for feedback on it. Getting feedback on an outline (rather than a draft) has several advantages.

First, early drafts are embarrassing to share. They are messy and full of awkward wording. An outline is easier to clean up and make presentable, and readers are less likely to get distracted by typos or quibble about exact wording in an outline.

Second, drafts are long; outlines are short. People are busy. Your fellow writing workshop members can easily give you feedback on an outline during a workshop meeting, or a friend can read an outline and give you feedback in 10 minutes over coffee. If you ask someone to read a whole draft, you may give them days or weeks to read it. And often, people just don't have time to read a full-length draft.

Third, readers can't discern your argument structure from an early draft. Even if you ask them to pay attention to the big ideas and ignore the exact wording, they probably won't be able to. All they see is pages of text. There's no way for them to identify the big, important ideas without reading the whole thing. If you want feedback on just the argument and not the details, then show people just the argument and not the details. In other words, show them an outline.

Reverse outlining is the single most useful editing technique we have discovered in the writing workshop. Many of us were taught in school to make an outline before writing a draft. That's fine, but writing is thinking. By the time we've completed a draft, the argument has often changed. Making a reverse outline—a new, topic-sentence outline of an existing draft—allows us to "zoom out" and take stock of the new understanding that has emerged, so that we can see what we need to do next. When members of the writing workshop experience breakthroughs in their writing, they are most often a result of reverse outlining, as in this experience described by Darby:

> *During my candidacy exam, one of my committee members pointed out a serious problem with the argument in my first dissertation chapter. I spent the whole summer wrestling with the argument. I read, and thought, and read, and thought. This went on for months and I didn't seem to be getting any closer to a solution. My advisor assumed I wasn't working, because it had been six months since he'd seen any writing from me. By the end of fall quarter, I was avoiding working on that entire section of my dissertation. I was making great inroads with other parts, and I was writing successful grants to fund another project. However, every time that I looked at*

the issue I had been trying to fix since the previous spring, dread and anxiety overcame me, and I quickly put it away.

One day, we spoke in the writing workshop about freewriting. I know that people generally find freewriting challenging, but over the last six months I've been practicing freewriting almost every single day and I've found that it gets significantly easier over time. In the workshop, I was always hearing the mantra that "writing is thinking," so I started trying to write through the problem. In one way, it was very successful. I started generating pages of material and having creative ideas again. However, each time I thought I was about to make a breakthrough, I hit a wall. My chapter swelled to 50 bloated pages held together by a crumbling structure. I started to feel anxiety every time I opened the document and the only time I was capable of working on it was during our quiet write-on-site time during the workshop meetings.

During one workshop meeting, I mentioned the problem I was having, and several members suggested that I try making a reverse outline of the existing draft. I started reverse outlining that night. I was pretty paralyzed by anxiety by that point, so it was difficult to work. But I managed to spend some time every day—whether it was five minutes or an hour—reading one paragraph at a time and writing a single sentence about what the paragraph said. I put each sentence into the document, in bold, at the beginning of its paragraph. Over the next few days, I generated the reverse outline through short periods of ninja writing, working through a few paragraphs at a time.

During my write-on-site group that week, I cut and pasted the bolded topic sentences into a new document. Reading through it, I was stunned. This argument had a completely different structure than the one in the original draft.

As I was reading through it, I started to fill in gaps, delete unnecessary premises, and restructure the argument. Utilizing only about 25% of my outline, a new argument came spilling out of my brain. Reverse outlining showed a hole in the argument, and by filling that hole, I was able to restructure my whole dissertation to make it a more manageable project!

Ultimately, reverse outlining has (at least) three fabulous benefits: (1) it illuminates the holes in your argument, (2) it highlights extraneous information, and (3) it provides a "sandbox" in which to test out alternative structures.

START CREATIVE AND THEN LET JUDGMENT KICK IN

As you move from the first, bad draft through successive drafts to the end, of course the work gradually gets better. But the difference between a first draft and a final draft is not just that the first one is bad and the last one is good. Early-stage writing requires a different attitude, different skills, and attention to things different from late-stage writing.

For one, the balance between creativity and judgment required from the writer gradually shifts from 99% creativity in the first draft to 99% judgment in the final proofread. The thing you must understand is that judgment strangles creativity. The way to be creative is to suspend judgment. Most of us find it much easier to be judgmental than creative, which is why proofreading is much easier than generating a first draft.

Because writing is so much like gardening, you can think of each writing project as a plant—perhaps a bonsai tree. Bonsai are small trees grown in pots and carefully pruned into graceful shapes. Like academic writing, they combine creativity with discipline.

Raising bonsai demands a balance between nurturing and pruning. You have to let your tree grow healthy and strong before you cut it back into the shape you want.

Imagine a person who has in mind a beautiful bonsai that they want to create. But this person doesn't know how to nurture; they only know how to prune. So they plant a bonsai seed, and as soon as it pokes its first green tendril up through the soil, they look at the tendril and say, "You're nothing like the bonsai I imagined!" and they pick up the pruning shears and chop the little tendril off at its base.

The little bonsai will certainly die. It can't survive if it is pruned too soon. The owner must first take care of the tree—water it, feed it, and give it sunlight, good soil, and good drainage—and gradually the tree will start to grow. Only after it has grown big and strong and unruly can the owner safely prune it back.

It is very common for writers to prune too much and nurture too little. This is the nature of writer's block—a person types a sentence, and instead of seeing it as a little sprout that has the potential to grow into something good, they compare it to their expectations for the finished product and see that it doesn't match. So they chop it off, deleting what they have drafted. They chop off tendril after tendril, and no draft is allowed to grow. Drafting new text requires that you put down your critical pruning shears and just nurture the writing for a while. Let it grow without judgment or evaluation.

Later in the writing process though, judgment and evaluation are needed. If you've been working on a grant proposal for the past month and it's due tomorrow, it's really too late to make major creative changes to the project. You might have a great new idea at the eleventh hour, but you don't have time to rewrite the whole proposal, so you have to suspend creativity and focus on pruning—tightening up and polishing up the draft you have.

START WITH STRUCTURE AND THEN MOVE TOWARD DETAIL

Another big shift that you make over the course of the writing process, closely related to the other two, is a shift in your attention from big issues to small ones. It's like building a house: You start with the blueprints, then prepare the plot of land, then construct the foundation, then build the frame of the house, then install the windows and doors, then put in the rough electrical wiring and plumbing, and so forth. It's not until the very end of the process that you put on the finishing touches, such as painting the walls and laying the carpet.

Early in the writing process, you need to figure out what points you will make and how they will fit together—this is like framing a house. Working with a topic-sentence outline is a good way to keep the focus on those big, structural issues. At later stages of the writing process, when the house is built and you are painting the walls, then it makes sense to work with a draft.

Revise for the reader

Many casual conversations among academics, on the topic of academic writing, follow the same pattern. First someone says that there's a lot of terrible academic writing. Everyone agrees. They trade stories about all the bloated, confusing, jargon-filled manuscripts and grant proposals they've had to review. Then they speculate on the reasons for all this bad writing. Are authors stupid, or just lazy? Someone suggests that authors write badly on purpose, to make themselves feel smarter. Someone else says that the authors are trying to hide the fact that they have nothing to say.

It's true that plenty of academic writing is incomprehensible, but not for the reasons people think. Most academic authors are intelligent, hard-working people who genuinely want others to understand their research. Their writing makes sense to them. It just doesn't make sense to readers. This is called the **curse of knowledge**. An important goal of revision is to overcome this curse by bridging the gap between the concepts required to understand your writing and the concepts your audience already has.

CONSIDER YOUR READER'S LEVEL OF PRIOR KNOWLEDGE

When you are an expert, writing about your own area of expertise, what you are actually doing is teaching. If you write about your research exactly the way you think about it, readers won't understand. They don't have the conceptual framework that you have—the framework that provides background and context for your work—the framework in which your ideas make sense. The curse of knowledge is that once you know something, it's hard to remember what it was like not to know it.

If you are a relative newcomer to resarch, you may not have a good sense of how broadly the concepts you are learning are shared across your subfield and your discipline. That's OK; these things get easier with time. The main thing to understand is that every research project can be described at multiple levels, depending on the prior knowledge of your intended audience. You have to tailor your description to start with what your reader knows, and build from there.

Consider the case of technical terminology. Every area of science and scholarship has special words and phrases that are used in very specific ways by the people who do that research, but are

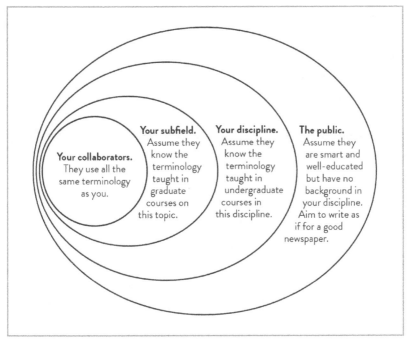

Figure 3.1

unfamiliar to other people. When you draft, you use whatever terms are easiest and most natural for you—which will probably be the special technical terms. But when you revise the draft to be understandable to readers, you will need to decide what to do with that terminology.

The first question to ask yourself is who the audience will be. Different readers can be assumed to have different levels of background knowledge. You can imagine readers as belonging to one of four groups: you and your collaborators, researchers in your subfield, researchers in your discipline, or the public.

When you are revising a draft and you come across a technical term, ask yourself how broadly the term is used. Is it known by most educated members of the public? Is it specific to your discipline or subfield? Or is it a word that you and your collaborators coined?

If it is a term that your readers may not know, you have two options. You can either define it the first time it is used, or you can look for a way to avoid it altogether. It depends on how many times the term appears in your draft. If it's only used a handful of times, perhaps you can rephrase to avoid it. If it's used a lot, you'll have to ask readers to learn it.

For example, let's say you're revising a draft of an article aimed at psychologists, and you come across this statement:

> After children have learned the meanings of "one," "two," "three," and possibly "four," they make the **cardinality-principle induction**.

The phrase "cardinality-principle induction" is understandable to people in the subfield of early childhood number-concept development, but it isn't widely used in psychology, so you can't just leave it there with no explanation. Should you define it, or try to find a way of expressing the same content in nontechnical words?

Say you search the document and find that "cardinality-principle induction" is used 10 times. That seems enough to justify asking the reader to learn the phrase, so you define it.

> After children have learned the meanings of "one," "two," "three," and possibly "four," they figure out that the last word of a correct count sequence corresponds to the number of items in the whole set counted. For example, a set that is counted "one, two, three, four, five, six," with no items skipped or counted twice, contains six items. This insight is called the **cardinality principle induction.**

Alternatively, let's say that when you search the document you find that the phrase "cardinality-principle induction" is used only twice. In that case, you won't ask the reader to learn it. Instead, you'll look for a way to say what you need to say without using that phrase.

> After children have learned the meanings of "one," "two," "three," and possibly "four," they figure out that the last word of a correct count sequence corresponds to the number of items in the whole set counted. For example, a set that is counted "one, two, three, four, five, six," with no items skipped or counted twice, contains six items.

Once you define a technical term, you can use it throughout that piece of writing. But readers will be annoyed if you make them learn a new word or abbreviation unnecessarily, so you should only do this if you need to use the word a lot. When you define a term, make sure to do so *the first time you use it.* The only exception is in a title or an abstract, where the strict word limit doesn't allow for definitions.

A few years ago in the writing workshop, the class was giving feedback on an abstract written by my graduate student James. Another student in the class read a sentence from the abstract aloud: "There were equal numbers of area-congruent and area-incongruent trials at each of seven discriminability ratios."

Lovely, I thought. A perfectly clear sentence. The student said, "So, this is an example of a totally incomprehensible sentence. It might as well be in a foreign language." The other students nodded in agreement, and James and I looked at each other, confused. What was the problem? That sentence could not have been any clearer.

That moment sticks in my mind not just because it was ironic—I was teaching a writing class and couldn't recognize unclear writing from my own lab—but also because it was such a good demonstration of the curse of knowledge. The sentence looked fine to James and me, because area-incongruent trials and discriminability ratios were things we talked about every day. But those words weren't familiar to the other people in the workshop.

In order to adequately describe his work to the other members of the workshop, James would have needed to say something like this:

> *People and other animals share a perceptual system that allows us to tell different numbers of things apart. For example, if you look at two apple trees and one has just a few apples while the other has a lot of apples, it's easy for you to see that the second tree has more. But if the two trees have similar numbers of apples on them, it's hard.*
>
> *How hard it is depends on how similar the numbers of apples on the two trees are—not their absolute difference, but their ratio. If one tree has twice as many apples as the other, it's easy to tell them apart. But if one tree has only 10% more apples, it's hard.*
>
> *To tell things apart is to "discriminate" them. Things that are easy to tell apart are said to be "highly discriminable," or to have "high discriminability." Things that are hard to tell apart have "low discriminability."*
>
> *If one tree has 5 apples and the other has 10, that's a ratio of 1:2, which is easily discriminable. The discriminability of 5 and 10 is the same as the discriminability of any other pair of numbers with a 1:2 ratio. In other words, 5 and 10 are as discriminable as 8 and 16 or 10 and 20 or 24 and 48. They all have the "discriminability ratio" 1:2.*

If one tree has 63 apples and the other has 70 (a ratio of 9:10), it's much harder to see which has more. But all pairs of trees with a 9:10 ratio are equally discriminable. So if one tree has 45 apples and the other has 50, they are just as hard to tell apart as if one tree has 90 and the other has 100. Those pairs all have the 'discriminability ratio' 9:10.

When we want to study people's accuracy at estimating numbers, we give them some trials with easy-to-discriminate ratios and other trials with hard-to-discriminate ratios. So when we say that participants completed trials at each of seven discriminability ratios, it means that they were given trials at seven different levels of difficulty.

That explanation is 356 words long. "Discriminability ratio" may sound like jargon, but it captures all that meaning in just two words. If I were writing a conference abstract with a 500-word limit, the explanation would take up way too much space. But if I were writing something like a handbook chapter, where most readers would not know what a discriminability ratio was, the explanation would be needed.

ASK YOUR PENGUIN HUDDLE FOR HELP

It's often difficult to know how widely a particular technical term is used. The curse of knowledge means that we all tend to overestimate the degree to which our knowledge is shared by other people. We think the terms used in our subfield are understood throughout the discipline, and we think the terms of our discipline are understood by the public. This is one place that your penguin huddle can be of great help.

When people in your penguin huddle give each other feedback on drafts, they should immediately flag words, phrases, and abbreviations that are unfamiliar. Don't be shy or embarrassed about saying that you don't know what a word means—it's a great service to your fellow writer. It's also rare: Outside your penguin huddle, most readers won't tell an author that they don't know what some of the words mean, because academics are trained to never let on that they don't understand something. So we all get trapped in the curse of knowledge, thinking that other people understand what we're saying when they don't.

This is why the trust and mutual respect you build in your writing group is so valuable. When you share your work, you are making yourself vulnerable to criticism. And when other members of the group give you feedback, they are also making themselves vulnerable. They are trusting that when they say they don't understand something, you (the author) will conclude that something is wrong with the writing, not with the reader.

To overcome the curse of knowledge, you must meet your readers where they are. Otherwise the work will simply fail to connect with audiences and won't have any impact. So listen to your penguin huddle, let them tell you what is clear and what isn't, and adjust your writing accordingly.

4

LITERATURE REVIEWS

Research does not occur in a vacuum; it always builds on prior research. The people who design and carry out a study need to know about prior research so that they can make the new study as useful as possible. Readers need to know about prior research too, in order to understand what contribution the new study makes. A piece of writing that summarizes the work already done in a particular area is called a literature review (often abbreviated "lit review").

Understand literature reviews

Lit reviews come in three types, serving slightly different purposes. The first is the stand-alone literature review, or "review article,"which provides an overview of literature on a particular topic. The second is the introductory literature review, which is included near the beginning of an article or book. This kind of lit review provides the context that readers need in order to understand the original research presented later in the article or book. The third is the student's literature review, which helps a student learn about a research area and allows a faculty committee to check the student's understanding.

THE STAND-ALONE LITERATURE REVIEW

The stand-alone literature review, often called a "review article," is an article-length survey of the research on a given topic. These come in two types. The first type is the review written by authors who are new to a research area and need to review the literature. Given that they have to read a bunch of things in the area anyway, they decide to generate a publication from the process. These reviews are like student literature reviews, but more polished and professional. Like student lit reviews, they summarize research from many different sources, discussing how each reading relates to a particular question or problem. These reviews are very helpful to people wanting to learn their way around a research area, although the analysis provided by the authors may not be very insightful, because the authors themselves are often new to the area.

The second type of stand-alone review article happens when a senior researcher is invited to write a review of the field in which they themselves have been working for many years. These review articles heavily emphasize the author's own work, along with the author's thinking about the topic. These articles are not good surveys of a field, but they are good surveys of one researcher's work in that field, and they often contain insightful discussion because the author has been thinking about the topic for a long time (e.g., Sarnecka, 2015; 2016).

THE INTRODUCTORY LITERATURE REVIEW

The introductory literature review is part of a larger document, such as an empirical article or a book. The purpose of the article or book as a whole is to present new, original research; the purpose of the lit review is to provide the background knowledge that the reader needs in order to understand that new research. The introductory lit review is typically the second thing in a big piece of writing. The very first thing (the first thing in an article's introduction, or the first chapter of a book) is the opening, which gets the reader's attention and introduces the big problem or question motivating the research. After the opening comes the lit review. There is no fixed length for lit reviews, but in the social and behavioral sciences they often account for something like 15-20% of the length of an article or book. (This is a very rough estimate, and of course there are projects in the humanities where the whole point is to discuss previous literature, in which case there may not be a clear distinction between lit review and original research.)

A lit review that fails to mention important prior research will likely be flagged by reviewers, who will tell the author to go back and read the missing work and add it. But a more common error that new researchers make is to put too much information in the lit review. They treat it like a student lit review, where the purpose is to show how much they have read. The purpose of an introductory lit review in a publication is not to prove that the author has read things; it is to provide the background and context needed for the reader to appreciate the new, original research being presented.

THE STUDENT'S LITERATURE REVIEW

The student's literature review is written by a researcher who is entering a new field of study (e.g., a doctoral student). The student literature review is not for publication, although it may be revised later into an introductory lit review for an article or book based on the student's graduate work. The purpose of having students write lit reviews is to help them structure the reading and writing that they need to do to familiarize themselves with the scholarly literature in their new discipline. A student lit review is not typically published. Instead, it is submitted by the student to a faculty committee. The committee reads it to check that the student is aware of the literature most relevant to their proposed work and understands the major issues in that field reasonably well.

In North American graduate programs, the process is often organized as an exam: Students ask several faculty members to serve as an exam committee; the committee helps the student put together a reading list of relevant literature; the student reads the literature and writes the review, which is then submitted to the committee for approval. In some programs there is an actual oral or written exam where the committee asks the student questions about the literature. These exams have various names, and often an abbreviation: qualifying exams ("quals"), preliminary exams ("prelims"), comprehensive exams ("comps"), concentration exam ("C-exam"), etc.

When you are learning your way around a new research area, reviewing the literature goes hand-in-hand with defining your research question. They happen together: You start with some general idea about what you want to do, and then you read some literature on that topic. The literature helps you understand what has already been done, which helps you hone your new research idea further. It's hard to come up with an original research idea that builds on the existing knowledge base in a field, *and* has not already been done, *and* is doable with the methods that exist, *and* is feasible in the amount of time you have available. It takes time to define a question like that, and reviewing the literature is an important part of the process.

Build your reading list

Reviewing literature involves three kinds of tasks: (1) building a reading list, (2) reading the literature, and (3) writing about the literature. These tasks are mixed together and repeated over and over again. List-building and reading are mixed because often when you read one article or book, it cites several others that are also relevant, and you add them to your reading list. Reading and writing are mixed because writing is thinking, and you digest the material by writing about it (this is called taking notes) both during and after reading. For the sake of clarity, this chapter is written as though the tasks were separate, but keep in mind that you will probably do all of them each time you sit down to review literature.

CHOOSE A PLATFORM

Before you start, decide how you will organize your reading list and notes. I like Zotero, which is free and integrates well with web browsers and with Google Docs. If your work includes a lot of formulas, code or other technical elements, you may find it more convenient to work in LaTeX or RMarkdown and use BibTeX to organize citations and references (all of these are also free). And of course there are bibliographic software packages that you can buy.

However you choose to organize things, what's important is that you keep track of your reading list and notes so that you can easily cite readings and generate bibliographies.

LOOK AT WHO IS CITED

The easiest way to start building a reading list is to start with a review article or chapter, look at the works cited in it, and decide which to add to your reading list.

You may be thinking, *Wait a minute. If someone else has already written a review of my research area, why do I have to write a new one?* There are several reasons. First, if you're a student, you need to learn about the literature before you can contribute to it. Writing is thinking, and the best way to learn about the literature is to write a literature review. Second, review articles get old. Each one captures the author's view of a particular research area at a particular point in time, but new research is published all the time and your lit review must be up to date. So you can start with an older review article, but you can't stop there. Third, there isn't a review article that covers exactly the areas of literature relevant to your interests and talks about them from your point of view. Your research will most likely draw on articles and/or books from a few different areas, and your point of view isn't quite the same as anyone else's, so your literature review will be unique too.

Nevertheless, a published review article or chapter is a great place to start. Let's call this Article Zero (just as the first patient in an epidemic is called Patient Zero). The reference list of Article Zero is full of candidates for your reading list. You don't have to read all of them, but skim the titles and add them to your list if they seem useful or interesting to you. Then, when you read those articles, do the same thing with their reference lists, and so on. You can also search in the other direction, using Google Scholar to find publications that have cited Article Zero in the years since it came out. This is especially useful if Article Zero is a few years old.

To take a silly, fictional example, let's imagine that you're interested in doing research on rodents and their behavior. You find a review article on rodent behavior research, which becomes your Article Zero. You read Article Zero and take notes on it, and then start to make your way through some of the articles and books in the Article Zero reference list. You soon realize that the literature on rats is many times larger than the literature on any other rodent species, so you decide to find some interesting phenomenon in rat behavior and investigate it in another rodent.

Reading about the rats, you come across some studies suggesting that rats' emotions are systematically related to their body temperature. You think this is really interesting and has big implications for how animal behavior could be affected by changes in global climate. After more reading, you start to think that hamsters would be a good species to study, and your reading list expands to include several sublists: (1) studies of how temperature affects animal behavior; (2) studies of rodent behavior; (3) studies of hamsters. One day, a more senior graduate student in your lab mentions that one of the storage closets in the lab contains a bag of tiny, rat-sized mood rings left over from an earlier study. The rings also fit hamsters, so you tentatively plan to do a study with hamsters and mood rings, measuring something about responses to the environment. Now you have a fourth sublist: studies where researchers used mood rings to measure something, preferably in rodents.

DECIDE HOW LONG YOUR READING LIST NEEDS TO BE

The scholarly literature in every field is enormous. If you try to read everything, you'll die of old age—if not boredom—before you get halfway through. So how do you know when to stop adding readings to your list? I suggest that you use your term plan to determine how long your list will be. For example, if you have allotted one semester (16 weeks) to review the literature, and you estimate that given your schedule, you can review 15 readings per week (three readings per day, five days per week) then your list should be about $16 \times 15 = 240$ items long.

This may seem like an odd way to think about a reading list. Of course the goal is not to read any particular number of items, but to become familiar with the literature relevant to your research question. And there are ways to know when you've become familiar with a topic—when you pick up a new reading and most of the concepts in it are already known to you, and the sources it cites are also known, then you're clearly familiar with the topic. But you can't use these indicators to decide when your reading list is long enough, because there are always uncountably many new topics to explore. All you can do is compose what seems like a good list, start reading and taking notes, and trust that if you've missed anything important, you'll hear about it eventually.

If you are a student, it may be useful to check in with your advisor about your reading list as it develops. If you have missed something important, your advisor may be able to tell you so. If you seem to be veering into irrelevant territory, your advisor may be able to redirect you. It's also fine to ask different people to look over different sublists. For example, if your advisor has expertise in mood rings but not hamsters, you can ask another faculty member—a hamster expert—to take a look at your hamster list.

TAME THE BEAST WITH A MIND MAP

Trying to learn your way around any area of scholarly literature can feel overwhelming. In that case, a mind map can be just the thing to help you organize your thoughts. A mind map is a pleasant, creative way to sketch out your growing lit review and start to organize the material. Mind maps are organized around a central idea or topic, with themes branching out from it. Subthemes are represented as twigs on the branches. You can draw your mind map on a computer or by hand. Don't worry if it's sloppy and incomplete and disorganized—that's fine! Just fill in whatever you can. Here are the steps to follow.

1. In the center of the page, write your own research topic (however you define it today).
2. Radiating out from the center, draw branches for the most relevant areas of literature. These roughly correspond to the sublists of your reading list.
3. Use very short phrases or single words.
4. Use images if you like them or find them helpful.
5. Add subareas to each branch as twigs.
6. At the smallest, twiggiest level, you can list individual readings.

Figure 4.1 shows a mind map created by longtime writing workshop member Ashley, while reviewing literature for a new series of studies on infant social cognition.

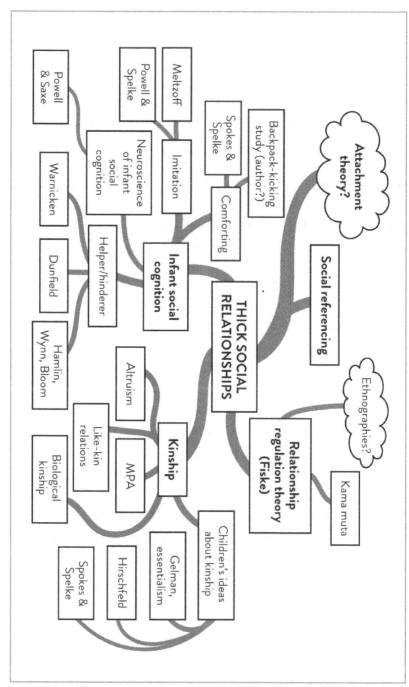

Figure 4.1

Read strategically

Reviewing scholarly literature is not like reading for pleasure. When you pick up a novel, you start at the beginning and read every word until you reach the end. That won't work with scholarly writing. First, it takes much too long. If you are aiming to review, say, 250 articles and books in a year, and you are taking classes or doing other work at the same time, you should be spending (at least for the initial read-through) no more than one hour on each book and no more than 20 minutes on each article. If you think this isn't long enough to absorb all the nuances and details of a book or article, you're right. Literature review is not about nuances and details—it's about getting an overview of the big ideas and main points, and moving on.

Of course there will be a handful of readings that you end up reading over and over again, and reading very closely. But at the beginning of the literature review process, you probably won't know what these are. You will only discover them as your research question becomes more clearly defined, because they will contain the theories or methods you decide to adopt in your own work. That's fine—you'll know when you need to read something very closely because it's highly relevant to your own work. But don't treat all the readings like that.

Imagine your field of scholarship as a big social gathering. The authors are all people standing around, talking with each other, in a giant ballroom. When you enter the ballroom, the party has already been going on for a long time. You wander around the room, stopping to listen to one person or another as they talk. Some of the conversations are more interesting to you, so you spend more time there. Some are less interesting, so you move on after a couple of minutes. Your goal is just to start getting acquainted with these people, to decide which conversations are interesting to you and which are not, which people you want to get to know better and which you don't.

There are hundreds of people in this ballroom. Does it make sense to run up to the first person you see and spend the rest of the evening hanging on their every word? Of course not. Most of the people in this room will become your acquaintances: You'll know their names and have a general idea of the work they do. A small subset of them will become your friends: You'll spend more time with them and listen more carefully to what they are saying, because it has implications for your own work. A very small handful will become your close friends—these are the ones whose work you read over and over again, the equivalent of staying up all night talking, one on one.

You should not try to absorb every word of every reading on your list, just like you would not try to become best friends with every person in the ballroom. The ballroom goes on forever, but your time and attention are limited. So practice reading lightly and strategically.

Although I read all the time for pleasure, somehow I got all the way through my undergraduate years without having to read much for school. As an undergraduate I studied Russian and Japanese, partly because language classes didn't require a lot of reading. When I started graduate school, I had never read a scientific paper. So my idea of reading was to sit down in a comfy chair with a cup of tea, put my feet up, open the work to page 1, and read until I reached the end.

In a PhD program, this didn't work at all. I would clear two or three hours in my schedule and try to tackle a stack of articles and book chapters. At the end of that time, I would have read only one article (maybe not even a whole one) and I would not have understood most of that. Week after week, I went to my classes feeling guilty. I was worried that other people would be able to tell that I was unprepared. I was angry at myself for not being able to keep up with the reading. I was angry at the professors for assigning such a ridiculous amount of reading in the first place.

One day I confessed my troubles to a professor in a different department, whom I trusted. (Thank you, Armand Lauffer of the University of Michigan.) He said something like, "You need to learn how to spend about an hour on a book. Study the table of contents, flip through and look at the figures, maybe read the first chapter, maybe the last chapter. In about an hour, you can get a pretty good idea of what the book says, and that's all you need."

At the time, I thought he was telling me to cheat. But I reasoned that skimming a book or article before *reading it would at least help me take in the information better, so I came up with a three-step plan. First, I would skim the article or book as Prof. Lauffer advised and write a summary paragraph. Second, I would actually read every word. Third, I would go back to the summary paragraph I had written and update it based on my new, more complete understanding of the reading. I would correct any errors and add any important details that I had missed.*

I followed all three steps for perhaps 10 or 20 articles, and noticed something odd: I almost never made any changes to the paragraph I had written after skimming. I was spending 15-20 minutes on the first step, and two to three hours on the second step, but the second step didn't seem to add much, if anything. I got everything I needed in the first 15 minutes just by skimming; the value added by reading every word was negligible. I realized that the professor was right, and I stopped bothering with the second and third steps. That's how I learned to read strategically.

There are times when skimming isn't appropriate. For example, when you review a manuscript or a grant proposal, you should read every word. But for the purposes of a literature review, skimming is just fine. You can always come back later and read it in more detail if necessary.

STRATEGIC READING, STEP BY STEP

Even when you set out to read strategically, it's easy to get sucked into details when you take notes. You read a sentence and think, *That seems like it might be important, I'd better write it down.* Before you know it, half an hour has gone by and you haven't even finished reading the introduction. You've also taken a page of notes that may later turn out to be irrelevant to your work.

A better way to start is to put down the pen or take your hands off the keyboard and give yourself five minutes to look over the reading *without writing anything.* (If your fingers are itching to take notes, set a timer for five minutes to help you resist the urge.) Then, pick up your pen or open your notes document and follow the steps below to pull the most important information out of the article or book in the time you have available.

There is a balance to be struck here: On the one hand, if you read too closely and take too many notes before determining that a book or article is really worth your attention, you will end up wasting a lot of time and feeling overwhelmed. On the other hand, writing is thinking. So when you do decide to read something closely, you will probably digest the information better if you take thoughtful notes at the same time. Taking notes while the material is fresh in your mind is a way of thinking it through. It is an opportunity to allow your impressions of the work to crystalize on the page.

So try to strike a balance: Be picky about what you read, but when you do decide to read something (e.g., the abstract of a paper or the preface to a book), read it with your complete attention and take notes on your impressions of it. To reprise the metaphor of a social gathering, be picky about whom you spend time with. But while you are talking to someone, try to give that person your complete and thoughtful attention.

READING AN EMPIRICAL JOURNAL ARTICLE

Follow these steps with pen or keyboard handy to pull out quotes that you might want to use later. As you read, take brief notes on both the content of the article and your reactions to it, including your thoughts about how it connects to your own work. For most articles, aim to finish with just a paragraph or two of notes. For the articles that turn out to be your favorite and most important ones, you may choose to write more, of course.

First, read the title. Make note of any words you don't understand and any questions the title raises in your mind.

Second, read the abstract. The abstract is a summary of the whole paper, and it's worth taking the time to read carefully, several times over if necessary. Again, make note of any words you don't understand or questions that arise.

Third, study the figures. Figures that illustrate methods or models should show you what the researchers did. Figures that illustrate results should show you what the researchers' hypotheses and results were. Again, make note of any undefined words or unanswered questions.

For 90% of the articles on your list, you are finished reading after these three steps. This is the equivalent of meeting a person in the ballroom and spending 10 to 15 minutes getting acquainted and making small talk before you excuse yourself from the conversation. It's perfectly acceptable and appropriate.

Of course, you can also stay and talk longer. If the article is genuinely interesting to you or seems relevant to your research, you can scan through the rest of the paper to find the answers to your questions. Here are some examples of common questions and where to find the answers.

What does [word] mean? Or, *what does [abbreviation] stand for?* All technical terms and abbreviations should be defined the first time they are used. But sometimes authors break this rule in the title and abstract, where word counts are limited. So look in the introduction for the definition of your mystery word or abbreviation. If you are reading the paper on a screen, you can save time by using the "find" function to search. (If the word or abbreviation is not defined in the paper, shame on those authors. You can decide whether to look it up online or just let it go. If you do look it up online, be careful, because technical terms are often used very differently across different subfields.)

What question, exactly, did the authors set out to answer? You can usually find this information in the last paragraph of the introduction. If the information is not there, the authors haven't organized their introduction properly. Again, you can choose whether to search further or let it go.

What precisely did they measure, and how did they measure it? This information is in the method section, along with information about the participants (if the experiment included human participants) and any materials or procedures used in data collection.

What did the authors find? (This is not the same thing as what they think the findings mean.)

How did they analyze their data? This information is in the results section.

What do the authors think their findings mean? This information is in the discussion.

READING A NONFICTION BOOK

Just as with an article, start by looking over the book for five minutes without writing anything down. Then pick up your pen or open your note-taking software and follow the steps below. At each step, just as with an article, make note of any words you don't understand or questions that arise. Pull out quotes that you might want to use later, and take notes on both the content of the book and your reactions to it, especially your thoughts about how it connects to your own work. For most books, aim to end up with just one to two paragraphs of notes restating the author's central claims and the main evidence for them.

First, examine the outside of the book (front and back). Study the title, the "blurbs" or comments on the covers, and the messages on the end flaps. Note the author's name and any biographical information about him/her. Is this person a researcher? A journalist? What else have they published?

Second, note the copyright date. You have to know when a book was written in order to put it in context. The author is a person in the ballroom described above; this book is what they said at some point in the past, as part of a conversation with others in that room. The conversations happening 20 or 50 years ago were different than the ones happening today, so you have to know when a book was written in order to understand what the author was responding to. Also take note of the book's publication history: A high number of editions, revisions, and reprints indicates that a book has been widely read.

Third, study the table of contents closely. This is an outline of the book.

Fourth, flip through the book and look at any visuals, such as figures and photographs. These are a fast and easy way to get a lot of information.

Fifth, flip through the end matter—indexes, bibliography, glossary, appendices, etc. In particular, look for complete references to cited research.

Sixth, read the preface, introduction, or foreword. This is where the author explains what they tried to do in the book. If a book has more than one of these, start with the shortest. Books with a long introduction typically also have a shorter preface and/or foreword. In such cases, read the shorter, earlier one (you can skip the acknowledgments), and skim the introduction. At this point, it's like you've been talking to the author for 10 or 15 minutes. You should be starting to get a sense of how well the book is written and whether it's worth more of your time.

Seventh, if there is an overall summary, conclusion, or general discussion, read it closely.

The last step is to look through the book for the answers to any questions you wrote down during the earlier steps. But don't drive yourself crazy doing this. If you've already spent an hour on the book, you might choose to leave the questions for another time. If the book turns out to be important to your research, you can always come back and look for the answers later. To return to the metaphor of people in a ballroom, you've already listened to this person talk for an hour. You may have some unanswered questions about things they've said, but you are not required to stick around until every question is answered.

The steps above are just one approach to literature review and note-taking. They are a starting point, but the only real rule of literature review is that you don't try to copy the whole article or book you are reading into your notes.

With a little experimentation, you will find a method that works for you. Here is a note-taking system recently developed by a member of our current writing workshop:

> *My process involves reading and taking notes on the document (but NO separate notes, because separate notes would take me forever and make me anxious). I do that in the evening. The next morning, I wake up and write down everything I remember over breakfast and coffee (without looking back at the document). I call this a brain-dump. Afterward (or later that day) I use my margin notes/highlighting/etc. to fill in citations and gaps in my summary. In many cases, the brain-dump + citations serves as a first draft of a few paragraphs for my dissertation (etc), but sometimes it just serves as a distilled version of the article for my records. I finally store my summary (with added citations) in Zotero so I have a great summary if I ever need to return to the article.*
>
> *This method will probably work better for humanities people than for scientists because we often get stuck spending forever reading and taking detailed notes, but sometimes lose the overall argument of the piece. In my method, that morning brain-dump ensures that I know the shape of the argument from the article, and it helps prune things that aren't important or relevant. It also takes way less time than taking detailed notes along the way. It ensures I can effectively weave the ideas from the article into my own work and it helps me understand how I'm in dialogue with current arguments in the field.*

Write the literature review

As noted at the beginning of this chapter, the tasks of reading and writing are mixed together, along with building a reading list, throughout the process of reviewing literature. But at some point the focus shifts from mostly reading and taking notes on sources to mostly working on the lit review document itself.

ASSEMBLE YOUR NOTES INTO A ROUGH DRAFT

Your notes are not photocopies of the readings. They pull out relevant quotations, summarize key ideas, and identify connections between the reading and your own project. The notes you take during reading are the first draft of your literature review. Just arrange the readings in some kind of order (maybe chronological, maybe grouped by topics, whatever makes sense to you) and slap a heading on each section. Then paste the notes from the readings into the document. *Voila!* A rough draft.

Returning to our imaginary hamsters-and-mood-rings study, let's say you've arranged your readings into subgroups titled *Temperature and Rodent Behavior; Animal Emotions; Studies of Hamsters;* and *Studies Using Mood Rings.* You paste in the readings and notes to make a very rough draft. The notes will form a series of brief and unconnected paragraphs like the following:

> Lawsky and Delaney (1964) used mood rings to measure rats' propensity to cry at sentimental movies. Found no such propensity; concluded that rats are cold-hearted creatures devoid of empathy.

Included measures of test-retest reliability for rat mood rings.

Pearl et al. (1968) created sentimental movies starring rat actors; showed that rat audiences were more sympathetic to rat protagonists than to human protagonists, as measured by mood rings and the number of tissues used by weeping rats. Lawsky et al. wrote commentary claiming that number-of-tissues measure was confounded, because rats were likely hoarding tissues as nesting material.

Lawsky, Delaney, and Herman (1975) measured television-viewing preferences in small mammals using daytime TV. Found that chinchillas, skunks, and a subset of gerbils enjoyed talk shows; squirrels and chipmunks preferred game shows (especially *Wheel of Fortune* and *Jeopardy*) but became hostile and agitated when their favorite contestants lost. Follow-up study showed that skunks became depressed after watching daytime dramas, although chinchillas did not. Studies did not include hamsters, but game-show results with squirrels and chipmunks did establish that rodent anger can be measured using mood rings.

Grossman, Liljeholm and Chernyak (1991) had guinea pigs wear mood rings for several weeks in an office environment; found that they were happiest on Fridays. Possible confound: Guinea pigs were given extra food on Fridays so that lab assistants could come in late on Saturday mornings. Authors conducted follow-up experiment with extra food given on Tuesdays; found that guinea pigs switched

preference to Tuesdays. Overall conclusion: Guinea
pigs are happy when they get extra food.

These paragraphs contain information about the readings, but
they don't hang together very well as a document. They need to
be organized into something more coherent, which means creating paragraphs with topic sentences; creating transitions between
sentences, paragraphs, and sections; and adding introductory and
concluding statements. These steps are difficult, but the difficulty
doesn't mean you are doing anything wrong. They're difficult
because a lot of the actual thinking and learning of reviewing literature happens in these steps.

ORGANIZE INTO TOPIC-SENTENCE PARAGRAPHS

First, start organizing your lit review into paragraphs with topic
sentences. Write topic sentences for the main points you want to
make, and let the reading notes be the supporting sentences. (For a
detailed discussion of this type of paragraph structure, see Chapter
8.) When you start writing topic sentences, you might realize that
several readings can be mentioned in the same paragraph because
they all support the same main point. Or you may realize that a
single reading makes several different points, and so should be mentioned in more than one paragraph.

Continuing with the hamster/mood-ring example, the first
and second paragraphs can be combined under one topic sentence
(shown below in bold), as can the third and fourth paragraphs. Once
the topic sentence of each paragraph is identified, it also becomes
easier to see which details are irrelevant and can be cut.

Mood rings have been used to reliably measure animals' emotions for more than 50 years. Lawsky and Delaney (1964) used mood rings to measure rats' propensity to cry at sentimental movies. ~~Found no such propensity; concluded that rats are cold-hearted creatures devoid of empathy.~~ Included measures of test-retest reliability for rat mood rings. Pearl et al. (1968) ~~created sentimental movies starring rat actors~~; showed that rat audiences were more sympathetic to rat protagonists than to human protagonists, as measured by mood rings and the number of tissues used by weeping rats. ~~Lawsky et al wrote commentary claiming that number-of-tissues measure was confounded, because rats were likely hoarding tissues as nesting material.~~

Mood rings have been used successfully with a wide range of small mammals. Lawsky, Delaney, and Herman (1975) measured television-viewing preferences in small mammals ~~using daytime TV.~~ Found that chinchillas, skunks ~~and a subset of~~ gerbils ~~enjoyed talk shows~~; squirrels and chipmunks ~~preferred game shows (especially *Wheel of Fortune* and *Jeopardy*) but became hostile and agitated when their favorite contestants lost. Follow-up study showed that skunks became depressed after watching daytime dramas, although chinchillas did not.~~ Studies did not include hamsters, but game-show results with squirrels and chipmunks did establish that rodent anger can be measured using mood rings. Grossman, Liljeholm, and Chernyak (1991) had guinea pigs wear mood rings for several weeks in an office environment; ~~found that they were happiest on Fridays. Possible confound: Guinea pigs were given extra food on Fridays so that lab assistants could come in late on Saturday mornings.~~ Authors conducted follow-up experiment ~~with extra food given on Tuesdays; found that guinea pigs switched preference to Tuesdays. Overall conclusion: Guinea pigs are happy when they get extra food.~~

ADD TRANSITIONS WITHIN PARAGRAPHS

The next step is to add words or sentences to glue sentences together within each paragraph, between the descriptions of readings, to indicate how each reading relates to the previous one and to connect the whole thing together into a coherent document. Transitions can be as short as one word (e.g., "Similarly," "Conversely," "Nevertheless," etc.) or as long as a whole sentence. In the example below, the transitions are bolded.

Mood rings have been used to reliably measure animals' emotions for more than 50 years. **One of the first studies to use this method was by** Lawsky and Delaney (1964), **who** used mood rings to measure rats' propensity to cry at sentimental movies. **This study** included measures of test-retest reliability for rat mood rings. **The method was next used by** Pearl et al. (1968) **to show** that rat audiences were more sympathetic to rat protagonists than to human protagonists.

Mood rings have been used successfully with a wide range of small mammals. Lawsky, Delaney, and Herman (1975) **used mood rings to** measure television-viewing preferences in small mammals, **including** chinchillas, skunks, gerbils, squirrels, and chipmunks. **Although** the study did not include hamsters, game-show results with squirrels and chipmunks did establish that rodent anger can be measured using mood rings. **Similarly,** Grossman, Liljeholm, and Chernyak (1991) measured guinea pigs' moods in two studies conducted in office environments, lasting several weeks each.

ADD CONCLUDING SENTENCES AT THE END OF PARAGRAPHS

Most paragraphs need a topic sentence, several supporting sentences, and a concluding sentence. So the next step in revising a rough draft of pasted-together reading notes is to add a concluding sentence (shown in bold) at the end of each paragraph.

Mood rings have been used to reliably measure animals' emotions for more than 50 years. One of the first studies to use this method was by Lawsky and Delaney (1964), who used mood rings to measure rats' propensity to cry at sentimental movies. This study included measures of test-retest reliability for rat mood rings. The method was next used by Pearl et al. (1968) to show that rat audiences were more sympathetic to rat protagonists than to human protagonists. **These studies established mood rings as a reliable measure in rats.**

Mood rings have been used successfully with a wide range of small mammals. Lawsky, Delaney, and Herman (1975) used mood rings to measure television-viewing preferences in small mammals, including chinchillas, skunks, gerbils, squirrels, and chipmunks. Although the study did not include hamsters, game-show results with squirrels and chipmunks did establish that rodent anger can be measured using mood rings. Similarly, Grossman, Liljeholm, and Chernyak (1991) measured guinea pigs' moods in two studies conducted in office environments, lasting several weeks each. **The success of mood-ring studies across rodent species bodes well for the potential use of mood rings in hamsters.**

Notice how the bolded sentences tie the information together and tell the reader why those previous studies are relevant to your planned research. For the purposes of your "angry hamster" research, it's not so important *what* the early studies with mood rings showed. Those studies are relevant because they showed that mood rings could be used to measure small animals' emotions—particularly anger, which is the emotion you want to measure. And although none of these studies featured hamsters, the fact that mood rings have been used successfully in quite a wide range of similar species implies that your research idea is reasonable.

ADD SHORT INTRODUCTORY AND CONCLUDING PARAGRAPHS FOR EACH SECTION AND LONGER ONES FOR THE WHOLE DOCUMENT

After completing the steps above, you should have a series of pretty good paragraphs. The remaining step is to write a short introductory paragraph for the beginning of each section, a short concluding paragraph for the end of each section, and a longer introduction and conclusion (maybe one long paragraph or a few normal-length ones) for the beginning and end of the whole document. Each introductory paragraph should present the themes of the section that follows it; each concluding paragraph should reinforce those themes.

Don't worry about the prose sounding graceful or elegant at this point. It's OK to write clumsy, boring prose in the early drafts. Remember, the early drafts are for you, the author, to help you figure out the argument. Polishing things up for the reader is a job to do in later drafts. For more on revising for readability at the paragraph, sentence, and word level, see Chapters 8-10.

5

SCIENTIFIC ARTICLES

Writing about your own original research is the bread and butter of academic life. In the sciences, empirical articles have a predictable structure known as IMRaD, which stands for introduction, method, results and discussion. The IMRaD structure is a great help and convenience, because authors know just where to put each piece of information, and readers know just where to find it.

In many PhD programs in the sciences, IMRaD articles can actually take the place of a dissertation. A traditional dissertation is structured like a book, with chapters. But in some PhD programs in the experimental sciences (including psychology), a student who has several (e.g., three) articles accepted by peer-reviewed journals is allowed to use those articles to fulfill the dissertation requirement. It's an efficient way to let students spend their writing time producing publications that will help them get jobs and grants, whereas a dissertation may be read only by a faculty committee.

In truth, though, five or six years (the typical length of a psychology PhD program in the United States) is usually not enough time for a brand-new researcher to learn the field, conceive of three new empirical projects, carry them out, and get them through the multiple cycles of submission, review, revision, and resubmission that typically precede acceptance at a journal. So most students end up describing their ongoing, not-yet-accepted-for-publication experiments in something like a traditional dissertation format. For example, Chapter 1 is a literature review; Chapters 2, 3, and 4 are three studies in various stages of completion; Chapter 5 is devoted to conclusions, reflections, and planned future research.

The point is that if you are in a field where the IMRaD format is standard, getting familiar with this format is an excellent use of your time. The IMRaD format is perfect for describing empirical studies, both for publication in journals and as chapters of a dissertation. If you are outside the sciences, in a field where the IMRaD format is not standard, this chapter will not be as useful to you as the others. But it may give you a sense of how to read IMRaD articles (should you ever want to) and it may help you identify the standard format in your own discipline, if one exists.

Understand the IMRaD structure

This IMRaD format is drawn in the shape of an hourglass because articles start out broad and general, get narrower and more specific in the middle, and then return to broad and general discussion at the end.

The width of the hourglass corresponds to the breadth of the audience for each part of the article. Only experts are likely to read the narrow, middle parts of the hourglass—the method and results sections. But nonexperts and researchers much further afield may be interested in the big, general questions that are asked in the introduction and answered in the discussion. This handy structure tells authors what information to include and where to put it and

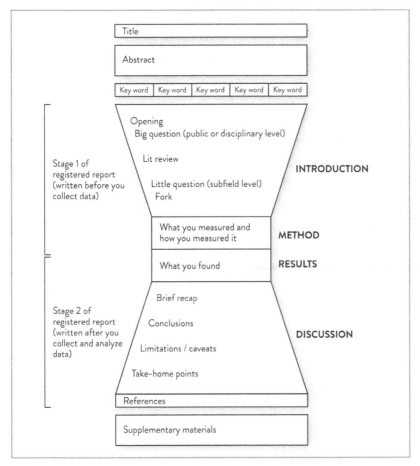

Figure 5.1

tells readers where to find the information they want. Figure 5.1 shows the parts of an IMRaD article.

CONSIDER A REGISTERED REPORT

Traditionally, researchers didn't start writing an article until after they had finished the whole study. The problem was that if the findings weren't exciting enough, journals didn't want to publish them (Buranyi, 2017; Sarnecka, 2018). In recent years, the psychology research community has addressed the problem of publication bias (i.e., the problem where journals don't want to publish boring findings) with a new type of article, the registered report.

For a registered report, you write the introduction and method sections before you collect any data. You send these sections to a journal, where they get reviewed. The reviewers might suggest changes, but once all the parties are happy with the introduction and method sections, you get an in-principle acceptance (sometimes called a "pre-acceptance") from the journal. Then you go ahead and do the study. As long as you follow the agreed-upon plan, your article is guaranteed acceptance in the journal. Writing a registered report is sort of like writing a PhD dissertation: You make a plan (the introduction and method sections), get your committee to approve it (in this case the committee is the journal editor and reviewers), and then do the work.

Even if you aren't writing an actual registered report to send to a journal, you can still preregister your study. You might do this if you like the idea of preregistration but want to send your work to a journal that doesn't offer registered reports. (For a list of journals that do offer them, go to the Center for Open Science Registered Reports web page and click on the tab that says "Participating Journals.") Writing a preregistration is similar to writing a registered report, except that no one reviews a preregistration. Also, it is likely that no one will hold you accountable if your published study deviates from your preregistered plan, because not many reviewers or readers take the time to go back and read preregistrations. Still, preregistration has the potential to make your thinking clearer and your decision-making process more transparent.

The Open Science Framework (OSF) is a great place for preregistrations. Additional places to register studies include ClinicalTrials.gov,

SocialScienceRegistry.org, Egap.org, RIDIE, ResearchRegistry.com, and others.

A PAPER PRESENTING MULTIPLE EXPERIMENTS

Customs differ from one discipline to another, but in psychology, papers presenting multiple experiments use a modified form of the hourglass structure as shown in Figure 5.2. The title, abstract, keywords, introduction, references and supplementary materials are all the same as in a single-experiment paper. The difference is in the method, results, and discussion.

First, there is a general method section. This describes the parts of the method that were the same for the whole series of experiments. For example, if participants for all experiments were recruited in the same way, that recruitment process is described in the general method section.

Then there is a separate method and results/ discussion section for each individual experiment. It starts by briefly explaining what question this particular experiment was meant

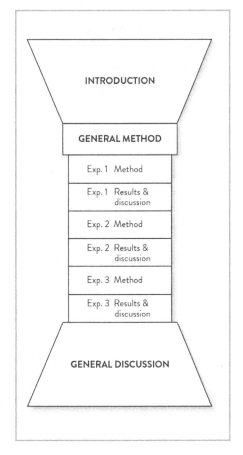

Figure 5.2

to answer, and then it describes whatever was unique to this experiment. (Often this results in wording like: *The procedure was the same as in Experiment 1, except that participants saw pictures of animals rather than vehicles.*) The method section for each experiment is followed by a combined results and discussion section for that experiment.

After all the experiments have been presented, there is a general discussion about all of them as a group. This includes the same information as the discussion in a single-experiment IMRaD paper.

A PAPER IN WHICH THE AUTHORS DID NOT COLLECT NEW DATA

Sometimes your contribution is not new data, but a new thing you did with data that were already published. For example, secondary analyses look at existing datasets in new ways; meta-analyses combine data from multiple previous studies; and modeling projects use existing datasets to build and test new formal models.

These papers are usually structured like an IMRaD hourglass, but instead of explaining in detail how the data were collected, they describe the datasets they used. For papers in which the empirical results are especially important (such as secondary analyses and meta-analyses), the datasets are described in detail. This is usually done in the first part of the method section, in the same place where the collection of new data would be described.

Some modeling papers use widely available datasets, such as census data or sports results, to build and test new statistical models. In this case the main contribution of the paper is the model itself, and the authors just need to say enough about the dataset to give people a general idea of the information it contains, along with a citation to the source. For example, they might say, "We used the Economist Intelligence Unit dataset (2012), which provides country, risk, and industry analysis for 200 countries worldwide." The full reference would appear in the reference list at the end of the paper. In these papers, the method section is used to present the model.

A PAPER PRESENTING BOTH NEW EMPIRICAL DATA AND A NEW STATISTICAL MODEL

Sometimes students ask me how to structure a paper for which they have collected new data answering an empirical question, and they have also come up with an innovative way to model those data. In this case, the variation on the standard hourglass would be similar to a multi-experiment paper, where the first "experiment" describes the data collection and the results (description and standard analysis of the results) and the second "experiment" presents the model and modeling results.

But don't write this kind of paper. It just confuses everyone. Most reviewers are either experts in a content area or experts in modeling. Very few can evaluate both parts of a paper like this, which complicates the peer review process. Most readers are in the same boat—they care either about the empirical findings or about the model, but not both. So no one is really happy with the paper. Why not write two papers instead? First publish a standard empirical paper with the new data, then publish a separate modeling paper with the previously published data. That way people are less confused, and you get two publications on your curriculum vitae (CV) instead of one.

Start by making great figures

If you do quantitative research—if you count or measure anything—figures are your friend. They pack a lot of information into a small space, and many readers study the figures before deciding whether to read the rest of the paper, so good figures engage readers and draw them in. But that's not all figures do. Just as writing is both a form of thinking and a means of communication, so are figures a way of both thinking and communicating about quantitative data.

PLOT YOUR DATA TO UNDERSTAND THEM BETTER

Just as the early stages of writing help you find out what you think, plotting the data you've collected helps you to understand it. So the first thing to do with a new dataset is plot the data in as many ways as you can think of. It's much easier to see patterns in data plots than in rows and columns of numbers.

For example, imagine that you are part of a research team studying the nut-collecting behavior of squirrels. You have placed trackers on dozens of squirrels, and hidden balance scales inside their nests, so that you can measure the number of nuts stored there. On October 1, you record the amount of time (in minutes) each squirrel spends collecting nuts, as well as the number of nuts they collect. This gives you the data in Table 5.1. Based on these data, do any squirrels stand out to you as particularly good or bad nut collectors?

S	M	N
AZ	33	5
AT	86	13
AR	59	9
AX	34	6
AV	90	12
AG	81	14
AL	65	9
AB	80	12
AI	53	7
AK	54	10
AE	88	15
AA	92	15

S	M	N
BC	99	18
BD	58	10
BH	25	2
BI	33	3
BJ	21	5
BK	34	4
BL	20	4
BM	41	5
BN	91	16
BO	58	10
BP	91	16
BQ	32	15

S	M	N
CA	71	13
CB	75	12
CC	41	8
CS	60	11
CD	68	11
CF	50	8
CG	30	6
CH	45	7
CJ	95	13
CK	75	4
CL	68	11
CQ	68	10

S = squirrel
M = minutes
N = nuts

Table 5.1

Now consider Figure 5.3, which is a scatterplot of the same data. It's immediately obvious that one squirrel (who happens to be Squirrel BQ) is a very efficient nut collector, gathering 15 nuts in only 32 minutes. Another squirrel (CK) stands out as very inefficient, working for 75 minutes to collect only four nuts. It's easy to miss these two outliers in the data table, but they stand out clearly in the scatterplot.

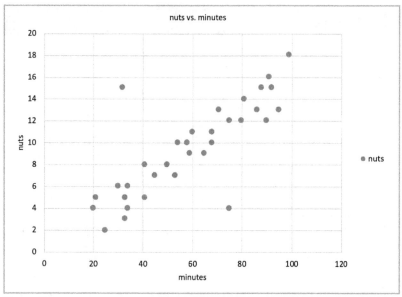

Figure 5.3

CONSIDER USING A FIGURE TO DESCRIBE YOUR METHODS

Figures can also be a great help in describing research methods. In my own field of cognitive-developmental psychology, a figure is often the simplest way to explain what the people in our experiments did. Compare the following text description of a task with the figure illustrating the same task. Which is easier for you to understand?

> **TEXT**
>
> Give-N task. Materials for this task included a plush toy and a set of 15 small plastic counters. The materials were arranged on the table in front of the

participant, who was instructed to create a set of a given numerosity (N).

FIGURE PLUS CAPTION

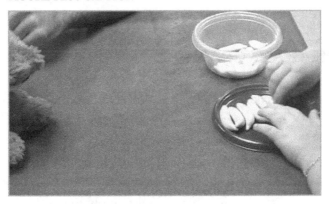

Figure 5.4   "Please give FIVE bananas to the dinosaur."

If you are presenting your research in a talk, consider using a video to show audiences what your participants actually saw or heard or did. Many phenomena that are difficult to describe in words or even still images are easy to understand on video (Gilmore & Adolph, 2017). Particularly for those of us who study human or animal behavior, videos are a wonderful way to bring the behavior to life for an audience.

USE FIGURES TO PRESENT YOUR RESULTS

If you have just a few numbers to present (let's say, eight values or fewer), a table may be fine. But when there are a lot of numbers, a figure works much better. One of my favorite examples is a visual essay breaking down the dialogue from 2,000 films by Gender and Age (Anderson & Daniels, 2016). A huge number of data points are presented in three interactive figures that invite readers to explore and learn from the data in much the same way as a good interactive museum exhibit. Figures are also beautiful—they give readers a break from text. (For inspiration, browse the plots on the R Graph Gallery.)

MAKE GOOD GRAPHS

Being able to make good graphs is almost as important for a quantitative researcher as being able to write. A detailed discussion of graph design is beyond the scope of this book, but the same principles of scientific communication that guide scientific writing also apply to graphs. In particular, making good graphs comes down to three basic principles: (1) Make the data stand out, (2) Don't mislead the reader, and (3) Design the graph to work in the circumstances where it will appear. Let's consider each of these in turn.

First, make the data stand out. When someone looks at the figure, the data should be the first thing to catch their eye. If the figure is crowded with background patterns, gridlines, or too many labels, the reader will have to search for the data. Figure 5.5 is a plot of the same squirrel data shown earlier, but with minor gridlines added and the data points reduced in size. The resulting plot is much harder to read than the original.

Make the data stand out.

Don't mislead the reader.

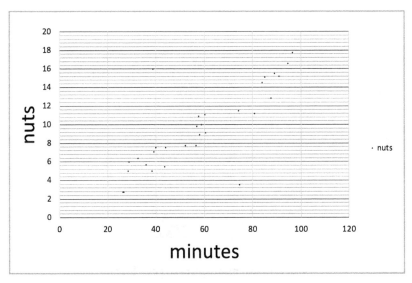

Figure 5.5

The second principle of good graphing is to avoid misleading the reader. Big differences should look big; small differences should look small. Let's say that the squirrel data in the scatterplot in Figure 5.5 come from squirrels with one of three personality types: angry, bold, or cheeky. If we graph the average number of nuts per hour collected by each type of squirrel, we get values of 9.4 for the angry squirrels, 11.0 for the bold ones, and 9.5 for the cheeky ones. We could plot those values as a column chart like the one in Figure 5.6.

The problem with this graph is that it misleads the reader because the vertical axis doesn't go all the way to zero. The bold squirrels collected only 17% more nuts than the angry squirrels, but in this graph, the "Bold" column occupies more than twice the area than the "Angry" column, implying that the bold squirrels collected more than twice the number of nuts. If the whole vertical axis from zero is shown (as in Figure 5.7), the resulting graph shows correctly that the differences between groups are relatively small.

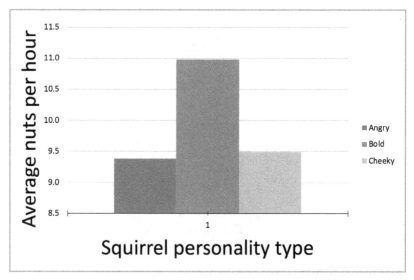

Figure 5.6

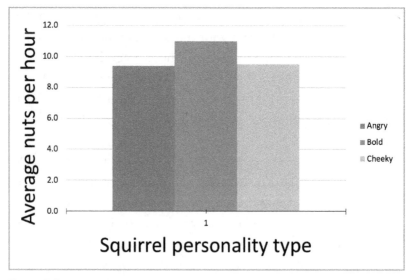

Figure 5.7

Other errors of graphing occur when the graph type just doesn't fit the data. For example, many graphing programs will give you the option of connecting the lines in a scatterplot to create a line graph. But in the case of these squirrel data, connecting the dots doesn't make sense. Every data point is a squirrel. There's nothing "between" Squirrel AA and Squirrel AB, so it doesn't make sense to draw a line between their dots. Take some time to think about the kind of data you have and how it makes sense to picture them. (For an excellent, free online tool that helps you match graph types to data types, check out the website "From Data to Viz.")

The third basic principle of good graphing is to design the graph to work in the circumstances where it will appear. If people will read the graph online, you can use color to convey information. But if the graph will be printed in black and white on paper, the figures need to be different. Readers can't distinguish shades of gray as easily as they can distinguish colors, so black and white figures need to rely on shapes or patterns, such as dotted versus solid lines, to make the data stand out.

Design the graph to work in the circumstances where it will appear.

Another consideration is how long the reader will look at the figure. Figures that appear in journal articles can include a lot of information, because readers can study them for as long as necessary. Figures that appear in talks will be seen just for the amount of time they are shown onscreen, so they should be simplified to show just those aspects of the data that the speaker wants the audience to notice. To illustrate this point,

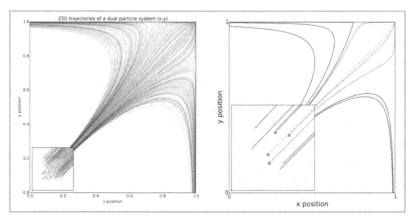

Figure 5.8

Rougier, Droettboom and Bourne (2014) show two versions of the same figure (Figure 5.8). The version on the left was designed to appear in a journal article, and the one on the right was designed for use in a talk. Many details have been removed from the second version, and a larger box and dashed line have been added to make it easier for the speaker to draw the audience's attention to specific details of the figure by saying, "Here in the box, you can see . . ." or "This dashed line represents . . ."

Longtime workshop participant Sierra, who after finishing her PhD went on to success as a data scientist in industry, shared the following reflection on the importance of figures:

> *I've been contacted by a few recruiters specifically for my experience in the writing workshop. One of my first industry interviews was for a biomedical company who needed the equivalent of a ghostwriter for scientific papers. During my interview, one of the interviewers pulled out two publications*

and laid them on the desk. One was mine and the other was from a student who had graduated from my lab a few years earlier. He opened both papers to a page with a figure on it and asked, "Why does your figure look different than the one in this other paper?"

I stared at him blankly for a while, trying to imagine how he wanted me to respond. There were so many possible answers to that question, and none of them seemed like the right one. I worried that he was trying to tell me that my figure was missing something important. I hesitantly listed a few of my answers.

Eventually, he took pity on me and clarified, "I mean, why does your figure look so much better than the other one? Do you just have really high standards for figure clarity? Or is that the standard in your lab?"

I could finally breathe again and said, "Well . . . it seems like you already have the answer given that the other paper is also from my lab. But yes, one of the things I practiced in the writing workshop was making figures that are easy to comprehend. I try to apply those standards to all of my figures."

Industry jobs drive home the point that your research is only as good as your ability to communicate clearly. Most industry jobs consist of understanding the needs of a stakeholder, using your skills to answer that question, and then explaining that answer to the stakeholder. In academia, we spend 90% of our time practicing analysis and only 10% of our time on practicing clear communication.

Being able to demonstrate soft skills like this is what will separate you from the rest of the candidates. In every interview, someone will inevitably ask a variation of "How *do you communicate complicated ideas to someone without your scientific background?"*

Because of my time in writing workshop, I am not only prepared to answer this question from a theoretical stand-point, but I can also mention that I've attended the workshop to specifically develop that skill. The writing workshop is one tangible way for me to show that I value clear communication and gives me endless examples of what I have done to improve my skills.

Of course it's not only people outside academia who appreciate clear, well-designed figures—it's people, period. The people who judge your submitted manuscripts and grant proposals will study the figures first, just like everybody else. So go ahead and spend as much time and effort as necessary to develop your graph-making skills. It's an investment that pays off.

Draft an article from meta-material to methods

This step includes everything in the top half of the **IMRaD** hour-glass—everything that would be included in Phase I of a registered report. The meta-material summarizes the whole project, whereas the introduction and method sections lay out the question or problem motivating the study, and how the researchers tried to answer or solve it.

META-MATERIAL

Meta-material, such as the title, abstract, and keywords, is text that helps people find the article online and gives them a little bit of information about it, so that they can decide whether they want to read it. As such, it deserves more time and attention per word than any other part of the article. The title and abstract are as a summary of the whole article. They are a good place to start drafting, because they help you focus on the main points to be made. They are also probably the last elements you will revise at the end. That's because the article will change a lot during the process of drafting and revision, and the final title and abstract need to represent the final version.

Title

Good titles state either the central finding of a study (e.g., "Saturated Fat Consumption Is Not Linked to Heart Disease") or the study's contribution (e.g., "*Ab initio* Calculations for the E2 Elimination Reaction Mechanism in Ricinoleic Acid").

Readers searching the literature enter some search terms and scroll through the results, clicking on titles that look promising. So when you choose a title, try to make it as clear and informative as possible. Pitch your title at the most general level you can without misrepresenting its content. The title is the face that your paper shows the world. Make it friendly if you can.

Abstract

The abstract is a brief (usually under 250 words) summary of the whole paper. After the title, the abstract will be read by the greatest number of people, so it's worth getting right. Expect to revise your abstract no fewer than 10 times.

The structure of the abstract mimics the hourglass structure of the whole paper, except that there's just a sentence or two for each section: a sentence or two for the big question; then a sentence or two each for the little question, the method, the results and the discussion. Here's a useful annotated example of an abstract from the biological sciences.

Keywords

Choosing keywords requires a balance. If you choose only general search terms (e.g., "fat" and "heart attack") your paper will be buried in a pile of 10,000 search results. If the terms you choose are overly specific ("electrocardiographically defined clinical endpoints") they won't help anyone find the paper because no one types those terms into a Google Scholar search.

Instead, choose a combination of general keywords (e.g., *children, preschool, numbers, counting*) and slightly more specific ones (*cognition, development, cardinality, magnitudes*). If there was something unusual or interesting about the method, you might add a keyword for that (e.g., *fNIRS* or *latent mixture model*).

DRAFT THE INTRODUCTION

This is where you set up the questions asked in the study, both broad and narrow. This is also where you review the literature to show how you got from the big (broad, theoretical) question to the little (specific, operational) question.

In a traditional article, you write the introduction after you already know what the results are. In a registered report, you write the introduction before you've started collecting data, so you don't know yet what the results will be. Once you get an in-principle acceptance for a registered report, you can't change the introduction anymore—the one that the reviewers approved is the one in the final paper, no matter how the results come out.

Opening

The first few sentences of your introduction should raise the general topic or problem of your study. Pitch your opening at the broadest, most accessible level you can. Even if your work is very technical, strive to make the first and last paragraph understandable to nonspecialists. Anecdotes can make effective openings, as can hypothetical situations (e.g., "Imagine that you are hiking in the alps . . ."); so can interesting facts or references to current events (e.g., "The world was amazed in 2016 to see video of antarctic penguins playing ice hockey with fish skulls. But how did they learn the rules?")

In the social sciences, one sometimes hears the advice to "start by talking about people, not about researchers." What that means is that the paper should start with an opening, rather than plunging right into the lit review. An example of an opening is, "Each time you visit a café, you must decide whether to order something familiar or try something new. This is known as an explore/exploit problem." An example of jumping into the lit review is, 'Barsever and Barsever (2013) developed a model that describes explore/exploit behavior in a café game." This rule is violated often: Many published articles have no opening and jump directly into a literature review. The fact is, a lot of published articles are badly written.

Big question

After introducing the general topic of your study in your opening, your next task is to raise the big question—the broad, general, theoretical question motivating the research. This is a question that readers should already care about. For example, say you're doing a study about the feasibility of an alternative to the cash bail system in county jails. Your specific question is about cash bail and its alternative, but your work is motivated by a much bigger, more general question—perhaps something like, "How do law enforcement policies victimize poor people?" or "How can we make law enforcement more fair?" Most of your readers will not have an interest in bail systems *per se*, but they will care about the bigger questions of poverty and fairness and the law. When authors don't identify the big questions motivating their work, it makes the work seem trivial.

Literature review

The introduction to an IMRaD paper includes a brief literature review connecting the big question (e.g., poverty, fairness, and the law) to the little question (e.g., "How good is this alternative to cash bail systems?") The literature review provides just the background and context that the reader needs in order to understand the new research being presented in the article. This is different from an article-length literature review of the type described earlier in this book. A common mistake made by early-career scientists is trying to put everything they know about a topic, everything they've ever read that could possibly be relevant, into the literature review of their article. Don't do that. Include only what the reader needs to know in order to understand the new research you are presenting.

Little question and fork

After the literature review comes the little question: the narrow, specific operational question addressed in the study. It might be something like, "When bail is replaced with nonfinancial release conditions, do fewer defendants appear at their scheduled court dates?" Big questions are intriguing, but not easily answerable. So we break them down into lots of little questions that can be answered.

The fork (picture a fork in a road, not a dinner fork) is a few sentences at the end of the introduction identifying at least two plausible outcomes for the study and explaining what each outcome would mean. For example, if you find that nonfinancial release conditions result in many defendants missing their court dates, that would imply that the new system is not a good alternative to cash bail. Alternatively, if you find that the number of defendants who show up for court is the same or better than with a cash bail system, this would imply that the new system works and should be widely adopted.

Many published articles lack forks, just as many lack openings. But a fork is even more important than an opening because it shows that the authors have thought the study through and aren't wasting time on a question whose answer is obvious. Too often, I've reviewed papers where the authors devoted time and resources to a study, only to conclude something obvious (e.g., that there is a correlation between owning a tennis racket and playing tennis, that anxious parents tend to have anxious children, or that kids who read a lot are good at reading).

It's easy to understand how this happens. Researchers, especially inexperienced ones, struggle to come up with study ideas. Their thinking goes something like, "X and Y are both things we can measure. Maybe they're related. Has anyone shown that they're related? No? Great! That's our study!" They don't stop to ask about the fork: Are there really two different plausible outcomes here?

Realistically, is it possible that X and Y are *not* related? If we show that they're related, what will we have learned? Identifying your study's fork requires you to think through these questions.

One good thing about registered reports is that they allow reviewers to catch forkless studies before the authors waste precious time collecting data that don't teach anyone anything. But you don't have to wait for reviewers. Get in the habit of looking for the fork in each study you do and describing it clearly at the end of the introduction.

To help you get started, try using the chart in Figure 5.9 to answer the questions about a study you are designing.

1. What is the broad, theoretical question motivating the study? This should be a question that readers care about.
2. What is the narrow, operational question you will ask in this study? In other words, what will you actually measure?
3. What is the fork in this study? In other words, what are two different ways that the results could plausibly come out, and what two different answers (to the original, broad question) would those patterns of results point to?

DRAFT THE METHOD SECTION

This is the section where you describe what you measured and how. If you analyzed data in a way that was complicated or innovative or otherwise special, describe that here too. Your method section should include enough detail for a reader of your article to evaluate whether you did the study correctly and whether your findings can be trusted.

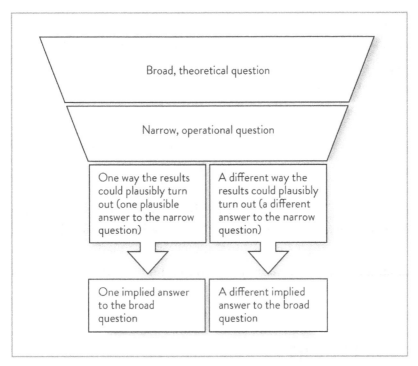

Figure 5.9

People sometimes say that the method section should include enough detail to allow a reader to replicate the study, but the truth is that method sections are not long enough for that. In order for someone to replicate your study, they probably need copies of your surveys, interview protocols, or experimental stimuli. They probably need the code that you used in data analysis, so they can reproduce your results from your data. And they need your data. That stuff can all be shared easily online, but you can't cram it all into a method section.

In a registered report, you specify the details of your method and analysis before data collection starts. This is an important safeguard against researcher degrees of freedom (Malecki, 2012) the flexibility that lets researchers try a bunch of different ways of collecting and analyzing data until they hit on something that seems to work or shows a significant effect. (Doing this is fine when it's identified as exploratory, but it's not fine when you pretend that you made those choices ahead of time and used them to test a hypothesis.)

Present and discuss your results

The first half of an **IMRaD** article is all about your questions: what they were, why they matter, how they fit into the existing literature, and how you tried to answer them. The second half of the article is all about your answers: what you found and what you think it means.

DRAFT THE RESULTS SECTION

This is the section where you describe what you found. Figures usually summarize findings better than text alone. If you have some (not too many) numbers to present, a table can work well. Don't present giant tables of statistical output if you can avoid it. (For some types of analysis, they may be unavoidable.) Take your cue from whatever you consider the clearest and best-written papers in your own research area.

Some people say that a results section should contain only results and no interpretation, because all the interpretation should be reserved for the discussion section. But the results need to include enough context that readers can follow what's being reported. For example, do not write this:

> Two-tailed binomial test: 16/19 participants, p = .004; 95% CI: .604-.966; probability of success = . 842; BF 27.05.

Instead, write this:

> Results from the replication matched those of Experiment 1.0, with 16 of 19 toddlers choosing the non-yielding or "winner" puppet (two-tailed binomial test p = .004; 95% CI: .604-.966; probability of success = .842). The Bayes Factor was 27.05, which is strong evidence in favor of the hypothesis that toddlers chose the nonyielding puppet either more or less than 50% of the time.

But again, conventions differ from one field to another, so you do what makes sense for your field.

For a registered report, there are two parts to your results section. First you report the outcomes of the registered analyses—all the things you said you were going to measure. Second, you can report "exploratory analyses"—analyses that were not described in the method section you originally submitted. Exploratory analyses are not cheating. You can include them in your results, but you should label them as exploratory (i.e., you shouldn't pretend that they were predicted ahead of time), and you should be careful not to base your conclusions entirely on the exploratory analyses, especially if it means ignoring the results of your preregistered analyses.

DRAFT THE DISCUSSION SECTION

The discussion section is where your results are unpacked and laid out for the reader. Following the hourglass structure of the IMRaD article, the discussion should be written for a broader audience than the results section.

Brief recap

Many readers come to the general discussion after reading only the title, the abstract, and the figures. So try starting the discussion by briefly recapping the big and little questions of the study and the main finding(s), to bring everyone up to speed. This is not obligatory, and you may decide that it's not necessary. But for very long or complicated papers, it can help readers keep track of what is going on.

Conclusions

Next you explain how the results point down one of the roads identified in the fork at the end of the introduction. In an ideal world, your results would clearly point to one road. But in real life results are often inconclusive, mixed, weak, or otherwise unsatisfying. If you are publishing this study as a registered report, those things won't matter because the work is already accepted. If you are trying to publish a regular article, you will probably face pressure from reviewers to do additional data analyses, collect more data, rewrite the introduction to tell a story with a more satisfying arc, and so forth.

To me, this is the clearest argument in favor of registered reports. If you've done rigorous work on a question that the reviewers agreed was important, then it should be published—boring or not. Scientific journals are not supermarket tabloids.

Of course journals agree with this in principle. But in practice, the giant bloodsucking parasites that are for-profit academic publishers are looking to make money, journals want to be cited, and authors want to be published in highly cited journals. That's because journal impact factors (average citations per article) have, despite a complete lack of objective evidence, become a proxy for quality of work.

Don't get me started on how statistically illiterate it is to use journal impact factors to evaluate individual papers, much less individual authors. As Stephen Curry (2012) lamented, "the stupid, it burns." But when enough people buy into an idea—even a bad idea, it becomes a social reality.

I have tenure, so I can say, "Forget impact factors. I'm all about noncommercial, fair open-access publishing." But you, dear reader, may be at the beginning of your career. And you will probably run into people who value journal impact factors when you apply for jobs and grants and promotions, because this foolishness is both widespread and institutionalized. So, publish wherever you want; I won't judge you. But there are steps we can all take to start changing this system even while we work within it.

First, post preprints of your articles on free servers such as Arxiv, PsyArxiv, or BioArxiv, so that everyone who needs to read them can do so. Second, support the grassroots movement to change how research is assessed, starting with the San Francisco Declaration on Research Assessment (DORA) It's time to change the evaluation practices for hiring and promotion so that publishing one impactful study with trustworthy results is more valuable to a person's career than publishing five flimsy papers with few data and unreliable conclusions. And once you get tenure, please join me in telling commercial academic publishers where they can stick their exploitative financial model and their dumbass impact factors. But I digress.

————

Back to registered reports. Even if you preregister your analyses, you can still add analyses that you thought of later, and you can report discoveries that you didn't go looking for. Depending on the kind of statistics you use, post-hoc analyses may not give you the same certainty as *a priori* predictions (many frequentist tests are only valid if the predictions are made before you look at the data), but you can still report everything and talk about what you think it means. Often, unexpected findings become the inspiration for future studies.

Note that a clear distinction between predicted and unpredicted results arises only in registered reports. That's because only registered reports force authors to make their predictions clear ahead of time. When you report unexpected results in a regular article, reviewers will probably pressure you to rewrite the article to provide a better "framing" for the results—in other words, to rewrite the paper to make it sound like the thing you found was actually the thing you went looking for.

The ending: Limitations and take-home points

No study is perfect; no study answers all questions; most studies include some caveats that readers should keep in mind. Some papers end by discussing a study's limitations, which is a shame. The end of a paper is a highly visible position, and it should be used to highlight the study's most important findings and implications.

In the words of Joshua Schimel (2012), instead of saying "yes, but," you should say "but, yes." That is, rather than talking about your study's most important take-home points and then ending the paper with its limitations, reverse the order. Present your findings along with any limitations or qualifications, then end the paper by recapping the main points that you want the reader to remember.

Ideally, the bottom of your hourglass will be the same width as the top, meaning that your final answers are at the same level of generality as your original questions. If the paper starts out with a broad question and ends up with a narrow answer, then your hourglass is wider at the top than the bottom. This makes it seem like you overpromised and underdelivered, and the reader will feel cheated. Conversely, if the paper sets out to answer a narrow question but arrives at an answer with much bigger implications, the hourglass will be narrow at the top and wide at the bottom, and the introduction will seem to undersell the importance of the results.

When you're writing a regular article, you're under pressure to avoid both of these problems and rewrite the introduction after you see the data so that the top and bottom of the hourglass are the same width. With a registered report, the introduction is written ahead of time and doesn't change based on the data, so papers may not have the same poetic balance. In other words, the stories won't be as good. Which is fine, because you're not writing a novel— you're writing science.

ADD REFERENCES AND SUPPLEMENTAL MATERIALS

References should be formatted according to the journal's guidelines. If you use a tool like BibTex or Zotero, then formatting the in-text citations and references is easy. If you do it the old-fashioned way, then by the time you get to the final draft of the paper, there are usually some missing references or extra references from citations that were added or deleted in later revisions. Make sure to double-check these as part of the final proofread.

An empirical study will also include materials that aren't described in the actual text of your paper but that you want to make available to readers. Some journals may ask you to archive supplemental materials on their website. Others will be happy if you post your materials, data, and code on a separate site (e.g., Open Science Framework, GitHub, etc.) and just include a link in the article.

The supplementary materials are for sharing information that is not important enough to go in the article but still of interest to some readers. If you used standardized measures to collect your data, you can just cite them like you would any other source. But if you designed your own measures, you should include them in the supplementary materials so that people can see exactly what you did and replicate it.

The same is true for video of your procedures: If the researchers in your study just asked people questions, or directed them to sit down at a computer or lie down in an fMRI machine, that's easy to describe. But if your researchers did something special like perform a puppet show (as our research assistants do in many of our studies with infants and toddlers), then you should include video of the puppet show in your supplemental materials.

You may also sometimes want to use the supplemental materials to present different variations of the main data analysis. For example, say that you administered a 100-question survey to participants and decided to exclude all the participants who completed the survey in under five minutes, because you don't think it was possible to really read and answer 100 questions thoughtfully in under five minutes. You assume that those people were just clicking through the survey and marking answers without reading them, so excluding their answers from the data analysis seems like a reasonable thing to do. (Actually, an even better solution is to include questions specifically designed to check whether participants are paying attention, and exclude people who fail those questions. But let's pretend that you forgot to include any questions like that.)

So you exclude all the people who completed the survey in under five minutes. But what if a reader thinks, "Hey! That's cheating! I think you just excluded those participants in order to get the results you wanted!" If you think that some readers might have that objection, you can do a separate analysis where you include all the participants, so that readers who are curious about it can see whether that would have changed the results. Of course, if you have posted your data at the time of publication (an open-science practice that many journals and funders now require), you can skip the alternative analyses. Anyone who wants to know what some other analysis would have shown can download the data and do the analysis themselves.

In addition to sharing data, it's good to share your code (the scripts that you used to program the experiment and to analyze the data) so that any reader who wants to can reproduce your analysis. (For this reason, it's good to use statistical software like R or Matlab, which saves a record of the scripts you used, rather than one like SPSS, which uses drop-down menus. Or you can use the free, friendly, and all-around awesome JASP, which gives you drop-down menus but also saves a complete record of everything you did.)

REVISE AND RESUBMIT

Assuming that your goal in writing an article is to publish it in a peer-reviewed journal, you will at some point submit an article for review and receive a decision of "revise and resubmit." This is neither an acceptance nor a rejection, but rather a request from the editor for you to do more work on the article before sending it back to the same editor to be considered anew. Some revise-and-resubmit letters are upbeat and encouraging, hinting that if you just make the requested changes, the paper is likely to get a favorable second review. But most seem deliberately discouraging. "You can try to rearrange this pile of garbage into a bouquet of flowers if you really want to, but the second version probably won't be any better, and we still probably won't accept it, is what those letters seem to say. Presumably these editors have been traumatized by authors who got a revise-and-resubmit decision, made only minimal changes to the manuscript, and then complained when it still wasn't accepted.

But authors like that are rare. More often, new researchers agonize over revising for resubmission because they feel that they have no control over the process. The reviewers' concerns and suggestions seem to have a divine force, such that they cannot be questioned or argued with. Authors feel like the research they've worked on so hard, for so long, is held hostage to the whims of these nameless, faceless people.

Even if the reviewers' comments are misinformed, or poorly considered, or irrelevant, authors feel like they have no choice but to do everything the reviewers say, or else their work will never see the light of day. In these cases, a few small changes in your perspective as an author can go a long way toward making the process feel calmer, less intimidating, and more within your control.

First, distinguish between the editor's comments and the reviewers' comments. Some editors (the good ones, when they are doing their job) will read through your manuscript and through the reviewers' comments and decide which of the reviewers' comments they agree with and which they don't. They won't say "I disagree with Reviewer 2's point about X," but they will mention in the action letter what the most important revisions are. That's code for, "Definitely make these changes; the others are negotiable." Not all editors do this in all cases; some just say, "Please address all of the reviewers' concerns," which is code for any or all of the following: "I'm too busy to read this"; "I don't know enough about this research to form my own opinion"; "I had to ask 12 people to review this in order to find three who agreed, and I'm not going to offend them by overruling any of their comments." In any case, it's always worth paying close attention to what the editor says, because it's the editor who ultimately makes the decision, not any individual reviewer.

Second, remember that this is your research, not theirs. You have been thinking about it longer than they have, and you care more about it than they do. You are the expert on this study. The worst thing they can do is decline to publish it. They can't force you to make changes you disagree with, or say things you don't believe, or do anything that you think makes the research worse rather than better. If you and they can't come to an agreement on revisions that everyone is happy with, so be it. You will add a line to the rejection collection and submit the manuscript somewhere else.

Third, go through the suggestions one by one and decide how to respond. Once you remember that this is your work and not theirs, you can see the feedback as a valuable opportunity to find out whether your argument was clear or not, and perhaps to get some ideas for improving it. Read each point raised by a reviewer, and ask yourself whether you agree or disagree. If you agree with the reviewer's point, go ahead and make the changes they suggest. If you don't agree, you don't have to do what they say. If the reviewer seems to misunderstand something, ask yourself how they got confused and whether the manuscript can be clarified so that other readers don't get confused in the same way.

Fourth, write a response letter explaining your decisions. After you've made all the changes you are going to make—the ones that you agree with, and that improve the work—write your response letter. Copy the text of the editor's action letter and the reviews into a new email, and respond point by point. First, thank the editor and reviewers for their help. (Remember, they are doing this for free.) Then, for each suggestion, either confirm that you followed it or explain why you chose not to follow it. In the cases where reviewers misunderstood something, thank them for bringing the issue to your attention, identify the misunderstanding, and explain what you've done to avoid confusing future readers.

6

PROPOSALS

Writing about research comes in three flavors: writing about research other people have done (Chapter 4), writing about research you have done (Chapter 5), and writing about research you plan to do, which is the focus of this chapter. Most writing about planned research is asking for money to support the work. But there are a few times when you might write about planned research in order to get something other than money, such as approval or guidance.

For example, if you do behavioral or clinical research with human participants, you will need approval from the Institutional Review Board (IRB) of your university. The IRB only wants to make sure you don't break the law or hurt anyone with your research, so writing for them is easy. Find someone who uses similar methods and ask for a copy of their approved IRB application to use as a model. If the people in your IRB office are friendly, ask if you can meet with one of them to go over your application before you submit it. They can often point out errors and give you a chance to fix them ahead of time, which will help your application make its way through the formal approval process faster.

Another time when you seek approval for proposed research is as a PhD student. Most graduate programs require students to submit a dissertation proposal describing the research they plan to do to complete their doctoral training. If you are in any kind of science, this proposal will contain the sort of information that appears in the introduction method sections of an IMRaD paper, including a brief literature review that explains the background of the proposed studies, the broad and narrow questions that the studies will answer, the fork for each study you are proposing, and a description of the methods you plan to use. This proposal is typically submitted for review by a group of three to five faculty members, who read it and offer feedback on ways to make it better. This process is anxiety-producing for students, but it shouldn't be. Faculty have nothing to gain by holding students back or inhibiting their success. PhD programs require student researchers to seek faculty preapproval for big projects because on their own, students often come up with plans that are poorly designed, poorly grounded in the existing literature, or not feasible to complete, given the time and resources available. PhD programs hope that faculty committees will catch problems with the proposed work ahead of time, so that the student can fix them before it's too late. This saves the student from spending years on a project that won't yield usable or publishable data. This is a great gift to the student. Outside of PhD programs, researchers don't get that kind of helpful feedback in the planning stages of a project.

At least traditionally they didn't. Registered reports now do for any researcher what the dissertation proposal process does for a PhD student, providing feedback on a study design while the project is still in the planning stage.

Asking for money

IRB, PhD proposals, and registered reports aside, the main reason academics write about planned research is to get money to do it. If you are in a field where people write books, you probably need money to travel somewhere to do the research for your book, and to pay your rent while you are there. If you write empirical articles, you may need money to travel to data collection sites, compensate study participants, hire research assistants, purchase lab equipment and supplies, and so on. The higher you rise in the academic food chain, the less time you spend doing research, and the more time you spend selling research ideas to funders. This is actually kind of a bummer if you enjoy doing research.

I, for example, love listening to little kids explain things. When I was a PhD student, I spent a lot of time doing just that, collecting data for studies of conceptual development. Now that I'm a professor, the data are collected by undergraduate research assistants, who are supervised by PhD students, who are supervised by me. Instead of talking to kids, my job is now to write about the research and bring in money to keep it going.

FELLOWSHIPS

A fellowship is money that goes to an individual researcher. It usually includes a salary or living stipend (i.e., money for rent, groceries, etc.) plus tuition and fees if the researcher is a student. Many fellowships also include a budget for research expenses, such as research-related travel and supplies. Fellowships that you get as a

PhD student are called predoctoral; they support you while you do the work to complete your PhD.

Fellowships that you get after finishing your PhD (but before you get a permanent job) are called postdoctoral. Postdoctoral fellowships support you while you get additional training that wasn't available in your PhD program and will make you a better researcher. For example, maybe you learned how to collect and analyze two kinds of data during your PhD. But there is a third kind of data that would enrich your research, and to learn how to collect and analyze that, you need to go to some other lab where they use that method. You might write a proposal for a postdoctoral fellowship to pay your salary while you spend a couple of years in that new lab, learning those new skills. There are also fellowships for faculty members, particularly in the arts and humanities. These cover the costs of traveling away from one's home campus for some period of time (usually a few months to a year) to do research and/ or teach somewhere else.

Different fellowship and grant programs ask for different information. For example, the National Science Foundation (NSF) Graduate Research Fellowship Program asks for a lot of information about you, the applicant: They want to know about your background, your future goals, and your research plan for the fellowship period. They require letters of reference and transcripts. The National Institutes of Health (NIH) predoctoral and postdoctoral fellowships also want to know about you, but they ask for more information about the training environment: Who will your mentors be, and how often will you meet with them, and what exactly will you do together? What are the benefits of the environment (the lab, the department, the scientific community) where you will be working? Will you take any classes?

GRANTS

In the sciences, researchers with their own labs apply for grants. For grants, the emphasis is less on you as an individual (although you still have to show that you are competent) and more about the research you are proposing. For example, a grant proposal to NIH includes a one-page statement of "specific aims" laying out the goals of the project and a research strategy section explaining the logic of the approach. Whereas a fellowship is proposed by one person, grants usually describe work that will be done by a team of researchers headed by the lead researcher (also known as the PI, for "principal investigator")

Grants also cover a much broader range of expenses than fellowships. The first one is usually one or two months' summer salary for the PI Officially, most faculty are paid to teach for nine months of the year. This leaves three months open during the summer during which faculty can be paid (by grants) to work on research. But grants don't just pay for a PI's time. They also include salaries for paid employees such as lab managers, lab technicians, postdocs, graduate and undergraduate student researchers, and statistical consultants. Other lines in a grant budget are for lab equipment, materials, and supplies used in research. Still others are for participant compensation (i.e., money that people get in return for participating in a study), money for one of the researchers to travel to a conference to present the results of the research, and various other expenses. So a grant proposal is a much bigger, more complicated document than a fellowship application.

AWARDS

Award is a general term for money given out by some institution, such as an academic department or a funding agency. When a university department gives $500 to a graduate student to help pay for their travel to a conference, that money often given a name like, "Exogeology Department Graduate Student Travel Award," or even "Prof. J.-L. Picard Award for Student Research," which not only gives the student $500, but also something snappy to put on their CV. "Award" is also the word that the big federal funding agencies in the U.S. use for the money they give out. So whether you get $500 from your own department or $5,000,000 from the National Science Foundation, either way it's called an award.

Understand the funding game

Many new researchers take funding decisions personally. They imagine that winning an award will make them feel valued and respected, and when they apply for an award and don't get it, they feel undervalued and maybe even unworthy. In other words, they imagine that the awards are all about *them*. This is the wrong way to think about awards. In truth, funders have a certain amount of money to disburse and certain funding priorities to pursue. The key to getting that money is writing a proposal that matches their funding priorities and happens to go to the right reviewer at the right time. That's why, once you have written a proposal, you should get as much use out of it as you can. Which means submitting the same proposals (maybe with slight variations) over and over again, to as many funders as possible.

PLAY THE ODDS . . .

The first and most important thing to keep in mind about applying for funding is that it's a numbers game. The first step in winning more money is applying for more money. Illustrating this point, Pier et al. (2018) asked each of 43 NIH reviewers to rank the same set of 25 grant applications (all of which had, in reality, been funded by the NIH). What did they find? "Results showed no agreement among reviewers regarding the quality of the applications in either their qualitative or quantitative evaluations."

No agreement! For every reviewer who ranked Application A as the best, there was another reviewer who ranked it worst. In the words of the authors, "It appeared that the outcome of the grant review depended more on the reviewer to whom the grant was assigned than the research proposed in the grant."

So for heaven's sake, don't take it personally when your grant or fellowship application is not funded. It's no more personal than rolling dice. A funded grant is like double sixes. How do you roll more double sixes? You just keep rolling. In the case of grants, that means polishing up your proposal, fixing any errors or weaknesses that are pointed out to you, and then resubmitting as many times as you are allowed, both to the same grant program and to others.

. . . BUT PLAY TO WIN

Playing the odds doesn't mean submitting bad proposals. The grant applications reviewed by Pier and colleagues (2018) were all eventually funded by the NIH, so it's safe to assume that they were all good. In an ideal world, every good proposal would be funded. In the real world there's never enough money, so what gets funded often comes down to luck. But of course, in order to make it into that final pool in the first place, your application has to be very strong. Proposals with any significant weaknesses get weeded out in the review process. Your job is to make your proposal as strong as possible to get it into that lottery of excellent proposals at the top.

DO YOUR HOMEWORK

You get money in science the same way you get money everywhere else—by selling something that people want to buy. In this case, your product is research. So it might help to think of yourself as a design-build contractor.

Let's imagine two contractors: Alphie and Betty. They've spent five years as apprentices at the same water-park building firm, and now they're each ready to strike out and start designing and building water parks on their own.

Alphie sits down at a drafting table and designs the water park of his dreams. He's a military history buff, so he decides on the theme *Arctic Naval Operations of World War II*. The park is divided into four areas named *Operation Claymore*, *Operation Doppelschlag*, *Operation Gearbox II*, and *Battle of the North Cape*. Alphie spends two months creating detailed designs for his park, which will cover 2,720 square feet and cost $750,000 to build. He goes to a municipal contractors' website and finds a list of cities looking to build water parks in the next couple of years. He sends his plan to all the cities and then sits back and waits for the money to roll in.

Betty takes a different approach. She starts by making a list of cities looking to build waterparks. She searches each city's website for information about their budget, timeline, space constraints, and any specific design criteria they have. She makes a list like the one shown in Table 6.1.

City	Due date	Size (ft²)	Budget	Notes
Escondido, CA	July 1, 2021	4,000	$1,250,000	Environment or conservation theme
Mexico City	Dec. 1, 2020	9,000	$2,475,000	
Montgomery, AL	Feb. 4, 2021	3,000	$825,000	
Ottawa, ON	Nov. 30, 2021	8,500	$644,000	
Quincy, MA	April 30, 2021	1,500	$300,000	Separate area for kids 2–5
Rock Hill, SC	June 30, 2021	10,000	$2,500,000	Pirate theme
Tulsa, OK	Oct. 15, 2020	8,000	$2,800,000	

Table 6.1

It's already October 1, so Betty eliminates the Tulsa project—there's no way she'll have enough time to prepare a proposal in the next 2 weeks. She divides the remaining projects into two groups: big and small, shown in Tables 6.2 and 6.3. These are sorted by due date.

The three big projects have similar sizes and budgets, so she decides to create a basic design for a big park and customize it for each of the three cities. She will also design a small park and submit slightly different versions of it to Montgomery and Ottawa. She decides not to submit a design to Quincy, because that project is so much smaller than the others that she would have to create a completely separate design.

Compare our two contractors. Alphie is thinking about what he wants to build and hoping someone will fund it. Betty is thinking about how to use her skills and expertise to create something that fits the funders' priorities, space constraints, budget, and timeline.

Big projects	Due date	Size (ft²)	Budget	Notes
Mexico City	Dec. 1, 2020	9,000	$2,475,000	
Rock Hill, SC	June 30, 2021	10,000	$2,500,000	Pirate theme
Ottawa, ON	Nov. 30, 2021	8,500	$644,000	

Table 6.2

Big projects	Due date	Size (ft²)	Budget	Notes
Montgomery, AL	Feb. 4, 2021	3,000	$825,000	
Escondido, CA	July 1, 2021	4,000	$1,250,000	Environment or conservation theme
~~Quincy, MA~~	~~April 30, 2021~~	~~1,500~~	~~$300,000~~	~~Separate area for kids 2–5~~

Table 6.3

Don't be an Alphie; be a Betty. Before you start designing your project, take the time to research funders and find out what they want. What kind of questions are they interested in? How long (time-wise) and how big (budget-wise) are the projects they fund? None of this is a secret—most funders openly announce their funding priorities, and their websites include abstracts of projects they've funded before. Read the priorities and take them seriously. Read the abstracts. If you have any questions at all, call or email the program officers. At some agencies (including the NIH), program officers are a huge untapped resource—they will give you a lot of great advice if you just ask them.

Write the proposal

When you've gathered all the relevant information, draft a work timeline that will let you resubmit versions of the same grant to multiple agencies, customizing it for each one. If your work gets funded by more than one agency, you'll have to negotiate with the program officers about how to split it up, but that's a good problem to have.

In general, start as early as you can—preferably several months before the submission deadline. This will give you time to draft the whole grant, get feedback from several colleagues (sometimes a program officer will even be willing to look at your "specific aims" or other brief outline of the proposal), make revisions, and still submit it by the deadline.

Funding proposals take shape through the same messy process as other kinds of documents. The first draft is terrible, the second is better, the third might be good enough to show a friend, and so on. When you have a draft but don't know how to revise it, reverse outlining (see Chapter 3) is a powerful tool. All of the advice elsewhere in this book about how to write clearly for a nonspecialist audience is brought to bear in writing funding proposals.

Because the applications are different for each funder and each program, the easiest way to start is to get a copy of a finished proposal for the program you are applying to and use it as a template. (If the proposal was funded, even better.)

No matter where you are applying, and what you are proposing to do, grant proposals always have a similar argument structure, which can be summed up in a single paragraph, or "blurb."

Here's how the blurb is described by my friend Teya Rutherford, a longtime member of our writing workshop, now an assistant professor at the University of Delaware. Teya recently received her fourth NSF grant—their prestigious CAREER award—and she wrote an excellent blog post about the application process.

> *When I work on any grant, I first start with the blurb. This is a short statement of the problem, the opportunity, and the proposed solution. When I help mentor graduate students in fellowship applications, like the NSF GRFP [National Science Foundation Graduate Research Fellowship Program], I advise them to write a short paragraph that covers (1) The problem—start broad and then narrow, (2) What people have done about it before and why it isn't enough, (3) What is the particular opportunity that will allow you to address shortcomings from #2, and (4) How will you do that? (Rutherford, 2019)*

Teya goes on to explain that she worked on the blurb (just the blurb) for her CAREER award proposal for three months—refining it, rewriting it, showing it to every colleague who was willing to comment. Only when she felt happy with the blurb did she move on to writing the rest of the (ultimately successful) proposal.

The blurb is a one-paragraph summary of the whole proposal, and the four points Teya identifies in the blurb are the four questions that every grant proposal must answer. Let's consider them one by one.

LAY OUT THE GENERAL AND SPECIFIC
PROBLEMS MOTIVATING THE RESEARCH

Nobody is going to give you money unless your research addresses some problem they care about. (You can find out which problems they care about by reading their website.) Sometimes funders, especially small ones, care about very specific problems. For example, say there's a private foundation that wants to fund research combating childhood obesity in the U.S. You have to show that your work addresses that problem. Sometimes the connection is easy to make—for example, perhaps you want to study the nutritional content of school lunch programs. Other times the connection requires a few steps. For example, maybe you want to study how much homework children are assigned. Then you need to make a convincing case that increases in homework might be related to increases in obesity.

Big funders, like the NIH, the NSF, the Institute for Education Sciences (IES), and the Defense Advanced Research Projects Agency (DARPA), support research on a wide range of topics. In this case, you have to identify a problem that you want to address and tell them why it matters.

Identifying the problem that your proposed research will solve (the rationale for the research) is similar to identifying the problem in the introduction of an **IMRaD** article (as described in Chapter 5). You start with the broad or general problem that you think the funder cares about (e.g., *Nearly 32% of American children are overweight or obese. One generation ago, the rate was only 17%.*) Then you draw a connection to the narrower, more specific problem that your research will actually address (e.g., *85% of children eat lunch at school; we're going to study the nutrition in school lunch programs* or *Over the past 20 years, schools have increased homework by 65%. We hypothesize that increases* *in homework cause increases in obesity by raising children's cortisol levels and reducing time spent in both outdoor free play and sleep.)*

If you are curing cancer or mitigating climate change, the importance of your research will be obvious. But if you do basic research (research where the goal is just to learn about something, with no immediate or obvious applications), then you'll have to convince reviewers that your work is worth their investment. This is always a challenge. On the positive side, your funding application will be reviewed by other scientists in the same field as you, and they value this work more than the average person does. On the negative side, funders don't want to spend their money on research that won't make any difference in the world. So if you are embarking on a career in basic research, start thinking now about what real-world problems you can connect your work to.

SUMMARIZE WHAT HAS BEEN DONE ALREADY AND WHY THE PROBLEM STILL ISN'T SOLVED

This is your literature review. It is an introductory lit review (as described in Chapter 4), meaning that its purpose is to provide the context that the reader needs in order to understand your argument. Specifically, its purpose is to describe what other people have done in the past to address the problem or answer the question you've raised, what they achieved (this is what you will build on), and what's still left to do (this is the gap that your research will fill).

This is not a student literature review, so its purpose is not to demonstrate what you know, although of course it does implicitly show that. But that's not its main purpose. The distinction is important because funding proposals have strict word or page limits. In a student lit review, you are free to include as much material as you like. Material can be included even if it's only marginally relevant, because more material just makes the review look more comprehensive, which is fine. The lit review section of a funding proposal, by contrast, should mention only those works that are clearly and directly related to the proposed project. Proposals have no room for extra words.

EXPLAIN YOUR UNFAIR ADVANTAGE

Your next task is to make the case for why your proposed research represents a special opportunity to make progress in this area where previous research did not. This is sometimes called the unfair advantage, as in *What is your unfair advantage? What is the advantage you have over other researchers that will let you do this work successfully where they could not?*

The word "unfair" is not meant to suggest cheating or lying or breaking rules, just that there is something special or unusual about you, or about your situation, that makes this research a unique opportunity for funders. Perhaps you have a new idea that had not occurred to anyone before. Perhaps you have skills that other researchers don't have. Perhaps you have access to something that is needed for this research but that other researchers don't have access to.

Continuing with the homework/obesity example, you might argue that no one has yet thought to study the connection between homework and obesity, although both have been increasing for years. Or you might emphasize your unique expertise and background on the topic of homework in elementary education, along with the expertise of your coinvestigator who is an expert on social and environmental causes of childhood obesity. Or you might present an agreement with the superintendent of schools in the district where you plan to do this work, showing that the district admin-istration, and the principals and the teachers, have all agreed to participate in this study where you will randomly assign teachers to give either a lot of homework or a little homework, and you will study the effects on students' health and weight. This agreement will allow you to do an actual experiment and collect causal data on a large scale, whereas other studies on this topic rely on merely correlational data. The point is that reviewers should read this pro-posal and think that it presents a unique (or at least unusual) oppor-tunity for the agency to fund some high-quality, important work.

At a minimum, you must demonstrate that you and the team you put together will be able to carry out the work you are pro-posing. If you are an established scientist with a long history of publishing in this area, then your track record will speak for itself. But let's assume you don't have that kind of record yet. How do you convince the reviewers that you can do this?

Highlight your strengths. Just like when you send out résumés for jobs, you want to present the best picture of your qualifications and accomplishments. You are probably too familiar with the infor-mation on your own CV to see it objectively, so make sure to draft your biosketch (or whatever CV-like document you have to submit for the proposal) early, and show it to someone such as an advisor or a senior colleague for feedback. Other people can often suggest improvements or clarifications that wouldn't occur to you.

If you're a scientist, build a team. The humanities are indi-vidual sports; the sciences are team sports. If you are in any type of science, don't try to play every position yourself. Instead, put together a great team. If you are applying for a predoctoral or post-doctoral fellowship, your team will be yourself and the people who will train you. They should have a strong track record of research themselves, and a strong record of training graduate students or postdocs. You should always work with your proposed advisor(s) to write a predoctoral or postdoctoral fellowship application. If you are considering working with a mentor, and they don't have time to at least read over a draft of your fellowship application and give you detailed comments, it means they don't have time to mentor you. Consider working with someone else.

Identify and contact community partners. If your work requires the help or cooperation of people or institutions outside your university, you will probably need letters of cooperation from them too. For example, in my lab we collect data at preschools and museums. So we include letters of cooperation from those preschools and museums in our grant proposals. The letters are on official letterhead and signed by the director of the school/museum (or other responsible person). They basically say, "We exist, and we have X number of children here, between the ages of Y and Z. We are happy to allow the Sarnecka lab to recruit participants and collect data for the proposed project."

Consider assembling an advisory board of experts in the area—people who won't actually do the work on your project but who will give you feedback on the research design and help you solve problems along the way. Just as you shouldn't propose to do a postdoc with a mentor who is too busy to help you write the proposal, you also probably shouldn't invite someone to be on your advisory board unless they have time to read and comment on a draft of your proposal. Some funding agencies ask you to include a letter of cooperation from each person on your advisory board. You should also include a plan for how the board will advise you. For example, you might put money in the budget to bring all the board members to your campus for a meeting at the beginning of the project and also plan to hold half-day meetings by teleconference every year while the project is being carried out.

You can't be an expert on everything, and you shouldn't try to be. When I was a new assistant professor, I didn't understand this. I remember having a conversation with an NIH program officer who said that I should include a budget for statistical consulting in my grant proposal. I was offended. "Statistical consulting?" I fumed. "What for? Do the reviewers think I'm statistically incompetent?"

I was offended by the idea of a consultant because I wanted to show that I could do everything myself. The NIH program officer was nudging me to adopt a more mature view. He knew that the reviewers wouldn't care whether I personally analyzed the data; they just needed some assurance that the analyses would be done right. I'm an expert in cognitive development, not statistics. Thus, I needed to show that there would be a statistics expert available. Today, I'm delighted to pay for statistical consulting. Why would I analyze data myself if someone else can do it just as well and save me the trouble? There's plenty of work that I can't delegate, so I'm happy to share what burdens I can.

PRESENT YOUR PLAN

Finally, you must present a plan for your research. This is analogous to the method section of an IMRaD paper, except that the methods described in a funding proposal are usually less detailed because proposals have strict word or page limits. Most proposals will include the following information in some form, maybe with different labels or in a different order, depending on the grant submission instructions.

*   A **method** section explaining what you are going to measure and how. This is similar to the method section of a scientific paper, but less detailed because space is more limited.

* A **budget** explaining all the costs associated with the project. For a big grant, this will include things like salaries, equipment, travel, participant compensation, etc. For a fellowship, the award is usually a fixed amount of money and you may just have to write a paragraph or two saying how you will use it. For a big grant, the budget is a separate document (usually a spreadsheet) that you work with an administrator at your university to prepare. (Most grants are technically awarded to the university, not to you.) If you get to work with a skilled and experienced administrator, count yourself lucky and treat that person with the greatest courtesy and respect. They can make your job a whole lot easier.

* A **budget justification**. This document explains each of the items listed in the budget. Again, your administrative support person should be able to help you with this.

* A **timeline** sketching out when everything will get done. This need not take up much space—maybe a couple of lines at the bottom of a page.

* A statement that you have the necessary **facilities** or environment to do the work. For example, if your research requires an fMRI machine or a scanning electron microscope or the use of a research station at the South Pole, you will have to confirm that you have access to those things.

* A **dissemination plan** explaining how you plan to share the results of your work with the scientific community, the public, politicians, or whoever you think should know about it. You do this by publishing articles, giving talks at conferences, etc. Publicly

funded agencies are especially interested in this, because their mission is not only to fund research but also to get the results out into the world.

———

A few years ago, I was serving as a reviewer on a panel for a federal funding agency. We reviewed a few dozen grant proposals, two of which described essentially the same work. One of these came from a well-known senior researcher whom I will call Prof. Hotshot. The other came from Prof. Hotshot's former PhD student, who had recently been hired into a tenure-track job at another university. I'll call this person Prof. Newbie.

Prof. Hotshot's proposal described the work in very general terms, starting at the public level and narrowing to the disciplinary level by the end of the introduction. The proposal included just enough methodological detail to reassure reviewers that the work would be done competently. Prof. Newbie, by contrast, spent most of the proposal describing the research methods in far more detail than necessary and not giving reviewers a big picture that they could get excited about.

The proposed work happened to be in my own subfield, so I was one of the only reviewers who understood Prof. Newbie's proposal. I could see that both proposals described essentially the same set of experiments.

I gave Prof. Newbie's grant a higher score just because I like to root for the underdog, and Prof. Hotshot had plenty of grants already. But the other reviewers rated Prof. Hotshot's proposal much higher. They said it was clear and convincing, unlike Prof. Newbie's proposal. The problem wasn't the work itself—the two proposals described the same work. The problem was that Prof. Newbie filled the proposal with overly technical and specific descriptions. The reviewers were bored, and they didn't see the connection between the proposed work and any big question or problem they cared about. That's what happens when you write about your work in overly technical terms.

PUT THE FINISHING TOUCHES ON YOUR PROPOSAL

Before you submit your grant, ask someone to proofread it carefully. Unless you are supremely well organized, you will have been working on this document for the past 72 hours straight, and the deadline will be four hours from now, and the thought of looking at the proposal one more time will make you want to throw your laptop into the nearest large body of water. So ask someone you trust—someone from your writing group, your roommate, your mom, etc.—to proofread the whole thing for typos, sentence fragments, missing words, and other errors that you can no longer even see because you've read the proposal so many times.

Also (and this should be obvious, but it's worth saying anyway), *follow the instructions to the letter.* If it says to put your proposal narrative in 14-point, purple Comic Sans font, with happy-face emoticons instead of page numbers and every 17th word in Japanese, then *do it.* The first thing funders do when they receive an application is check to make sure it meets all the technical requirements (formatting, length, all documents complete, etc.). Applications that don't conform are tossed immediately. So follow the damn directions.

Finally, try not to wait until the very last minute to upload your proposal. First, submitting usually takes longer than you think it will. Say for example that the granting agency requires you to submit the proposal as a .pdf. But when you convert your working document to the .pdf format, the one-page summary no longer fits on one page. Now it's one page plus one sentence that spills onto a second page. So you have to go back and change something—cutting words or changing the margins or the font—but that creates other problems, which take additional time to solve, and so on. Second, for really big deadlines for really big agencies, the websites sometimes crash during the last hour or two before the deadline.

The agencies often extend the deadline when this happens, but you can't count on that, and either way it creates a headache you don't need. So do yourself a favor and pretend that the deadline is a day or a week earlier than it actually is. Put the earlier deadline on your calendar and try to forget that it's not the real one. When your fake deadline rolls around and you're not ready to submit, having that extra time will be like finding money in the pocket of a jacket you haven't worn since last year—a lovely surprise gift from your past self.

7

PRESENTATIONS

Part of being a researcher is presenting your work in person. This can be as informal as your answer when someone asks what you work on or as formal as giving the keynote speech at a conference. Listening to a live presentation should be an easy and painless way for academics to learn about each other's work, but not all presentations are easy to understand. Some difficulty is probably unavoidable when researchers try to convey complex information, but much of the difficulty is unnecessary and could be avoided if presentations were designed and delivered better. I've suffered through countless presentations in my own subfield that I could barely follow. In most cases the research itself was fine, but the presentation was bad. This chapter tells you how to create academic presentations that audiences will understand and enjoy.

The elevator pitch

From the time that you enter a PhD program, people ask what you study. "What kind of research do you do?" asks the family member at the holiday gathering. "What will your PhD dissertation be about?" asks the woman cleaning your teeth at the dentist's office. "Please start by introducing yourself and telling us what you work on," says the faculty member leading the seminar. After a while, the one-sentence summary of your work feels like a natural suffix to your name and departmental affiliation (e.g., "Barbara Sarnecka, Cognitive Sciences, I work on language and number concept development in early childhood.")

A slightly longer and higher-stakes version of that brief summary is the elevator pitch. Imagine that you are at an academic conference and you find yourself riding up in the elevator with Dr. Famous, who is a big deal in your field. You introduce yourself to Dr. Famous, who politely asks you what you work on. Knowing that you only have a couple of minutes before the elevator ride is over, what do you say? The answer is your elevator pitch.

A good elevator pitch has two parts: The **headline** and the **elaboration**. The headline is a concrete, one-sentence summary of your work. When Dr. Famous asks what you do, you give the headline and then **stop talking**. If Dr. Famous asks a follow-up question or signals that they want to hear more, then give the elaboration, which should take no more than one minute. Again, after you say your piece, be quiet. Let Dr. Famous ask you questions to guide the rest of the conversation. Table 7.1 gives examples of polished elevator pitches contributed by successful scholars in a variety of disciplines.

Although the elevator pitch is brief and informal, it's not easy to produce a good one spontaneously. So make time to practice these with your writing workshop at least once per term, and recognize that there's likely to be a lot of awkwardness and nervous laughter as people try to describe their research in just a sentence or two. But it's well worth the effort because the end result, a smooth elevator pitch, is a real asset.

Name (Discipline: Subfield)
Headline
Elaboration (only if they ask)

Ashley (Psychology: Developmental Social Cognition)

Toddlers like winners, and they don't like bullies.

We showed toddlers a puppet show where two puppets have conflicting goals and one of them wins. Then we ask who they like better, and toddlers choose the winner. But when the winner knocks the other guy out of the way, then they don't like the winner anymore.

Duncan (Philosophy: Epistemology)

I'm interested in explaining how knowledge is possible, contrary to radical skeptical arguments that suggest otherwise.

I claim that the radical skeptical problem is more challenging than many have supposed, but that even in its strongest form it can be resisted. They key to my solution is to realize that it is in fact two logically distinct problems in disguise. The solution involves showing that two apparently competing current anti-skeptical proposals are in fact not only compatible but mutually supporting—at least provided they are each targeted on the right element of the sceptical problem. I call this dual account of both the skeptical problem and its resolution the biscopic response.

Emily (Neuroscience: Cognitive Neuroscience)

We are learning how brain stimulation can promote stroke recovery.

Clinicians are beginning to look to noninvasive brain stimulation as a tool to improve outcomes after stroke. But the effective stimulation protocols and how they promote plasticity are unknown. My goal is to identify how brain connectivity is impacted by stimulation, which may be beneficial in developing interventions for stroke patients.

Table 7.1 (continued on next page)

Heidi (Political Science: International Relations)

I study how and why groups of countries—called international organizations—succeed and fail to resolve conflicts around the world. Examples of these organizations include the United Nations, NATO, and the European Union.

My research involves interviewing and conducting survey experiments on large numbers of political and military elites (such as high-level military officials and ambassadors) so as to understand how bureaucratic problems within international organizations help or hurt their ability to be effective. Few studies have taken such a close look at the people within these organizations and how—as individuals—they affect the organizations' performance.

Greg (Chemistry: Synthetic Organic Chemistry)

We can help cure cancer by doing some very cool chemistry and make a lot of money.

[This example is written from the perspective of a scientist working in industry, not academia.]

Nature has this amazing cure for cancer, but it's really rare and hard to find in the jungle. In the lab we've figured out a way to improve on an old and expensive synthetic technique, so much so that it is now profitable to make. With current demand forecasts we reckon we can provide a real rate of return higher than any other new drug on the market.

Lisa (Linguistics: Natural Language Processing)

I use insights from how people use language to help machines decode subtle information that people communicate via language text, such as intentions, tone, and identity.

A lot of current approaches to natural language processing don't leverage the insights from psychology about why people communicate the way they do in certain contexts or the more sophisticated representations from linguistics that capture the abstract knowledge that humans have about language. Many of my recent projects have incorporated features that both (i) draw from the psychology of language use and (ii) harness

Table 7.1 (continued)

linguistic abstract representation. I've used these features together with state-of-the-art symbolic machine learning algorithms to automatically detect intentions like deception, tone-like politeness, and whether a single author can truly write as if they were multiple characters (who each have their own styles).

Oren (English Literature: Poetics)

I am interested in connections between the way poems try to portray a human mind in action and the way that contemporary philosophers think about and debate the nature and structure of minds and thought; I'm interested in why these two disciplines haven't recently had much to say to each other, and also in what each has to offer the other.

For example, I'm interested in why scholars of poetry have recently been interested in the problem of "melancholia," while philosophers have been more interested in the problem of "akrasia." Both concepts arguably describe a similar problem: the inability to move on from an unproductive state of feeling or action. Both can be found in the long history of art and thought. So why has it come to pass that one is "poetic" and the other "philosophical"?

I argue that these concepts illuminate a fundamental schism between a philosophical tradition that views "weakness of the will" as an aberration in need of rational justification and a poetic tradition that views the mind's plight (and maybe even its particular virtue) to lie in its insurmountable irrationality. So I read Thomas Hardy's elegiac poetry (in *Poems 1912-1913*, for example) to consider the question of what difference it might make to see mourning as a case of akrasia (remaining stuck in mourning despite knowing better) rather than a melancholy (remaining in the grip of loss and lack because there is nothing better to know).

Rahul (Developmental Biology: Gene Expression)

I'm really interested in how IRES function.

There's increasing evidence that up to 10% of eukaryotic mRNAs use IRES. And while we have a reasonable idea of how viral IRES work,

Table 7.1 (continued on next page)

there's really no basis to understand how their cellular counterparts function. There's no consensus sequence that can predict the presence of an IRES, and IRES-transacting factors are not known. We have a powerful system to study this problem that bypasses the artifacts in cell culture approaches and allows us to use genetics as well.

Sarah (Law: Tax Law)

Tax forms actually make law.

The structure of tax forms—not the instructions, but the structure of the forms themselves, the order in which the user adds, subtracts, divides, and so forth--can resolve ambiguous law, usually without anyone noticing. This raises issues for tax law, and also is an example of some potential problems with computational law, even in the absence of a computer.

Table 7.1 (continued)

Being able to describe your research briefly and clearly makes it much easier to have conversations with people—not only famous people, but also your peers—who are interested in similar topics. The person standing next to you in line for coffee at a conference could be a potential collaborator. If you can easily and comfortably explain what you work on, it could start a conversation that leads to collaborations, invitations to present your work, job opportunities, and other benefits. So practice your elevator pitch.

The poster

Let's assume that you know what information goes on an academic poster. (If not, check out Hess, Tosney & Liegel, 2013; Graves, 2019; or Purrington, 2019.) The traditional scientific poster format does not do a good job of communicating information. Most posters are densely covered with text, and it takes a lot of time and effort from the reader to figure out what the researchers actually found. Many people dislike poster sessions. The presenters feel disappointed that no one wants to read their poster, and the visitors just feel exhausted. No one learns much.

TRY A MORRISON-STYLE POSTER

Happily, there is a much better way to do it. PhD student Mike Morrison (2019) has applied modern principles of graphic design and user experience to create a much better poster format. It takes no more time or effort to create than the old format, and it communicates the key information much more clearly and easily, even to people who just glance at it from across the room. Morrison's invention gets the official Writing Workshop Seal of Approval. (Five out of five penguins!) Figures 7.1 and 7.2 are examples of posters made in the traditional style and Morrison's new style, respectively.

MAKE IT A CONVERSATION, NOT A SPEECH

Once you have designed a beautiful poster, you will have to present it. The key is to let your presentation be guided by the listener's questions. When you give a poster, you are usually speaking to just one or two people at a time. Don't launch into a monologue like a telemarketer; have a conversation like a normal human being. Follow the same principle as in the elevator talk: Prepare a headline of just one or two sentences, and let the rest of the conversation take the form of a question-and-answer session, where the visitor asks questions and you answer them.

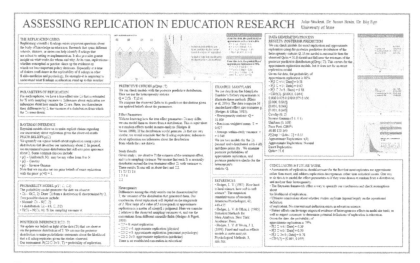

Figure 7.1 Traditional wall-of-text poster

This is the big advantage of posters—you don't have to antici-pate the right level of description for your listener, because your listener is standing right there and will (if you let them) tell you what the right level is. Some people want to talk about big ideas; others want to talk about technical details. The poster is there to provide a few key sentences and important visual information. The main source of information is you, having conversations with people.

The talk

The curse of knowledge is a big problem in talks. If you pitch a research article too high (in other words, if you make it too dif-ficult for nonexperts to understand) the only consequence is that fewer people will read it. People who don't have the background to decode it will simply find your article boring and put it down. But those who really need to know what it says can still work their

Figure 7.2 Morrison's billboard-style poster

way through it by looking up terms they don't know, and rereading sentences as many times as necessary, and discussing the paper with knowledgeable others.

Talks are a different story. Audiences at a talk can't control how fast you throw information at them. They can't pause your presentation like a video, and most people are too polite to raise their hand and ask you to repeat or explain things they didn't understand. If a person at your talk loses track of your meaning, they will watch quietly for another couple of minutes and then start checking email on their phone. At the end of the talk, they will applaud politely and ask no questions.

Most academic talks and posters should be pitched at the disciplinary level (see Chapter 3). This is the right level when you are speaking at a conference or in a university department where the audience is mainly other researchers in your field. Presentations to broader audiences (e.g., to faculty from across the university, or to a nonuniversity audience) should be pitched at the public level.

On rare occasions, if you are speaking to a small group of researchers who all work in the same area as you, you may be able to pitch a talk at the subfield level. No talk should be pitched at the lab level. Early-career scientists (particularly graduate students) often make the mistake of attributing too much insider knowledge to their audience. They get used to talking about their work with people in their own labs, and they don't realize that the rest of the world doesn't have the same background knowledge. This is the curse of knowledge in action.

TELL A STORY

A lot of academic and scientific talks are boring. Not just boring to outsiders, but boring to other researchers in the same area. When you can't hold the attention of people who spend all their time thinking about this stuff, you're doing something wrong. Because bad academic talks are boring, one of the most common pieces of advice you hear is that you must grab the audience's attention and hold it. But how are you supposed to do that? The answer is simple: by giving your talk the structure of a story.

Popular story types like romances, murder mysteries, police procedurals, and even jokes all grab and hold people's attention in the same way: They create some kind of tension and then relieve it. The simplest example of this is the joke, which in its classic form consists of a *setup* that creates tension and a *punchline* that relieves it. Here's an example, with the setup in regular type and the punch-line in bold:

> The Dean is hospitalized after a heart attack. As she is lying in her hospital bed reflecting on her near brush with death, an attendant arrives with a

lovely bouquet of flowers. The card reads, **"By a vote of 26 to 3 with 2 abstentions, the faculty wish you a speedy recovery."** (secundem_ artem, 2012)

Other genres also rely on tension to keep people reading. Romantic or sexual tension is created when lovers want to be together but are kept apart. The tension is resolved when they get their happily ever after. Adventure stories and thrillers create tension by putting characters in danger. The tension is resolved when the characters are once again safe. Murder mysteries and police procedurals create tension through curiosity and unanswered questions: Who committed the crime? How will they be caught? How high up does the conspiracy go?

All of us who grew up with popular fiction, TV and movies expect these rules to be followed. We know that the joke will have a punchline, the lovers will get together, and the mystery will be solved. Waiting for the tension to be resolved is what keeps us invested in the story. The way to structure a research presentation like a story is by raising some problem or question at the beginning, and then resolving it over the course of the presentation.

Finding the story in translational or applied research

This is easy. You're already working on something people care about; you just have to show them how your particular research connects to the big problem you are trying to solve. Let's imagine that you are trying to cure cancer. You could start your talk as in the fictional example that follows. (Here and throughout the chapter, the rectangles on the left are slides, and the text on the right is what you might say while the slide is visible.)

This opening connects a big problem the audience cares about (curing cancer) to the specific question your research addresses (How can we optimize the process of making Talinexatol?). If they want to learn the answer to the second question, they will keep listening to your talk.

Finding the story in basic research

If you do basic research, you have to work a little harder to make your audience care about the question you are trying to answer, but you can do it. After all, there's some question in there that interested you, right? So you just need to help your audience see it too.

The easiest way to raise a question in your audience's mind is by presenting them with a puzzle—something surprising or counterintuitive that piques their curiosity. It could be some surprising facts about the world, or just an apparent contradiction. Consider this example from the philosopher Duncan Pritchard (2019, personal communication):

> We standardly take ourselves to know a great many things, but there are some apparently compelling philosophical arguments which purport to show that knowledge is impossible. I'm interested in working out how these arguments go awry, and in the process discovering something important about the nature of knowledge (and related notions, like reasons, evidence, and so on).

This is definitely basic research, and Pritchard introduces it by way of an apparent contradiction: *As human beings, we think we know*

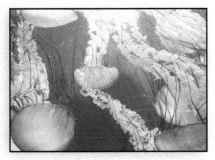

Figure 7.3

Does anyone know what this is? Right, it's a jellyfish. It's actually the rare, deep-sea jellyfish scyphozoa talinexae, and right there [pointing to picture] inside its gut is a substance called Talinexatol, which is great at fighting cancers of the mouth and foot in humans. The problem is this guy is so hard to find and lives so deep in the ocean, we just can't get enough Talinexatol for medical use.

Figure 7.4

The good news is it's possible to make Talinexatol in the lab. The bad news is it's a very long process. Time-consuming, labor-intensive, expensive, and not very efficient.

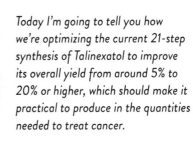

Figure 7.5

Today I'm going to tell you how we're optimizing the current 21-step synthesis of Talinexatol to improve its overall yield from around 5% to 20% or higher, which should make it practical to produce in the quantities needed to treat cancer.

stuff. But some philosophers say we can't know anything. What's up with that? Of course when you start your talk with an unanswered question, puzzle, or contradiction, you implicitly promise that you will resolve it by the end of the talk. If it's a really big question, you probably can't answer it completely. But you should at least be able to show how your work gets us closer to an answer.

Using brief stories to make points within a presentation

Even if you can't figure out a way to structure your whole presentation like a story, you can use stories make smaller points within it. This will still make for a better talk than if you didn't have any stories.

My former student Ashley studies how people think about social hierarchies, which includes how they feel about winners and losers. In order to introduce the idea that adults like winners, Ashley sometimes shows a photo of her father, wearing what appears to be a baseball cap with two brims facing in opposite directions. She puts the picture up on screen and says something like,

> *This is my dad. Can you see what's unusual about the hat he's wearing? Yes, it's actually two hats sewn together. It's a UC-Berkeley hat on one side and a UCLA hat on the other. My brother went to UCLA, and I went to Berkeley. In this picture, my dad is watching the the UCLA-Berkeley football game. And here's the key question: Can you guess which team is winning?*

Ashley points out that the UCLA side of the hat is facing forward in the picture, and she explains that her dad supports whichever team is ahead, turning his hat around to show his changes of allegiance. She then goes on to present other examples and experimental data showing that adults like winners. But she introduced the idea with a story and an image that were relatable and fun.

As another example, my student Emily studies a classic decision-making problem called the explore/exploit problem. She often introduces this problem by giving audiences a hypothetical explore/exploit task. For example, she might say,

> *Imagine that after this talk, you decide to go out for dinner. Do you go to your favorite restaurant, or try a new one? To go to your favorite restaurant is to exploit a known resource; to try a new place is to explore. Exploring is considered riskier than exploiting, because you might not like the new restaurant. But it also has potentially greater rewards because you might like it even better than your old place.*

To introduce the idea that different people follow different strategies of exploring or exploiting resources, Emily uses the example of her own parents. (I swear I don't tell my grad students to mention their parents in their talks— Emily says she got the idea from Ashley.) She describes how they follow a near-perfect exploitation strategy, eating dinner every Saturday night at the same Legal Sea Foods restaurant in Boston, sitting in the same booth, and ordering the same meals. She shows pictures of her parents, the restaurant, the booth, and the meals. It only takes a few seconds, but it's charming; it makes everyone in the audience smile; and most importantly it clearly illustrates an exploitation strategy that they can understand.

If you happen to study psychology or any aspect of human perception or behavior, you're in luck. Your audience is made up of (relatively) normal humans, so you can often demonstrate the phenomenon you study by having them do some version of your experiment for themselves.

For example, those who study number estimation often do a demonstration in which they flash an image (e.g., a flock of birds) up on screen for a second or so and ask the audience to yell out how many birds they saw. In this way, they can easily demonstrate that there is almost no variation for small numbers (if I show two birds, everyone yells out "Two!") and lots of variation for large numbers (if you show 20 birds, people yell out numbers ranging from about 15 to 25).

If participants in your experiments listened to a series of musical notes and then judged whether they were mostly ascending or descending, play the notes for your audience and ask them to make the same judgement. If your participants had to decide which of two witnesses was telling the truth, play the two videos for your audience and ask them to decide. Of course not all experiments with human participants can be demonstrated neatly in a talk. But if you can do this, it's a great way to bring the research to life.

Stories must be relevant

If you do use something like a demonstration, an anecdote, or an example, make sure it really does illustrate the phenomenon you want to talk about. The danger with stories and examples, because they are so attention-grabbing, is that audiences get invested in them. So if your opening story or example implies that your talk will be about one thing, but your talk turns out to be about something else, people will feel annoyed and cheated.

Emily (of the Legal Seafood parents), way back when she was a new graduate student, was presenting a study of children's propensity to take risks. "Risk" was operationalized as a choice between two spinners, which were like simplified roulette wheels. One wheel gave the child a single sticker with every spin. The other wheel gave the child two stickers on 50% of spins and no stickers on the other 50%. Choosing the second wheel is considered a "risky" strategy. (This is a child-friendly version of a task long used to studying decision-making in adults.)

Looking for a fun way to introduce the idea of kids taking risks, Emily started a talk about this work with a picture of kids climbing a tree. She said something like, "Kids make decisions about risk and reward all the time. For example, these kids have decided that the fun of climbing this tree is worth the risk of falling." Then she went on to present the study with the roulette wheels.

Afterward, some people in the audience complained, saying that if you wanted to study why kids climb tall trees, the roulette task wasn't a good way to do it. Of course Emily never intended to study why children climb trees. She had merely picked the tree example as a way of introducing the topics of kids and risk. The problem was that the tree-climbing example had been so engaging that some people in the audience really wanted to know how children decide which trees are too high to climb, and they were disappointed and irritated when Emily's work turned out to be about a different kind of risk.

My point is this: Examples, demonstrations, and stories are like flashing lights and sirens. They really grab people's attention, so use them carefully.

If you can't find a story, at least create a list with depth

Research presentations that don't tell stories usually just present a bunch of information in some kind of logical order, which is essentially a list. The presentations may be very well organized, but they aren't stories unless they raise a question at the beginning and answer it by the end. Because lists don't create tension and then relieve it like a story does, they don't hold an audience's attention as well.

But let's assume that, for some reason, you really can't think of any way to make your talk into a story. In that case, at least create a list with general or abstract points backed up by specific details and concrete examples, so that the list has some depth. For example, imagine that for some reason I have decided to tell you my grocery shopping list. I have several options.

1. I could just read you the list: almond flour, butter, eggs, cheddar cheese, salt, pepper, heavy cream, baking powder.

2. I could give the list some depth and coherence by adding another layer (sections of the store) and ordering the list from the section with the most items to the one with the fewest. Then the list would be something like DAIRY: butter, cheddar cheese, eggs, heavy cream. BAKING AISLE: almond flour. SPICES: black peppercorns. For that kind of list I might start my talk with an outline, saying something like, "I have to get things from three sections of the store: Dairy, Baking, and Spices."

3. I could make it a story. I could start with an image of scones and say something like, "A couple of weeks ago, my friend texted me a picture of these gorgeous black pepper and cheddar cheese scones. I found this really annoying." [First question raised in audience's mind: Why was I annoyed?] "You see, my friend knows that I recently gave up eating flour and sugar. So it seemed like she was taunting me and my pitiable sconeless existence. But of course, she's too good a friend for that. It turns out there's no flour or sugar in these scones at all." [First question answered. Second question raised: How do you make scones without flour?] "It turns out

they're made with almond flour. I decided to make them immediately. The scones required almond flour, butter, an egg, shredded cheddar cheese, salt, pepper, baking powder, and heavy cream. I already had the salt, pepper, baking powder, and egg, so I went to the store to get the rest of the ingredients."

Looking over these three options, you can see how No. 2, the list with structure and depth, is better than No. 1, the flat list. But No. 3, which has a story, is more interesting than either of the first two. In fact, I'm pretty sure that reading No. 1 and No. 2 didn't make anybody want to go to the store and buy that stuff. But No. 3 probably inspired at least some readers to make the scones. (You can find the recipe at Gourmet Girl, 2013. You're welcome.)

GIVE THE AUDIENCE ONE THING TO FOCUS ON AT A TIME

This and telling a story are the two most important principles of a good talk. It's amazing how often speakers violate this simple rule. They hand out printed material for the audience to read during their talk, guaranteeing that no one will listen to them. Or they show text on the screen and then say something else while the audience is reading the text. They put up tables full of data when they only want the audience to look at two cells; they fill their slides with weird backgrounds and animations and expect the audience not to be distracted. The key to giving a good talk is to direct the audience's attention to *one thing at a time.*

Only show text that you want people to read

Many academic speakers not only put too much text on their slides, they compound the error by showing text and then talking over it—that is, continuing to speak while the audience is reading the text. If you put text in front of people, they will read it. They can't help it. The words on the page will grab their attention more than the words you are speaking. So if you put text on a slide, either read it aloud or shut up and let the audience read it themselves. But for heaven's sake, don't show a bunch of text and then expect people to ignore it while you continue speaking.

Let's imagine another silly, fictional example: you are doing a research project where you build a robot that can crochet stuffed toys. In particular, you have designed this robot to be self-aware and to recognize representational art, and you hypothesize that it will crochet faster and make fewer errors when it makes a toy robot

> If you put text in front of people, they will read it.

TARGET OBJECTS

Robot	Mummy
• Main color is gray.	• Main color is white.
• 'Amigurumi' construction with plastic eyes.	• 'Amigurumi' construction with plastic eyes.
• Figure includes head, body, arms, legs, applique heart.	• Figure includes head, body, arms, legs, applique smile and loose bandages.
• Finished object approx. 10cm x 6xm x 4cm	• Finished object approx. 10cm x 6xm x 4cm

Figure 7.6

As you can see here, the robot and mummy are very similar. They're both made of just one color with basically the same construction: Both have a head, a body, two arms, two legs ,and two plastic eyes. And they both have a little detail in a constrasting color: The robot has a pink heart and the mummy has a black smile, as well as some loose bandages.

Figure 7.7

As you can see here, the robot and mummy are very similar. They're both made of just one color with basically the same construction: Both have a head, a body, two arms, two legs, and two plastic eyes. And they both have a little detail in a constrasting color: The robot has a pink heart and the mummy has a black smile, as well as some loose bandages.

(with whom it feels a kinship) than when it makes an otherwise similar toy mummy. How do you describe the toy robot and mummy to your audience? You could do it with text, as in Figure 7.6, but in this case you are asking your audience to listen to your stream of spoken language while they simultaneously read (because they can't help it) the conflicting text on the screen. A much better idea is to use images, as in Figure 7.7. Then you can talk and the audience can listen, because they won't be reading at the same time.

———

Here are the first few slides from a talk I gave about registered reports. Notice how the slides mostly have images, with text used only to highlight key words and phrases. Notice also how the text is revealed a little bit at a time, and I read the words as soon as I show them. (The only exception is the text in the citations.) I also use a plain white slide (in PowerPoint and Keynote you can just press the "W" key) to turn the screen blank when I want the audience to look at me and just listen to what I'm saying. (You can also use the "B" key in PowerPoint and Keynote to turn the screen black, but sometimes that makes people think that the talk is over or the projector is malfunctioning, so I prefer white.) All of these techniques serve the same function, which is to keep the audience's attention where I want it.

Figure 7.8

Raise your hand if you've ever put a lot of work into a project, like you've worked on it for months, and then you didn't end up getting a publication out of it.

[Pause for show of hands.]

Yes, all of us, right? Happens all the time. How much time do we all waste doing studies that get . . .

Figure 7.9

REJECTED for things like lack of novelty, lack of impact, or because the reviewers didn't like the methods? It's incredibly frustrating, right? And not just for authors. Sometimes as a reviewer you say, "This is not a well-formed question. It misrepresents the topic." Or you say, "It's a good question, but these methods can't answer it."

And as an author, sometimes I get rejections that say, "This should have been a between-subjects design" or "You didn't do the right control here," and you know what? Maybe they're right.

And I think, "Thanks a lot, reviewer, where were you when I was designing this study? I could have used this feedback two years ago."

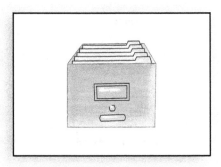

Figure 7.10

And then there are the studies that didn't get rejected because you never submitted them.

You had a good idea, you did the study, but the effect you expected to find just wasn't there. So you didn't have a finding. Which meant you didn't have a paper.

And let's be honest: You didn't just do one analysis and find a null result, and drop it in a file drawer. After working on it for six months? No way.

Figure 7.11

You probably tried a whole bunch of different analyses. "What if we exclude outliers that are 3 standard deviations from the mean? How about 2.5? 2?"

"What if we control for age, sex, right-handedness, bilingualism, and task order? No? How about just the first three? What if we split up the groups? Merge the groups? Analyze the high and low performers separately? Use just the first block of trials from each subject?"

The fact is, when you have a big dataset, there are a million different ways you can analyze it. And if you try enough different analyses, you've got a pretty good chance of finding something, even if there's nothing there. Statistician Andy Gelman calls this the "Garden of Forking Paths" problem. It's also called "researcher degrees of freedom."

Figure 7.12

And when you looked for X, didn't find it, looked some more and found Y instead, did you write a paper saying that? No.

Or if you did, reviewers rejected it. They told you you had to come up with an explanation for Y, and write the paper explaining why Y was predictable all along.

In other words, to publish the study, you had to do what's called . . .

Figure 7.13

HARKing, which stands for . . .

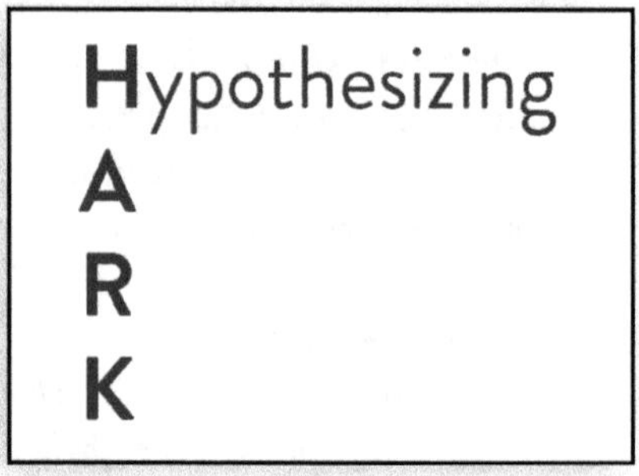

Hypothesizing
A
R
K

Figure 7.14

Hypothesizing

Hypothesizing
After the
R
K

After the

Figure 7.15

Hypothesizing
After the
Results are
K

Results are

Figure 7.16

Hypothesizing
After the
Results are
Known

Known

Figure 7.17

It's like the story of the Texas sharpshooter, who shoots a bunch of holes in a wall and then draws targets around them to make it look like he's a great shot.

Figure 7.18

If you agree that there must be a better way to do things, then I have good news for you. The Journal of Numerical Cognition *is now offering . . .*

Figure 7.19

registered reports!

Figure 7.20

After the meeting was over, I created a separate, stand-alone version of the talk to post online. For the stand-alone slides, I added the text that I had spoken aloud at the meeting. Here's the first slide:

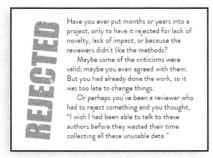

Figure 7.21

Maybe it's because academics are used to writing papers, or maybe we're afraid that once we get up in front of the audience, we'll forget what we were going to say. But many speakers prepare stand-alone slides for live talks, putting everything they plan to say on the slides themselves. At best, this makes for a boring talk as you read the slides along with the audience. At worst, it makes for a confusing and irritating talk as you talk over the slides while the audience tries to read them. If you are really afraid of forgetting what you wanted to say, put your talk on note cards that you can read from. But don't put it on your slides.

Reveal quotations one clause (or one readable chunk) at a time

One time when it does make sense to put text on slides is when you quote someone. If it's a long quotation, animate it to appear one clause at a time and read each clause as soon as it appears.

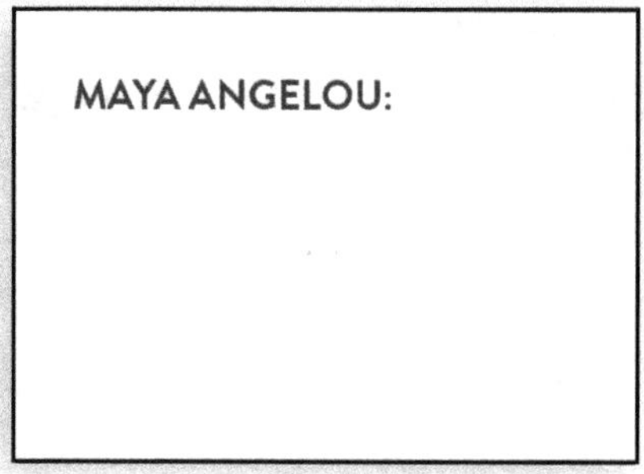

MAYA ANGELOU:

Figure 7.22

This brings us to a quote by the great American poet Maya Angelou, who said,

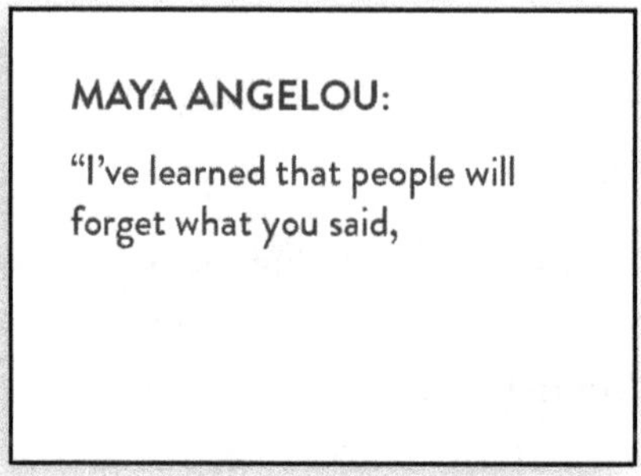

MAYA ANGELOU:

"I've learned that people will forget what you said,

Figure 7.23

"I've learned that people will forget what you said,

MAYA ANGELOU:

"I've learned that people will forget what you said, **people will forget what you did,**

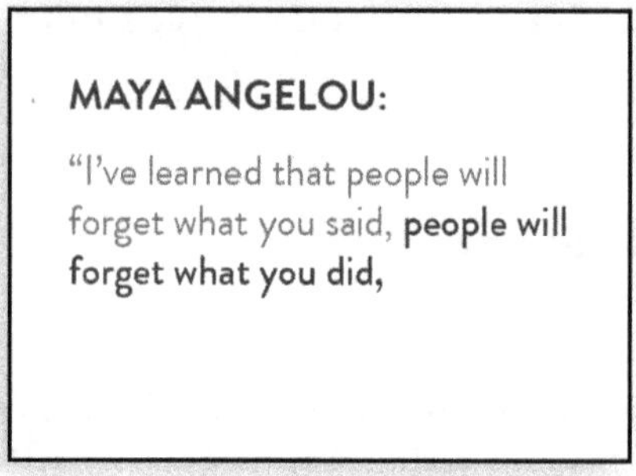

Figure 7.24

"people will forget what you did,

MAYA ANGELOU:

"I've learned that people will forget what you said, people will forget what you did, **but people will never forget how you made them feel.**"

"but people will never forget how you made them feel."

Figure 7.25

Reveal data in tables as you mention them

Just as quotations should be shown one chunk at a time in order to manage the audience's attention, so should the data in tables. Tables may be revealed by the cell, row, or column, depending on how much time you want the audience to spend looking at them.

In the example below, a comparison of dog breeds, the first column of the table is revealed one cell at a time as the breeds are introduced. Then the data are revealed one column (one variable) at a time.

Don't show rows and rows of data if you only want to talk about a values or comparisons. Instead, present the relevant information as a figure or just quote the data points you need.

BREED			
 Beagle (n = 50)			

The study compared dogs from three breeds. We had beagles,

Figure 7.26

BREED			
 Beagle (n = 50)			
 Boxer (n = 44)			

Figure 7.27

boxers,

BREED			
 Beagle (n = 50)			
 Boxer (n = 44)			
 Dalmatian (n = 47)			

Figure 7.28

and dalmatians.

BREED	Smart		
 Beagle (n = 50)	4		
 Boxer (n = 44)	4		
 Dalmatian (n = 47)	4		

Figure 7.29

They were all smart. On a scale of one to five, with five being the highest, all of these breeds are about a four.

BREED	Smart	Good with kids	
Beagle (n = 50)	4	5	
Boxer (n = 44)	4	4	
Dalmatian (n = 47)	4	4	

Figure 7.30

And all of these breeds are pretty good with kids.

BREED	Smart	Good with kids	Health
Beagle (n = 50)	4	5	1
Boxer (n = 44)	4	4	2
Dalmatian (n = 47)	4	4	4

Figure 7.31

Where they differed was in their health. Beagles are great dogs, but they do have a lot of health problems. Boxers are a little better, and dalmatians are pretty healthy.

Exceptions to the read-aloud rule

As a general rule, you should read all the text you show as soon as it appears on screen. The exception is text that must be included by law or custom, but that you don't want the audience to focus on. For example, if you refer to your own or someone else's published research, you should put citations on your slides. If you use an image, you should credit the source of the image. If you use a figure with error bars, you should include a label saying what the error bars represent (standard deviations, standard error, confidence intervals, etc.) To omit these bits of text would be unprofessional, but you don't have to read them aloud. You can put the words in a small font and unobtrusive color (e.g., gray instead of black) and assume that the audience will glance at them only briefly.

Figures and video in talks

As discussed in Chapter 5, figures pack a ton of information into a small space. That's good for a paper but bad for a talk. For simple figures, you can slow the flow of information to a manageable rate by presenting the figure one element at a time.

Our main outcome measure was practice time: the number of hours each student spent practicing the violin each week.

Figure 7.32

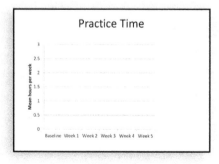

We asked them to record their practice time for one week as a baseline measure, and then we followed each family for five weeks.

Figure 7.33

Figure 7.34

Student 1 earned 10 minutes of video games for every 10 minutes of violin practice; Student 2 earned a spoonful of ice cream for every 10 minutes of practice; and Student 3 was told that her parents would be very disappointed in her if she didn't practice for at least two hours.

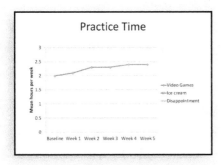

Figure 7.35

Student 1 kept up her practice over the five-week period of the study, and even increased it from 2 hours to almost 2.5 hours by the end.

Figure 7.36

Student 2 stayed right around two hours of practice time per week.

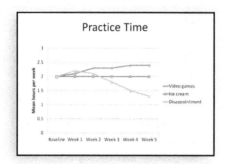

Student 3 practiced slightly more than the other two for the first week, but her practice time steadily decreased over the period of the study, and by the end she was practicing only about 1 hour and 20 minutes per week.

Figure 7.37

A note about accessibility: One of the most common reasons that speakers fail to connect with audiences is that the audience has trouble hearing or understanding the speaker. This can happen because the microphone setup in the room is poor or there is ambient noise, or because audience members have hearing issues, or because the language of the talk is not their first language. To make your talk as accessible as possible, always caption your videos. (Websites like Kapwing let you automatically add captions to video for free.) If you are giving your talk in a room with a reliable internet connection, you can go one step further and auto-caption the talk itself. Just create your presentation in Google Slides and click the captions button when you start presenting. These are small efforts that make a huge difference in the audience's experience.

Practice your presentation

Even if you don't think of yourself as a performer, you are one when you give a presentation. So prepare your presentations early and rehearse them. The more important a presentation is, the more rehearsal it deserves.

My colleague Lisa Pearl, a cognitive scientist and linguist, offers these timelines as examples.

> *I gave an hour-long invited talk on Nov. 15. I started putting it together on Oct. 1, based partially on material I had presented before. I finished a complete draft by Nov. 1 and practiced the hell out of it (i.e., some part of it out loud every day) until I was happy. As another example, for my 30-minute advancement presentation as a grad student, I started putting it together two months in advance and practiced the entire talk out loud every day for three weeks prior.*

Realistically, few speakers are as prepared as Lisa. (This is a woman who prepares all of her lectures for each academic year during the preceding summer.) But even if you are not as well organized as she is, you can improve your own presentations by starting a little bit sooner and rehearsing a little bit more. Even practicing your talk once is better than throwing it together on the plane on the way to the conference. So practice your presentation with anyone who will listen.

CHECK THE TIMING

Time your practice presentation to make sure you will not exceed your allotted time. Going over time is rude to the audience, to the next speaker, and to the organizers. It makes you look unprepared and unprofessional. Feldman and Silvia (2010) suggest using no more than 80% of your time for the talk itself, leaving 20% to answer questions. We've all been to presentations where the speaker gets the five-minute warning when they still have 20 slides left. So they break into a sweat and start babbling like an auctioneer, racing to cram everything they wanted to say in the minute or two they have left. This mess is completely avoidable if you practice your timing beforehand.

CHECK THE TECH

Make sure the images show up, the animations work, the videos play, and the audio is audible. If you will travel to give the talk, build in backup systems. When you travel, keep a backup of your slides. For example, you could keep one copy on your laptop and another copy online or on a USB drive, in case you need to transfer them to another computer. If you will be running the talk from your own laptop, make sure to bring all the adapters you will need; don't count on the conference organizers to provide them. If you do have to transfer your slides to another computer, click through them beforehand to make sure that the images show up properly and that the audio and video files have sound.

PRACTICE ANSWERING QUESTIONS

Most academic talks have a question-and-answer session at the end. Practice answering questions when you practice your talk. Many inexperienced speakers fear the question-and-answer session. They're afraid that the audience will stump them with hard questions that expose weaknesses in their work, but that rarely happens. By the time you give a talk about your work, you've been thinking about it for a year or two at least. The audience has only been thinking about it for a few minutes during your talk, so you know a lot more about it than they do.

Most questions fall into one of three categories: (1) The person asks you to clarify some aspect of your work; (2) they ask how your work relates to something else, which usually turns out to be their work; (3) they ask something bizarre that doesn't make any sense. No matter what kind of question it is, follow the same guidelines for responding.

First, smile and nod. Try not to look defensive or angry, even if that's how you feel. Act like every question is reasonable and every questioner is well-intentioned.

Next, repeat the question. This serves several functions. First, it's likely that not everyone heard the question, so by repeating it into the microphone (or loud enough for everyone to hear), you are including everyone in the conversation. Second, repeating the question allows you to make sure that you heard and understood it correctly. Third, if the question didn't make sense, this gives you a natural opportunity to reframe it as one you can answer. For example, let's say you've just finished giving a talk about your work training dogs of different breeds to find people who are trapped under rubble after earthquakes. Someone raises a hand and asks, "How is this related to deregulation of the concrete industry in California?"

Your first thought may be that it's not related, but try to find any hint of a reasonable question in it. For example, you could say, "You raise a good point—if deregulation leads to lower standards for concrete quality, that could make the damage from earthquakes much worse. In that case, search-and-rescue work will be more important than ever."

Sometimes people will ask you to speculate about something that's really outside the scope of the work. In this case, you have two options: Speculate, but be clear that you are speculating, or refuse to speculate, but talk about what information could be used to answer the question.

———

When I talk about my research on people's fears of letting children play unsupervised, people often ask what I think the effect of constant surveillance will be on the long-term development of this generation of children. I might say, "Well to be clear, we didn't measure effects on children. We just measured adults' reasoning. But if I were to speculate about the long-term effects on children's development, I guess I would say . . ." Or if I don't want to speculate, I might say something like, "Well no one knows, because no previous generation of children has been raised like this. What we really need, to answer that question, are large-scale longitudinal studies that follow these kids for decades."

———

Finally, if you get a truly bizarre question and you have absolutely no idea how to respond, you can just look thoughtful and say, "Hmm, I guess I need to think about that some more. Let's talk later." But that's like a get-out-of-jail-free card. You can only use it once per talk.

8

PARAGRAPHS

Many academic writers don't pay enough attention to paragraphs. Writers tend to organize documents at the section level (introduction, method, etc.) and to edit individual sentences. They don't think as much about paragraphs, which is a shame, because readers really notice paragraphs.

The visual cue separating one paragraph from another (a blank line or an indent) signals to the reader that the writer has finished making one point and is beginning a new one. If you imagine the author speaking to the reader, the paragraph breaks are points where the author stops talking. These breaks also give the reader a chance to breathe—to pause and let the point sink in.

Writing that is organized as a series of tight, coherent paragraphs will strike readers as being clearer and easier to understand than writing that lacks such organization. The same clarity can help make the writing process easier, because organizing your writing into topic-sentence paragraphs allows you to switch back and forth between outlines and drafts, which is magic when you are developing a complicated argument. If you have been making topic-sentence outlines as described in Chapter 3, then you're already using paragraphs well. (Yay, you!) If not, consider taking a moment to go back and refresh yourself on the basics.

Understand "hamburger" paragraphs

Most paragraphs should start with a topic sentence that expresses the paragraph's main point. Sometimes the topic sentence is preceded by a transition sentence, leading the reader from the previous paragraph into this one, but if so, the topic sentence should come right after that. The topic sentence is followed by several supporting sentences, and the whole thing ends with a concluding sentence, which relates back to the theme presented in the topic sentence. Sometimes the closing sentence will be followed by a transition sentence leading the reader into the next paragraph. One easy way to check for coherence in a paragraph is to read just the topic sentence and the concluding sentence. If they aren't on the same theme, the paragraph has wandered off track and needs some attention.

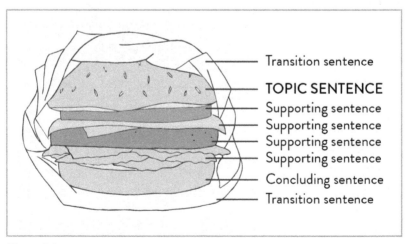

Figure 8.1

This paragraph structure is summarized in a delightful metaphor related by Morton Ann Gernsbacher (2013): the hamburger. The topic sentence is the top half of the bun; the supporting sentences are the fillings (hamburger patty, tomatoes, cheese, lettuce, etc.); the concluding sentence is the bottom half of the bun. The topic sentence and concluding sentence should match in the same way that the top and bottom halves of a bun match. Transition sentences at the very beginning and end of the paragraph can be represented as the wrapper.

Here's how the hamburger structure looks in a real (albeit satirical) paragraph. The topic sentence and concluding sentence are in bold.

> **A new paper published in *Science* has concluded that no further research is needed.** The announcement, made in the discussion section of the paper, comes as a shock to millions of scientists across the world. Lead author Sara Jackson explains: "We were writing the discussion section of our paper and could think of no useful avenues for further research. We pretty much covered all bases. We then thought for a moment and concluded that this was probably the case for the rest of science as well. **So, we simply suggested that no further research is needed, at all, anywhere, ever."** (Dr. Psyphago, 2013)

The hamburger structure is extremely useful for academics. Most academic writing consists of claims and evidence, or of general statements backed up by specific examples, or of abstract statements that are fleshed out in concrete situations. The hamburger structure has a place for each type of information. For arguments made up of claims and evidence, each claim is a topic sentence. The evidence for the claim goes in the supporting sentences, and the claim is restated in the concluding sentence.

Similarly, each general statement can be a topic sentence. Specific examples that illustrate the statement can go in the supporting sentences, and the principle can be restated in the concluding sentence. In some cases, each element may require a few sentences to express. In that case, the hamburger structure can be applied to a whole section, with a topic paragraph, supporting paragraphs, and a concluding paragraph, each of which has its own hamburger structure (fractal hamburgers!) Abstract statements and concrete examples can be handled the same way, with the abstraction expressed in the topic sentence or paragraph and concrete examples in the supporting sentences or paragraphs.

NONHAMBURGER PARAGRAPHS

There are occasional paragraphs that don't need topic sentences. For example, many documents, or sections of documents, begin with an introductory paragraph that functions like a table of contents, presenting the topics or themes of the section. These paragraphs often do not have a hamburger structure because they are really lists in paragraph form.

There are also transitional paragraphs, which serve to signal a shift in topic between one section of a document and the next. These typically don't have a hamburger structure. Instead, they start by referring to the section that just ended. Then they draw some connection or raise some question that leads the reader into thinking about the next section, and they end by introducing that section.

There are also serial paragraphs—those that function as a series and all refer back to a single topic sentence. This happens when a claim, generalization, or abstraction requires only one sentence to express, but the evidence, examples, or details needed to support it require so much space that they have to be broken up into separate paragraphs just to give the reader's eye a break. This is a little bit of a cheat, in the sense that the information could really be one long paragraph, but there's nothing uglier than a giant block of text with no visual breaks, so long paragraphs are sometimes broken down into shorter ones.

If you are making a reverse outline and you come across a paragraph without a topic sentence, the usual answer is to write one. But for these kinds of paragraphs, which actually don't have a hamburger structure, it's fine to use a placeholder such as (*introductory paragraph*), (*transitional paragraph*) or (*Paragraph 2 of series*).

USE PARAGRAPH STRUCTURE WHEN REVISING

Here is an example of how thinking about paragraph structure can help you revise an early draft. This is based on a real application essay that someone in the writing workshop presented for feedback a few years ago. The application was for a pedagogical fellowship program, which gave PhD students intensive training and mentorship in teaching techniques. The program also helped students get teaching experience at community colleges. The application essay prompt was very general (e.g., "Tell us why you would be a good candidate for this fellowship"), and the draft presented by the student in the workshop consisted entirely of general statements, with very few details or examples. It went something like this:

From the time I entered graduate school, I have viewed teaching as an important part of my academic work. I actually find teaching rewarding. I had the opportunity to teach my own class last summer, and I didn't do only what was required; I made extra efforts to help my students be successful. I don't just see teaching as something I have to do in order to fund my research. I know that's a minority opinion at this university, where most of the graduate students and faculty consider research to be the only thing worth doing. But I don't feel that way; I consider teaching important and worthwhile. Students have a better experience in my classes because of the work I put in.

Unlike some of my colleagues, I do everything I can for my students. Even when it means spending time that I could be using for research, I go the extra mile to teach better, because I care. I would also say, with all due humility, that I am good at teaching. Students enjoy my classes, and they also learn a lot. To me, that's the sign of a good teacher. Although many of my peers see research as their highest priority and teaching as secondary, I see teaching as being just as important as research. It's rewarding for me to know I'm a good teacher, but I would like to be better still. This pedagogical fellowship will give me the training I need to do that.

The draft above is broken into two paragraphs, but it seems like the author just put the break in the middle of the page. There's no structure to the paragraphs: no topic sentences, no supporting sentences, no conclusions. Our job in revising is to find the main points, which can then become the topic sentences of their own paragraphs. Bolding the main points gives us something like this.

From the time I entered graduate school, I have viewed teaching as an important part of my academic work. I actually find teaching rewarding. I had the opportunity to teach my own class last summer, and I didn't do only what was required; **I made extra efforts to help my students be successful.** I don't just see teaching as something I have to do in order to fund my research. I know that's a minority opinion at this university, where **most of the graduate students and faculty consider research to be the only thing worth doing.** But I don't feel that way; I consider teaching important and worthwhile. Students have a better experience in my classes because of the work I put in.

Unlike some of my colleagues, I do everything I can for my students. Even when it means spending time that I could be using for research, I go the extra mile to teach better, because I care. I would also say, with all due humility, that **I am good at teaching.** Students enjoy my classes, and they also learn a lot. To me, that's the sign of a good teacher. Although many of my peers see research as their highest priority and teaching as secondary, I see teaching as being just as important as research. It's rewarding for me to know I'm a good teacher, but I would like to be better still. This pedagogical fellowship will give me the training I need to do that.

Now let's take each of these main points and consider whether they would make good topic sentences for paragraphs.

1. I make extra efforts to help my students be successful.

This seems promising. The supporting sentences can give examples of what the author has done to help students.

2. most of the graduate students and faculty consider research to be the only thing worth doing

This is a theme in the draft (it is repeated several times, in different ways), but it doesn't seem worth keeping. It made the author sound petty for criticizing other grad students and faculty, and it is also self-congratulatory, as though the author expects to be praised just for saying they care about teaching. It's also insulting to the people who run the teaching fellowship program because it implies that most people view teaching as unimportant.

3. I am good at teaching.

This is another of the author's themes, and it seems useful if it can be rephrased in more objective terms. The sentence that follows it in the draft is "Students enjoy my classes, and they also learn a lot." That's a claim that can be backed up with evidence from student evaluations. So the revised topic-sentence outline is something like this.

1. I make extra efforts to help my students be successful.
2. Students enjoy my classes, and they also learn a lot.

The next step is to figure out what the supporting sentences will be. To do this, the author needs to start drafting again—filling in details and examples. Out of this, a new draft will emerge. For example, the new draft of just Paragraph 1 might look like this:

I make extra efforts to help my students be successful. For example, more than half the undergraduates at University of California, Irvine, are first-generation college students. First-generation students are more likely than other students to also be parents, and child-care emergencies can cause them to miss class. So I announce at the first meeting of every discussion section that students are welcome to bring children of any age with them to discussion, and I've been able to persuade some of the professors I worked with to make the same announcement about lecture. Also work schedules. A lot of first-gen students have jobs off campus, with hours that change every week with only a few days' notice, forcing them to miss class sometimes. To help these students, I've convinced the professors I worked with to let me video record the lectures, and I post the lectures on the course website after class. Then students can watch them later. That's also been good, actually, for nonnative English speakers. Because around 20% of the students in some of my classes didn't speak English as a first language. Having the lectures recorded really helped them. We also started adding captions to lecture videos in real time using the new captioning feature on Google Slides, and that has been great for everyone—for nonnative speakers, for hearing-impaired students, and for students at the back of a noisy lecture hall. So I find that things we do to help one group of students often end up helping others too.

Based on this new draft, the author may realize that their extra teaching efforts have really been aimed at particular groups of students: first-generation students, nonnative English speakers, and students with disabilities. It turns out that there's enough material on each of these topics to fill its own paragraph, so the structure of the essay changes again, as Paragraph 1 is split into multiple paragraphs.

(Introductory statement) I make extra efforts to help my students be successful.
1. I make special efforts to support first-generation students.
2. I make special efforts to support nonnative English speakers.
3. I make special efforts to support students with disabilities.
4. Students enjoy my classes, and they also learn a lot.

All you have to do is continue to apply this technique through multiple cycles of revision until you have a strong, persuasive piece of writing. As always, if you're not sure what's working and what's not, ask your penguin huddle for advice.

Manage information flow within the paragraph

In order to write paragraphs where information flows smoothly, you must pay attention to the information structure of the sentences. Many of us learned in school that sentences have subjects and predicates. Those are grammatical terms. But in terms of information, it's more useful to think in terms of topics and comments. The topic of a sentence is the thing being talked about; the comment is what is being said about it (McCarthy, 1991, p. 55). For example:

Topic	Comment
Penguins	form huddles.
Huddles	are formed by penguins.
Prosecutors	hold a lot of power.
A lot of power	is held by prosecutors.
The Lannisters	always pay their debts.
The Lannisters' debts	are always paid.

Table 8.1

The topic and comment of a sentence are usually the same as its subject and predicate, but not always. In the sentences below, the topic appears in a separate phrase at the beginning, and the subject and predicate are both part of the comment.

Topic	Comment
As for penguins,	they huddle to stay alive.
Speaking of criminal justice reform,	prosecutors have a lot of power.
In *Game of Thrones*,	the Lannisters always pay their debts.

Table 8.2

PUT OLD INFORMATION BEFORE NEW

Most supporting sentences contain both old and new information. The old information (also called "given" information) is something that has already been mentioned earlier in the piece. The new information is being introduced for the first time. For example, in the paragraph below, the main topic (foxtails) is introduced as new information in the topic sentence. In each of the subsequent, supporting sentences, foxtails and foxtail seed heads are old information, appearing in the topic position.

> A ubiquitous danger for dogs in the western half of the United States is the **foxtail**. **This plant** has barbed seed heads that can work their way into any part of a dog or cat, from the nose to between the toes and inside the ears, eyes, and mouth. **They** can even simply dig themselves directly into a patch of skin. **Foxtails** present a danger beyond simple irritation. Because **these tough seeds** don't break down inside the body, **an embedded foxtail** can lead to serious infection for a dog. **It** can even lead to death if left untreated.

Readers expect old information to appear in the topic position, at the beginning of a sentence. They expect new information to appear in the comment position, at the end (Brown, 1983; Halliday, 1967). You can make this expectation work for you. Identify the old and new information in your sentence, then move things around as needed so that the old information is at the beginning of each sentence and the new information is at the end.

CREATE TOPIC CHAINS

You can use this technique to construct sentences that link together, creating paragraphs where information flows smoothly from one sentence to the next. A strong, clear link is formed when the topic of a sentence refers to something already mentioned, preferably in the previous sentence. If a string of sentences all share the same topic, the structure looks like this.

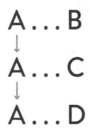

We can see this structure in the sentences below, from an article by Cowell (2018). The topic (protesters/organizers) is consistent across the three sentences.

Topic	Comment
Fifty years ago, hundreds of nationalist **protesters**	gathered on Duke Street in Londonderry.
Their demonstration, organized by the Northern Ireland Civil Rights Association—inspired in part by the civil rights movement in the United States—	had been outlawed when unionist opponents announced plans for a rival march.
The **organizers**	resolved to protest anyhow, fired by a long-simmering discontent with what was perceived as widespread discrimination.

Table 8.3

CREATE COMMENT-TOPIC CHAINS

The other easy way to link sentences is to have the comment of one sentence become the topic of the next one.

$$A \ldots B$$
$$\downarrow$$
$$B \ldots C$$
$$\downarrow$$
$$C \ldots D$$

This structure is shown in Table 8.4. Topic (A) is states. Topic (B) is laws, first mentioned in the comment portion of Sentence 1, and then used as the topic of Sentence 2. Topic (C) is prosecutors, first raised in the comment of Sentence 2, and then used as the topic of Sentence 3.

	Topic	Comment
1	Starting in the 1990s, many U.S. **states (A)**	passed **laws (B)** mandating minimum sentences.
2	These **laws (B)**	inadvertently shifted power from judges to **prosecutors (C)**.
3	Now, in many cases when **prosecutors (C)** decide what charges to bring, they	effectively decide **sentences (D)**.

Table 8.4

Both topic chains and topic-comment chains are easy for readers to follow. Topic chains work better when the writer has a lot of information to convey about a single theme, or variations on that theme. Topic-comment chains work better when the writer needs to walk the reader step-by-step through the events in a story or the moves in an argument.

MIX TOPIC CHAINS AND TOPIC-COMMENT CHAINS AS NEEDED

In the paragraph below (from Hogenboom, 2015), both types of links are used. Topic (A) is emperor penguins. They are the topic of Sentences 1, 2, and 3. Topic (B) is huddles and huddling behavior, which is mentioned for the first time in the comment of Sentence 3, and becomes the topic of Sentences 4, 5, and 6. Topic (C) is subsets of penguins doing specific huddling behaviors. This is mentioned for the first time in the comment of Sentence 6, and becomes the topic of Sentences 7, 8, 10, and 11.

	Topic	Comment
1	**Emperor penguins (A)**	are one of nature's great survivors.
2	**They (A)**	can endure the frigid cold of an Antarctic winter, when temperatures plummet to –20 °C or below.
3	To prevent themselves from freezing to death, **they (A)**	**huddle (B)** together in tightly packed groups to conserve heat and shelter themselves from the intense winds.
4	Now it seems these **huddles (B)** can actually be	too good at keeping the emperor penguins warm.
5	In the time-lapse below, you can see that penguin **huddles (B)**	constantly rotate.
6	The most obvious **behaviour (B)**	is that **penguins on the outskirts (C)** regularly muscle their way inside the huddle.
7	**That (C)**	is easily understandable.
8	**Those on the outside (C)** of the huddle	face the direct hit of Antarctica's icy wind chill.
9	But there is something else going on.	
10	The **penguins on the inside (C)**	get too hot, so after a while they need a little room to cool off.
11	**Penguins seeking to lose some body heat (C)**	actually break huddles apart, say researchers in a new paper in the journal *Animal Behaviour*.

Table 8.5

Make it clear what you're referring to

As discussed in discussed in Chapter 3, academic writers must always grapple with the curse of knowledge. When a person knows a lot about a topic, it's hard for them to remember what it was like to not know it. Imagining what it's like to be another person is tricky at the best of times, and the longer you've been working with a set of concepts, the more natural those concepts seem.

My 13-year-old son James and I start each day by walking our dogs. As we walk, James likes to tell me about whatever video game he is currently enjoying. I am happy to hear about whatever interests him, but there is such a curse-of-knowledge problem that most of the time I understand very little of what he is saying. I asked him to sit down with me briefly for the following conversation:

BARBARA: *OK, so tell me about* Dark Souls. *Just, like, the stuff you talk about on the walks when we're walking together.*

JAMES: *Well, I'm currently working on a tracer build, where I use the gold tracer and the dark silver tracer. They're basically supposed to be together as weapons. One is really good for backstabs and also toxic, and one of them is very good for bleed when wielded in the off hand. The problem is, they're very late-game items, so I don't get them until I beat the very hard boss in the DLC which is already difficult to get to, so I'm going to get another guy to give them to me—to give my own ones to me, that is—and I'll give mine to him.*

BARBARA: *What's the advantage of getting him to . . .*

JAMES: *Because you get it on a low-level character. So you're getting very strong gear very early. You're not supposed to get these things until way later in the game, so it's like . . . like playing* Civilization *or something, and starting off with a nuclear warhead.*

BARBARA: *And how is that achieved by somebody giving you something, and you giving somebody else the same thing?*

> JAMES: *He gets the tracers for his character and I get the tracers for my character.*
>
> BARBARA: *But can't you just give them to yourself?*
>
> JAMES: *No, you can't give things to yourself across characters. Otherwise it would be way, way easier.*
>
> BARBARA: *So, this is basically a workaround for you to give something to yourself? You find another player and you give the items to his character, and he gives the same items to your character?*
>
> JAMES: *Yes, exactly.*

As this example shows, the curse of knowledge is easiest to overcome in a conversation, where questions can be asked and answered. The person asking questions can identify gaps in their own knowledge, and the expert can answer them. This is why it's a good idea to structure your elevator pitches and poster presentations as conversations rather than monologues. Having your listener right in front of you is a huge advantage to communication.

With writing, the curse of knowledge is a much tougher problem because the writer must anticipate the gaps in the reader's knowledge. And not just one particular reader, but many readers. This requires you to start where your readers are, whether that's the public, disciplinary, or subfield level (again, see Chapter 3), and build up each new concept piece by piece. In practical terms, that means defining each technical term or abbreviation the first time you use it (see Chapter 10). But it also means being careful about how you refer to things throughout the text. Unclear reference is both a symptom of the curse of knowledge and a perennial source of confusion in academic writing.

TO REFER TO A DIFFERENT THING, USE A DIFFERENT WORD

You make things much harder for your readers by using different words to refer to the same thing, or by using the same word to refer to different things. So please, pick a word and stick to it. It's hard for readers to follow your meaning when you don't use words consistently.

For example, after the 2018 U.S. congressional elections, a senator was being interviewed on the radio. She had just lost her reelection campaign, and she was talking about what's wrong with Washington. She referred to several different groups of people, but always using the same word: "people." Her comments went something like this:

> People want to know that you have their back. They want to know that you care about what's happening to them, and you're working to make their lives better. And people in my state understand that you can't get anything done if you won't compromise. That's just the reality. But compromise is hard, because people are afraid to take tough votes. People from the deep blue and deep red states are afraid that their base will turn on them if they compromise. And you know, I get that. Because people don't call my office and say, "Senator, please compromise." Compromise isn't what gets people excited. And honestly, journalism is part of the problem, too. Celebrity gossip is always going to get more clicks than a budget bill, so even when we do get something done, people write about the

celebrity. They don't say, "Hey, the senate did something good today."

The senator wasn't trying to be unclear, and she probably didn't realize that she used the word "people" to mean several different groups of people within just a few sentences. If she had replaced each instance of "people" with a more specific word, her comments would have been much clearer:

> ~~People~~ **Voters** want to know that you have their back. They want to know that you care about what's happening to them, and you're working to make their lives better. And ~~people~~ **voters** in my state understand that you can't get anything done if you won't compromise. That's just the reality. But compromise is hard, because ~~people~~ **senators** are afraid to take tough votes. ~~People~~ **Senators** from the deep blue and deep red states are afraid that their base will turn on them if they compromise. And you know, I get that. Because ~~people~~ **constituents** don't call my office and say, 'Senator, please compromise.' Compromise isn't what gets ~~people~~ **the public** excited. And honestly, journalism is part of the problem, too. Celebrity gossip is always going to get more clicks than a budget bill, so even when we do get something done, ~~people~~ **journalists** write about the celebrity. They don't say, "Hey, the senate did something good today."

TO REFER TO THE SAME THING, USE THE SAME WORD

The opposite problem also occurs: A writer may use different words to refer to one thing. Many writers were told a long time ago (perhaps in high school) that using the same word over and over again results in boring writing. I'm sympathetic to the high school teacher who had to read 31 stultifying sonnets in a row, at least 14 of which rhymed "love" with "dove." But when you want readers to understand your research, clear communication is more important than variety.

Here's an example from my own work. This paragraph is about children's early understanding of words like "one," "two," "three," and "four," which are referred to by several different terms in the paragraph. None of these terms is wrong and all of them are used in the scientific literature on this topic. But when they are all used in the same piece of writing, the reader will naturally wonder whether the author is referring to different things.

Understanding That **Numbers**
Are About Quantity

One of the first things children may learn about **number words** is that they relate to quantity. A set of five objects can be shaken up, turned upside-down, stirred with a spoon, arranged in a line, and so on, but it will still be a set of five objects. The **numeral** for a set of objects only changes when the quantity changes—that is, when objects are added or removed. To find out when (i.e., at what number-knower level) children understand this, Susan Gelman and I tested 54 children on a task called the

Transform-Sets task (Sarnecka & Gelman, 2004). In this task, children were shown a set of five or six objects labeled with a **number name** (e.g., "I'm putting *six* buttons in this box."). Then some action was performed on the set (shaking the whole box, rotating the whole box, adding or removing an object), and the children were asked, "Now how many buttons? Is it five or six?" We found that even subset-knowers knew that the original **number** should still apply when the box had been shaken or rotated, but the **number word** should change when an item had been added or removed. In other words, even before they knew exactly what the words *five* and *six* meant, children already knew that those words should only change when an item was added or removed from the set. This is an example of subset-knowers having partial knowledge of the meanings of higher **numerals** before they understand the full, cardinal meanings.

Here's the same paragraph, using just one label ("number words") every time. It might still be hard to understand (especially for readers with no background in psychology), but the difficulty comes from engaging with new ideas, rather than from trying to figure out which words mean the same thing and which don't.

Understanding That **Number Words** Are About Quantity

One of the first things children may learn about **number words** is that they relate to quantity. A set of five objects can be shaken up, turned upside-down, stirred with a spoon, arranged in a line, and so on, but it will still be a set of five objects. The **number word** for a set of objects only changes when the quantity changes—that is, when objects are added or removed. To find out when (i.e., at what number-knower level) children understand this, Susan Gelman and I tested 54 children on a task called the Transform-Sets task (Sarnecka & Gelman, 2004). In this task, children were shown a set of five or six objects labeled with a **number word** (e.g., "I'm putting *six* buttons in this box."). Then some action was performed on the set (shaking the whole box, rotating the whole box, adding or removing an object), and the children were asked, "Now how many buttons? Is it five or six?" We found that even subset-knowers knew that the original **number word** should still apply when the box had been shaken or rotated, but the **number word** should change when an item had been added or removed. In other words, even before they knew exactly what the words *five* and *six* meant, children already knew that those words should only change when an item was added or removed from the set. This is an example of subset-knowers having partial knowledge of the meanings of higher **number words** before they understand the full, cardinal meanings.

BEWARE OF "THIS," "THAT," AND "THEY"

If you start a sentence with a bare pronoun such as "this," "that," or "they," make sure it's very clear what the pronoun refers to. These pronouns can refer to anything from theories and arguments to people, objects, and events. If there's any doubt about what a pronoun refers to, add a summary word or replace the pronoun with a noun to remove any ambiguity. Tables 8.6 and 8.7 give examples of ambiguous uses of "this" and "they," along with potential replacements.

COMPLETE THE COMPARATIVES

Another source of ambiguity is the comparative ("higher," "lower," "better," "worse," "more," "less," etc.). Whenever you make a statement using a comparative, the reader asks, *Compared to what?* Similarly, when you write that someone preferred something, the implicit question is *Preferred it over what?* As a writer, you know what's being compared, but your readers might not. So get in the habit of noticing comparative expressions and checking for ambiguities. Table 8.8 gives examples of ambiguous comparatives and ways to disambiguate them.

Use signposting as needed

"Signposting" means writing about your writing, rather than about your topic. When an author writes, "In this chapter, I will make three arguments . . ." That's signposting. It helps readers keep track of where they are in your argument, just as actual signs help people

Ambiguous	Researchers discovered that the penguins were interested in chess mainly because they believed the black and white pieces to be tiny enchanted penguins whom the researchers had enslaved. **This** was . . .
Clearer	The researchers discovered that the penguins were interested in chess mainly because they believed the black and white pieces to be tiny enchanted penguins whom the researchers had enslaved. **This discovery** was . . . OR The researchers discovered that the penguins were interested in chess mainly because they believed the black and white pieces to be tiny enchanted penguins whom the researchers had enslaved. **This belief** was . . . OR The researchers discovered that the penguins were interested in chess mainly because they believed the black and white pieces to be tiny enchanted penguins whom the researchers had enslaved. **This enslavement** was . . .

Table 8.6

Ambiguous	This discovery was soon followed by one even more surprising: The penguins had been studying chess strategy for several months, hoping to win the freedom of their small comrades in a tournament with the researchers. **They** . . .
Clearer	This discovery was soon followed by one even more surprising: The penguins had been studying chess strategy for several months, hoping to win the freedom of their small comrades in a tournament with the researchers. **The penguins** . . . OR This discovery was soon followed by one even more surprising: The penguins had been studying chess strategy for several months, hoping to win the freedom of their small comrades in a tournament with the researchers. **The researchers** . . . OR This discovery was soon followed by one even more surprising: The penguins had been studying chess strategy for several months, hoping to win the freedom of their small comrades in a tournament with the researchers. **The chess pieces** . . .

Table 8.7

Ambiguous comparative	Ambiguities	Revised to remove ambiguity
Older HIV-1 individuals showed a **higher** frequency of dementia.	Higher than young people with HIV-1? Higher than old people without HIV-1? Higher than the frequency of other diseases in older HIV-1 adults?	Older HIV-1 individuals showed a **higher** frequency of dementia **than** their HIV-negative peers of the same age.
Men with coronary artery disease have **lower** levels of androgens.	Lower than men without coronary artery disease? Lower than women with coronary artery disease? Lower levels of androgens than expected? Lower than their levels of something else?	Men with coronary artery disease have **lower** levels of androgens **than** men with normal coronary angiograms.
Is state-sponsored terrorism **more** common? An empirical study of group ideology, organization, and goal structure	More common than terrorism sponsored by nonstate actors? More common than other state-sponsored activities? More common now than it used to be?	Has state-sponsored terrorism become **more** common **in the 21st century?** An empirical study of group ideology, organization, and goal structure.
Children **prefer** prosocial individuals in affiliated groups.	Prefer them to antisocial individuals in affiliated groups? Prefer them to prosocial individuals in nonaffiliated groups?	Within affiliated groups, children **prefer** prosocial **over** antisocial individuals.

Table 8.8

keep track of where they are in a city. Signposting is mainly used either to lay out the structure of an argument or to help readers make transitions between sections, paragraphs, and sentences. Its purpose is to help readers make a one-way trip through your argument—that is, to read it from beginning to end and understand it, without having to stop, go back, and reread to figure out what's going on.

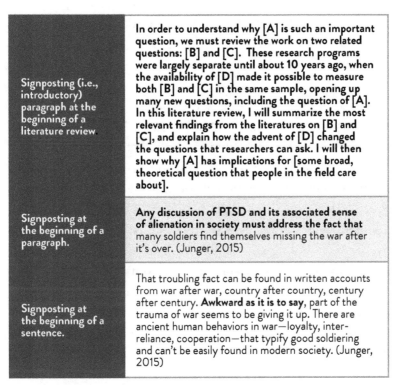

Signposting (i.e., introductory) paragraph at the beginning of a literature review.	In order to understand why [A] is such an important question, we must review the work on two related questions: [B] and [C]. These research programs were largely separate until about 10 years ago, when the availability of [D] made it possible to measure both [B] and [C] in the same sample, opening up many new questions, including the question of [A]. In this literature review, I will summarize the most relevant findings from the literatures on [B] and [C], and explain how the advent of [D] changed the questions that researchers can ask. I will then show why [A] has implications for [some broad, theoretical question that people in the field care about].
Signposting at the beginning of a paragraph.	**Any discussion of PTSD and its associated sense of alienation in society must address the fact that** many soldiers find themselves missing the war after it's over. (Junger, 2015)
Signposting at the beginning of a sentence.	That troubling fact can be found in written accounts from war after war, country after country, century after century. **Awkward as it is to say**, part of the trauma of war seems to be giving it up. There are ancient human behaviors in war—loyalty, inter-reliance, cooperation—that typify good soldiering and can't be easily found in modern society. (Junger, 2015)

Table 8.9

USE PLENTY OF SIGNPOSTING IN EARLY DRAFTS

Signposting in the early stages of writing has many benefits for the writer. It forces you to clarify the structure of your argument and the logical connections between your ideas. In the words of academic writing expert Rachael Cayley (2015),

> The act of describing—as bluntly as you wish—the order of what is going to happen in your writing is so useful. If you push yourself to write a road map for your text, you will gain insight into what you did

(or didn't do). Maybe you meant to do something and then didn't end up doing it. Or maybe you did something and need to explain why.

Explicit signposting often feels clumsy and awkward, but don't worry about that at the drafting stage. You may find yourself writing sentences like, "This is the literature review, where I will summarize prior research on how international organizations understand failures of communication. Then I will explain how my research is different." You might feel that this signposting is stating the obvious, and that it lacks style. That's OK! Remember that the early stages of writing are for the writer. You can always revise or edit out unnecessary signposting later on. But early in the process, while your argument is still taking shape, go ahead and signpost the heck out of it. It will help you keep track of what each part of the document is trying to achieve. Table 8.9 shows examples of signposting (in bold) at the beginning of a document, a paragraph and a sentence.

REVISE TO LEAVE SIGNPOSTS IN JUST THE TRICKY SPOTS

Once you move on to revising for the benefit of the reader, you can take out the unnecessary signposting. There's no need to start every paragraph and sentence with signposting. Think about how you give people driving directions. If the route includes a long, straight stretch of road, do you describe every intersection along the way? Do you say, "Turn left onto Main Street, and then continue straight past 1st Avenue; and then past 2nd Avenue; and then past 3rd Avenue; and then there will be construction on the road between 3rd and 4th Avenues, but you don't need to do anything. You just keep driving straight and ignore the construction. Pass 4th Avenue; and then continue on past 5th Avenue; and then actually turn right on 6th Avenue . . ."?

Of course you don't give directions like that. You don't say anything about the long stretches where the driver can keep going in a straight line. You only mention the intersections where the driver has to make a turn, or where there's something tricky or potentially confusing. So you would probably say something like, "Turn left onto Main Street and continue for six blocks, passing through the construction zone; then turn right on 6th Avenue."

The same only-if-needed rule applies to signposting bigger sections of writing too. You don't need to tell readers how a document is structured if the structure is completely predictable, as in IMRaD articles and most grant or fellowship proposals. It's only when the structure is not obvious that readers benefit from signposting.

The topics in this chapter—hamburger paragraphs, information flow, clear reference, and signposting—may seem diverse, but they are all tools that you can use to build an argument that is easy to follow. Researchers spend years becoming experts in our fields. To write about our work in a way that others without that expertise can understand and learn from, we need tools like these. The next chapter is about principles of clear writing that apply at a whole different level: the sentence.

9

SENTENCES

Sentences are the bite-sized pieces of written language that we produce and consume. Elementary-school children are admonished to write in complete sentences; most writing guides spend more time on sentences than on other levels of organization; and informal writing advice tends to focus on the sentence level as well. This is because a lot of language processing (i.e., people interpreting language) happens at the sentence level.

There is a large and active subfield of psycholinguists research called "human sentence processing," which studies the mechanisms at work in our brains when we construct meaning from sentences. But you don't have to study psycholinguistics to write well. The difference between good sentences and merely grammatical ones comes down to just two things: **readability** and **imageability**.

Readability is a general term for the ease with which a reader can understand a written text. In some contexts, the word "readability" includes things like legibility (e.g., whether the font is big enough to see clearly) and word frequency (e.g., whether the text contains rare and fancy words that the reader doesn't know). But the present chapter is concerned with readability as it relates to syntax: It's about how to construct sentences that are as easy to process as possible, so that the reader's attention and memory can be devoted to understanding the content of the research.

The "imageability" of a sentence is how easily a reader can form a mental image of its content. Imageability is traditionally discussed as a property of individual words, but this chapter is about imageability at the sentence level. The more your sentences give rise to clear images in the reader's mind, the more engaging your writing will be.

Understand readability

To understand why some sentences are easier to interpret than others, remember that for most of human history, language meant face-to-face communication. Prehistoric humans did not read or write, and the parts of our brain that let us do those things actually evolved to do other things. We read and write using brains that evolved with real-time, back-and-forth communication, and that sometimes makes reading and writing difficult.

When two people are talking and one becomes confused, there are many ways to signal the confusion. A person can furrow their brow, pause before speaking, ask a question, etc. In academic writing, the author does not get the benefit of immediate feedback from the reader. So academic writers have to anticipate difficulties that might arise in understanding and try to avoid them before they happen.

SEE THE DIFFERENCE BETWEEN WRITTEN AND SPOKEN LANGUAGE

The naturalness of spoken (or signed) language is reflected in the ease with which children learn it. Unless they have developmental disabilities, children learn to speak perfectly just by being around older children and adults who speak. In contrast, most children don't teach themselves to read and write. Spoken language is natural in a way that written language is not. So when we try to understand what makes written language difficult to process, we need to look at how it differs from speech.

First, written language is composed mostly of complete sentences. But spoken conversations are composed of utterances, many of which are not complete sentences. If you've never read a transcript of real-life conversation, you may be surprised at how short and choppy the utterances are. Table 9.1 shows an excerpt from a real conversation—File 02 from the Santa Barbara Corpus of Spoken American English at talkbank.org. This was an after-dinner conversation among four friends in San Francisco, California. All four were in their late 20s and early 30s. Harold and Jamie are a married couple, Miles is a doctor, and Pete is a graduate student from Southern California.

1	JAMIE:	How can you teach a three-year-old to tap dance?
2	HAROLD:	I can't imagine teaching a . . . yeah, really
3	MILES:	Who suggested this to him?
4	HAROLD:	I have no idea. It was probably my sister-in-law's idea because I think they saw that movie
5	JAMIE:	Tap?
6	HAROLD:	what was the

Table 9.1 (continued on next page)

7	MILES:	they had
8	HAROLD:	the movie with that really hot tap dancer
9	JAMIE:	oh, that kid
10	MILES:	He was actually here two weeks ago and I missed him.
11	JAMIE:	at the, at the jazz, tap thing or whatever
12	HAROLD:	Was he a little kid?
13	MILES:	No he's 16 now.
14	JAMIE:	No he's like . . . Yeah he's a teenager. But he teaches these classes in New York.
15	MILES:	That boy . . . he's supposed to be awesome.
16	JAMIE:	yeah
17	JAMIE:	really fast
18	MILES:	Hmm
19	HAROLD:	But I'm sure that was the . . . the impetus.
20	MILES:	Have you seen him?
21	JAMIE:	No . . . I just read an article on him.
22	MILES:	You . . . you probably read the same *Examiner* article I read.
23	JAMIE:	Yeah probably yeah
24	MILES:	talking about how Gregory Hines said he doesn't realize a human being can't tap that fast?
25	JAMIE:	Right, right
26	PETE:	(laughing)
27	JAMIE:	Yeah.
28	MILES:	And they were talking about how he's teaching these classes.
30	PETE:	Hmm
31	MILES:	and I guess he really goes fast, and
32	JAMIE:	yeah

Table 9.1 (continued on next page)

33	MILES:	and he
34	JAMIE:	He doesn't explain anything precisely
35	MILES:	He has to double it down to like one-fifth speed or something before they can g— pick it up— (laughs)
36	HAROLD:	Well I'm sure Thomas is all over it.
37	JAMIE:	Probably
38	HAROLD:	I mean he has a bro—
39	MILES:	could have seen him
40	HAROLD:	I guess that means his broken leg is doing OK (laughs).
41	PETE:	I was wondering about that. I was imagining a broken arm or something.
42	JAMIE:	Oh yeah
43	PETE:	But it was his leg?
44	HAROLD:	Yeah.
45	PETE:	That's like— I guess that he was being hauled around in a little wagon and stuff.
46	HAROLD:	Right . . . He healed very quickly.
47	JAMIE:	I guess kids' bones just like grow back really fast.
48	PETE:	Mm-hmm
49	HAROLD:	Yeah. I think they're really soft to start with.
50	JAMIE:	They're made of rubber. Th— that's it.

Table 9.1 (continued)

As this example illustrates, everyday language—the kind our brains evolved to process—is made up mostly of short utterances. When we hear an utterance, we store it for processing in our verbal working memory (also called phonological working memory), which can only hold as much language as we can pronounce in about two seconds. That's fine for speech, because two seconds is plenty to process the short chunks of language that make up spoken conversations.

The problem is that when we process written language, we still use the same two-second working memory buffer. Written sentences can be far longer and more complex than spoken utterances. Unless they are well constructed, they can quickly overwhelm the reader's working memory capacity. When that happens, the reader is forced to go back and reread individual phrases and clauses in order to reconstruct the meaning of the whole sentence. In other words, a reader cannot make a one-way trip through a badly constructed sentence.

SHORTEN SENTENCES TO INCREASE READABILITY

One easy way to avoid overwhelming the reader's working memory is just to keep sentences short. The classic Flesch-Kincaid Readability Tests (Farr, Jenkins, & Paterson, 1951; Kincaid, Fishburne, Rogers, & Chissom, 1975) calculate the readability of a text from the number of words per sentence and the number of syllables per word. Shorter words and shorter sentences equal higher readability.

Don't make the mistake of equating short sentences with unsophisticated thinking. The following is by one of the founders of cognitive psycholinguistics, George A. Miller (1956). This article is one of the most famous in the field, but the average sentence length in the first paragraph is only 19.3 words.

> My problem is that I have been persecuted by an integer. For seven years this number has followed me around, has intruded in my most private data, and has assaulted me from the pages of our most

public journals. This number assumes a variety of disguises, being sometimes a little larger and sometimes a little smaller than usual, but never changing so much as to be unrecognizable. The persistence with which this number plagues me is far more than a random accident. There is, to quote a famous senator, a design behind it, some pattern governing its appearances. Either there really is something unusual about the number or else I am suffering from delusions of persecution.

LEARN WHAT MAKES LONG SENTENCES READABLE

It is possible to write long sentences that are still clear and readable. One of the best science journalists working today is Natalie Wolchover, who has won multiple awards for her writing in statistics, physics, and mathematics. Her sentences are often long, but always clear. The first five sentences of this *Quanta* article have an average of 32.6 words, but are still very readable:

> Physicists at the Large Hadron Collider (LHC) in Europe have explored the properties of nature at higher energies than ever before, and they have found something profound: nothing new. It's perhaps the one thing that no one predicted 30 years ago when the project was first conceived. The infamous "diphoton bump" that arose in data plots in December has disappeared, indicating that it was a fleeting statistical fluctuation rather than a revolutionary new fundamental particle. And in fact,

the machine's collisions have so far conjured up no particles at all beyond those catalogued in the long-reigning but incomplete "Standard Model" of particle physics. In the collision debris, physicists have found no particles that could comprise dark matter, no siblings or cousins of the Higgs boson, no sign of extra dimensions, no leptoquarks—and above all, none of the desperately sought supersymmetry particles that would round out equations and satisfy "naturalness," a deep principle about how the laws of nature ought to work. (Wolchover, 2016)

These sentences demonstrate several rules worth following: (1) Put the subject and the main verb close together near the beginning of the sentence. (2) Put long structures at the end of the sentence. (3) Avoid multiple negations. Each of these will be covered in turn in the following section.

Write readable sentences

The old-fashioned way, and still probably the best way to learn to write well, is to read a lot of excellent writing—preferably in your own field—and develop an ear for the kinds of sentences you like best. But that takes time, and you probably already have a long reading list to tackle, and it's not easy to find great writing anywhere in academia, much less in your own field. So here are a few principles of readability to get you started.

PUT THE SUBJECT AND MAIN VERB CLOSE TOGETHER, NEAR THE BEGINNING OF THE SENTENCE OR CLAUSE

A clause requires a subject and a verb. A sentence may include just one clause (e.g., "I drink tea every morning") or more than one (e.g., "I drink tea every morning and I walk my dogs every afternoon.") In order to interpret a clause, the reader must first find the subject and the verb. Then other elements such as modifiers, prepositional phrases, subordinate clauses, etc. are added to the subject-verb backbone to get the meaning of the whole clause.

Think of a sentence as a jigsaw puzzle that the writer is handing to the reader, one piece at a time. The subject and verb of the main clause are like the sides and corner pieces of the puzzle. They must be assembled before the other pieces can be put in place. If the writer gives the reader a lot of nonside, noncorner pieces before the subject and verb, the reader has to hold those pieces in memory while waiting for the subject and verb to arrive. It is easiest for the

	Utterance or clause File 02.cha, Santa Barbara Corpus of Spoken American English, talkbank.org	Word count	Words before the main verb (in bold)
1	How can you **teach** a three-year-old to tap dance?	9	3
2	I can't **imagine** teaching a . . . yeah, really	7	2
3	Who **suggested** this to him?	5	1
4	I **have** no idea.	4	1
5	It **was** probably my sister-in-law's idea because I think they saw that movie	13	1

Table 9.2 (continued on next page)

6	Tap?	1	(no verb)
7	what **was** the	3	1
8	they **had**	2	1
9	the movie with that really hot tap dancer	8	(no verb)
10	oh, that kid	3	(no verb)
11	He **was** actually here two weeks ago and	8	1
12	I **missed** him.	3	1
13	at the, at the jazz, tap thing or whatever	9	(no verb)
14	**Was** he a little kid?	5	0
15	No he's 16 now	4	2
16	No he's like . . .	3	2
17	Yeah he's a teenager.	4	2
18	But he **teaches** these classes in New York.	8	2
19	That boy . . . he's supposed to be awesome.	7	3
20	yeah	1	(no verb)
21	really fast	2	(no verb)
22	Hmm	1	(no verb)
23	But I'm sure	3	2
24	that **was** the . . . the impetus.	5	1
	MEAN	4.9	1.5

Table 9.2 (continued)

reader to make a one-way trip through a sentence when the subject and verb are provided early on, as a frame into which the other pieces can be fit.

People do this naturally in spoken language. Table 9.2 shows the first 24 utterances of of the conversation shown in Table 9.1. The main verb of each clause is bolded. The utterances are short, and many are not clauses at all (i.e., they don't have a subject and a verb.) But when subjects and verbs are present, they usually appear close together, near the beginning of the clause.

If the writer gives the reader a lot of words to store temporarily, either before the subject or between the subject and the main verb, the reader's working memory buffer can quickly become overwhelmed. That's why, in good science writing, most clauses have the subject and main verb close together near the beginning.

Table 9.3 shows the sentences from the Wolchover (2016) article presented earlier. These sentences are long but still readable, because they get to the subject and verb relatively quickly.

In contrast, Table 9.4 shows some sentences that violate the rule. Although the mean length of these sentences (32.6 words) is the same as those in the Wolchover excerpt, these sentences require the reader to hold an average of 26.4 words in memory before the subject and verb arrive. Notice how much harder it is to make a one-way trip through these sentences.

PUT LONG STRUCTURES AT THE END

The "end weight" principle says that in general, sentences are easiest to read when longer structures occur later than shorter ones. When a sentence contains a series, the longest element in the series should go at the end. In the examples in Table 9.5, line breaks have been inserted to make it easier to compare the lengths of elements,

Utterance or clause Wolchover, N. (August 9, 2016) What no new particles means for physics. *Quanta Magazine.*	Word count	Words before the main verb (in bold)
1	Physicists at the Large Hadron Collider (LHC) in Europe have **explored** the properties of nature at higher energies than ever before, and they have found something profound: nothing new.	29	10
2	It**'s** perhaps the one thing that no one predicted 30 years ago when the project was first conceived.	18	1
3	The infamous "diphoton bump" that arose in data plots in December has **disappeared**, indicating that it was a fleeting statistical fluctuation rather than a revolutionary new fundamental particle.	28	12
4	And in fact, the machine's collisions have so far **conjured** up no particles at all beyond those catalogued in the long-reigning but incomplete "Standard Model" of particle physics.	28	9
5	In the collision debris, physicists have **found** no particles that could comprise dark matter, no siblings or cousins of the Higgs boson, no sign of extra dimensions, no leptoquarks—and above all, none of the desperately sought supersymmetry particles that would round out equations and satisfy "naturalness," a deep principle about how the laws of nature ought to work.	60	6
	MEAN	32.6	7.6

Table 9.3

Sentence (All sentences have only one clause.)	Word count	Words before the main verb (in bold)
1	Based on data from animals indicating that the basilar-membrane response to a tone of a given frequency is linear at a place with a characteristic frequency (CF) well above the tone frequency (Yates, 1990; Yates et al., 1990; Ruggero, 1992; Ruggero et al, 1997; Rhode and Recio, 2000), Oxenham and Plack **assumed** that the response to the 3-kHz masker at the 6-kHz frequency region was linear.	50 (excluding citations)	35
2	According to experts in the field, the need for all 34 cities in Orange County to start building affordable and permanent supportive housing for nearly 7,000 homeless people should **be** a wake up call.	34	29
3	Relying on anecdotes and false information, with little or no evidence to back up claims of vaccine danger, antivaccine activists have **infected** an entire generation of parents with fear.	29	21
4	Extending lifespan, increasing resistance to age-related diseases in rodents and monkeys, and improving the health of overweight humans, intermittent fasting (IF; reduced meal frequency) and caloric restriction (CR) **show** great promise.	31	28
5	Arguably more troubling is the fact that the fundamental labor rights of increasing numbers of workers are being **violated**.	19	18
	MEAN	32.6	26.4

Table 9.4

	Longer structures at the end (original, better version) **vs. at the beginning** (revised to be worse)
End	For seven years this number **has followed me around,** **has intruded in my most private data,** and **has assaulted me from the pages of our most public journals.**
Beginning	For seven years this number **has assaulted me from the pages of our most public journals,** **has intruded in my most private data,** and **has followed me around.**
End	In the collision debris, physicists have found **no particles that could comprise dark matter,** **no siblings or cousins of the Higgs boson,** **no sign of extra dimensions,** **no leptoquarks—** and above all, **none of the desperately sought supersymmetry particles that would round out equations and satisfy "naturalness," a deep principle about how the laws of nature ought to work.**
Beginning	In the collision debris, physicists have found **none of the desperately sought supersymmetry particles that would round out equations and satisfy "naturalness," a deep principle about how the laws of nature ought to work,** **no leptoquarks—** **no sign of extra dimensions,** **no siblings or cousins of the Higgs boson,** **and above all,** **no particles that could comprise dark matter.**

Table 9.5 (continued on next page)

End	The kitchen in the cottage was always too small. It had **a linoleum floor,** **a fridge that hummed and snorted,** and **a sticky yellow fly strip dangling from the ceiling.** (Bill Barich, "O'Neill Among the Weakfish." *Traveling Light*. Viking, 1984)
Beginning	The kitchen in the cottage was always too small. It had **a sticky yellow fly strip dangling from the ceiling,** **a fridge that hummed and snorted,** and **a linoleum floor.**
End	Lifting his head and sniffing, Caldwell experiences a vivid urge **to walk on faster,** **to canter right past Hummel's,** **to romp neighing through the front door and out the back door of any house in Olinger that stood in his way,** **to gallop up the brushy brown winter-burned flank of Shale Hill and on, on, over hills that grow smoother and bluer with distance, on and on on a southeast course cutting diagonally across highways and rivers frozen solid as highways until at last he drops, his head in death extended toward Baltimore.** (John Updike, *The Centaur*. Knopf, 1963)
Beginning	Lifting his head and sniffing, Caldwell experiences a vivid urge **to gallop up the brushy brown winter-burned flank of Shale Hill and on, on, over hills that grow smoother and bluer with distance, on and on on a southeast course cutting diagonally across highways and rivers frozen solid as highways until at last he drops, his head in death extended toward Baltimore,** **to romp neighing through the front door and out the back door of any house in Olinger that stood in his way,** **to canter right past Hummel's,** **to walk on faster.**

Table 9.5 (continued)

which are bolded. The first sentence in each pair follows the end weight principle by putting longer elements in a series at the end. The second sentence in each pair has the same elements but in reverse order, so that the longest element is first.

AVOID MULTIPLE NEGATIONS

In order to interpret a negative statement, the reader must first represent a positive statement (e.g., *This tea is delicious*), hold it in working memory, and then negate it (e.g., *This tea is not delicious*). When the resulting negative statement is itself negated (e.g., *I'm not saying that this tea is not delicious*), the burden on working memory is even greater. In this way, sentences with multiple negations quickly become confusing, leading to a phenomenon called "misnegation," where writers or speakers wind up saying the opposite of what they mean.

As linguist Mark Liberman (2009) observes, "Whenever we combine negation, concepts of possibility or difficulty, and thresholds on a scale of evaluation, people seem to get their wires crossed." Writing for the group blog Language Log, Liberman has compiled hundreds of examples of misnegations. Table 9.6 lists some of my favorites.

In order to help readers make a one-way trip through your writing, keep the number of negations per sentence low. Negation can be explicit (as in the word "not") or it can be implicit in the meaning of a word—often a word starting with one of the prefixes in Table 9.7. When multiple negatives occur in the same sentence, you can revise to avoid confusion by swapping out one or more of the negative words for positive ones. Table 9.7 gives some examples of negative words and potential positive substitutes.

Writing is a creative human endeavor, and as such it defies absolute rules. Following these suggestions will help most academic writers produce more readable sentences than if the rules were not

Misnegation examples
No head injury is too trivial to ignore. (cited by Kai von Fintel, 2004)
It is **impossible to underestimate** the value of the early diagnosis of breast cancer. ("Scan promises early cancer detection," 2001)
The photograph was prominently displayed and occupied almost the entire right-handed side of page 15. Readers of the newspaper **could not fail to miss** the article. (Bowcott & Watt, 2017)
Thousands march in Berlin to **protest against anti-racism** (SCMP News, 2018)
Late Friday, by voice vote, the Senate took an initial step to move ahead on the nomination. **Barring no major revelations from the FBI**, the Senate could vote on confirming Kavanaugh next weekend, days after the start of the high court's session. (Kim, Wagner & Dawsey, 2018)
Nestle is revered as being the best in the business. **I challenge anyone to refute that the company is not the most efficient producer in North America** (cited in Liberman, 2004)
No one, least of all my family and close friends, would deny that I am somewhat hidebound, stuck up to my nethers in mud. I mean, don't get me started on the subject of mobile phones and **the inability of so many of their owners not to comprehend that they are incapable of walking and using these devices at the same time.** (Bouquet, 2018)
The Skilling indictment demonstrates in no uncertain terms that **no executive is too prominent or too powerful and that no scheme to defraud is too complex or too fancy to avoid the long arm of the law.** (Flood & Ivanovich, 2004)

Table 9.6

followed. But there may also be times when you choose to break the rules in order to achieve a particular effect. If you apply these rules most of the time, readers will come to expect these structures in your sentences. You can then break the rules to surprise the reader, or get their attention. For example, the principle of end weight is so widely followed that readers expect it. Violating it can be used for humorous effect (e.g., "These are my cats: Honeybun, Little Miss Fluffball, Assistant Professor Whiskerface, and Mo.")

Prefix	Negative	Potential substitute	Prefix	Negative	Potential substitute
DE-	deactivate	turn off, close	**NON-**	nonobvious	subtle
	decompose	rot, break down		nonresident	outsider
	deconstruct	take apart		nonstop	constant
	decontaminate	clean, purify		nontrivial	important
	decrease	shrink	**NOT**	not allow	prevent
	deform	warp		not careful	rash, negligent
DIS-	disagree	argue		not different	same
	disbelieve	doubt		not dissimilar	similar
	discontinue	stop		not include	omit
	dishonest	lying		not many	few
	dishonor	shame		not notice	overlook
	disinfect	clean, purify		not often	seldom, rarely
	displease	annoy		not stop	continue
	distrustful	suspicious		not the same	different
IL-	illegible	sloppy		not unless	only if
	illegitimate	bogus		not unlike	like
	illogical	wrong	**UN-**	unaided	alone
IM-	immature	childish		unafraid	brave
	impatient	antsy		unanticipated	surprising
	imperfect	flawed		unbelievable	shocking
IN-	inaccurate	wrong		uncertain	dubious
	incorrect	wrong		unconventional	fresh
	insignificant	petty		undamaged	whole
	inconsistent	off and on		unexpected	novel
IR-	irrelevant	moot		unfocused	scattered
	irresponsible	risky		unforgettable	memorable
	irregular	strange		unforeseeable	random
NON-	noncomprehension	confusion		unkind	mean, harsh, cruel
	nonconformity	oddity		unstimulating	boring
	nonobvious	subtle		unrelated	separate
	nonresident	outsider		untrue	false
	nonstop	constant		unusual	rare
	nontrivial	important			

Table 9.7

Understand imageability

Humans are a highly visual species. Our visual system doesn't only take in information about the outside world; it also functions as a way of representing and organizing information within the brain. In addition to the verbal working memory that is always used in language processing, human beings also have another kind of working memory, which holds visual and spatial information. The "imageability" of a word or sentence is the ease with which readers can form a mental image of its meaning (Paivio, 2013; Richardson, 1975; Segal, 1971). Imageability is closely related to concreteness, because concrete words like "dog" are more imageable than abstract words like "loyalty" (Paivio, Yuille & Madigan, 1968).

There is plenty of evidence that imageability and concreteness affect how we process words. Concrete words are easier to learn and remember than abstract ones (Palmer, MacGregor & Havelka, 2013), and concrete nouns are processed faster and more accurately than abstract nouns in a variety of cognitive tasks (Jessen et al., 2000; Strain & Herdman, 1999). Children learn highly imageable words earlier than less-imageable ones (McDonough, Song, Hirsh-Pasek, Golinkoff & Lannon, 2011) and when they learn to read, they find highly imageable words easier to read (Coltheart, Laxon & Keating, 1988).

Other evidence comes from aphasic patients—people who lose language abilities after a stroke or other brain injury. These patients find it easier to complete sentences with highly imageable words than with less-imageable words (Berndt, Haendiges, Burton & Mitchum, 2002). One study found that "across nouns, verbs, synonymous and associative relationships, a clear and consistent pattern emerged: concrete words were always comprehended more successfully than abstract words." The authors concluded that "concrete words succumb less quickly [to dementia] by virtue of their richer and more detailed semantic representations" (Hoffman, Jones, & Lambon Ralph, 2013). All of these studies show that words high in imageability and concreteness are better represented in the brain—that they are in fact *more meaningful*—than words low in those qualities. The message for academic writers can be summed up in the title of one article: *Be concrete to be comprehended.*

Write imageable sentences

Visual imagery keeps readers engaged, which is of huge benefit to academic writers because it's so easy for academic writing to be dry and boring. The problem for academics is that we deal in abstractions: causes, effects, theories, models, data, and so on. The challenge is to connect these topics to visual imagery in a way that engages readers and doesn't distort the content too much. One obvious solution, at least for presenting data, is to make a figure (as discussed in Chapter 5). But sentences themselves can be made more imageable through the use of concrete subjects and actions.

DESCRIBE CONCRETE SUBJECTS DOING ACTIONS THAT READERS CAN PICTURE

The core of every sentence is its subject and its main verb. In many nonimageable sentences, the subject is an abstraction and the verb is equally abstract: often a variant of "be" or "have." To make the sentence more imageable, change the subject to something concrete (like a person), and the verb to something less generic—preferably an action the reader can visualize. Table 9.8 shows examples, with the subjects and main verbs bolded.

Sentences beginning with the words "There is" or "There are" are low-hanging fruit. They can almost always be rewritten with a more concrete subject and at least a slightly more interesting verb, as shown in Table 9.9.

Abstract subject, insipid verb	Concrete subject, interesting verb
The incumbency **advantage** of authoritarian regimes is in their control of public resources	**Authoritarians stay** in power by controlling public resources.
The **policy** of refusing treatment based on immigration status **has** the potential for widespread negative health effects.	When we leave sick people untreated because they don't have visas, **we endanger** everyone's health.
It is argued that the static model of adult neuropsychology is inapplicable to the explanation of atypical pediatric development.	Adult **brains differ** in many ways from the brains of children with developmental disorders, and **cannot serve** as a model.

Table 9.8

Sentence beginning with "there is/there are"	Revision
There is an airplane safety assessment committee, made up of engineers who are revising the standards for safety assessment of airplanes and their related systems.	**Engineers** on the airplane safety assessment committee **are revising** the standards that technicians use to assess the safety of airplanes and their related systems.
There are five factors that moderate the contribution of early peer victimization to subsequent depressive symptoms.	Some **children** who are bullied **become** depressed; others don't. This **paper identifies** five factors that make a difference in how children recover from victimization by peers.
There is a tendency to assume progress in reducing poverty and then to be shocked when it does not materialize.	**Voters assume** that cities are making progress in reducing poverty and are shocked when progress does not materialize.
There are "freeloaders," who wish to benefit from herd immunity without being vaccinated themselves.	**"Freeloaders" benefit** from herd immunity without being vaccinated themselves.

Table 9.9

FOLLOW ABSTRACTIONS AND GENERALIZATIONS WITH CONCRETE OR SPECIFIC EXAMPLES

Sometimes you can't avoid abstract and general statements, because they are the whole point of what you're trying to convey. If so, by all means make those statements. But support them with concrete examples and specific details to help readers connect them with real-world phenomena. In the examples below, each abstract or general statement is bolded and and is followed by supporting examples or details.

> **There is considerable heterogeneity in the exposure of European countries to the asylum crisis.** Whereas some countries, like Germany and Sweden, process a large number of asylum applications per capita, others, like the United Kingdom and Czech Republic, share a comparatively small responsibility. **Yet the migrant crisis has been so severe that it has resulted in political conflict and social tensions widely across Europe,** including extreme right-wing parties mobilizing citizens around asylum issues, frequent arson attacks on asylum centers, and the partial closing of Schengen borders (Bansak, Hainmueller & Hangartner, 2016).

> **New technologies are increasing learners' access to content.** Students can now listen to lectures via podcast while commuting to internships. Clinicians in remote and rural areas can access training and academic support that were previously

inaccessible because of geographic isolation from the large central hospitals and academic centres in the main cities.

KNOW WHEN TO USE THE ACTIVE VERSUS THE PASSIVE VOICE

In most English sentences with an action verb, the subject performs the action. These sentences are said to be in the "active voice.' If you rewrite the sentence so that the subject is acted on, the sentence is said to be in the "passive voice." (See Table 9.10 for examples.)

A standard piece of advice for writing clearly is to use the active voice rather than the passive voice whenever possible. This is good advice, which is why it has become standard. Active constructions are typically shorter than passive ones, which makes them easier to process. Passive constructions also place the direct object before the verb and the subject, forcing readers to hold more words in memory before they can process the whole sentence.

Perhaps most importantly, passive constructions allow the subject to be omitted entirely. For example, the passive sentences in Table 9.10 could be rewritten with no subjects: *Food was refused*; *a protest is being organized*; *a union will be formed*. Of course this ability

Active voice	Passive voice
The octopuses refused their food.	Food was refused by the octopuses.
The squid are organizing a protest.	A protest is being organized by the squid.
The predatory mollusks will form a union called 'Cephalopods for Justice'.	A union called 'Cephalopods for Justice' will be formed by the predatory mollusks.

Table 9.10

to describe actions without actors is exactly what politicians and bureaucrats love about passive constructions: They enable sentences such as the infamous "Mistakes were made." Many other people dislike passives for the same reason, seeing them as a way that speakers avoid taking or assigning responsibility for actions.

Hiding the actor is usually not helpful in academic writing, because it makes sentences less concrete and harder to process. But there are times when deemphasizing or omitting the actor makes sense. For example, sometimes you don't know who the actor is (e.g., "During the night of May 14, 2019, the Aquarium of the Pacific was broken into, and all of the octopus and squid were fitted with tiny swim caps bearing the 'Cephalopods for Justice' logo.") At other times, the actor may be irrelevant (e.g., "Fewer than 150 cephalopod-sized swim caps were produced in the United States last year.")

Passive constructions are also indispensable when the most important person in a sentence is the patient—the person to whom something happened. When two or more sentences in a row focus on the same patient, passive constructions allow a writer to keep that patient in the topic position, creating a topic chain, as described in Chapter 8. Table 9.11 shows a series of passive sentences that flow well because they all have versions of the same topic (in bold).

Topic	Comment
The union	will be known by the acronym CFJ.
Its goal	will be to provide all cephalopods with knitting supplies on demand.
CFJ	may eventually be incorporated into the larger Fiber Arts Union of the Aquariums (FAUA).
Alternatively, **it**	may be left to stand on its own.

Table 9.11

Topic	Comment
This **crisis**	arose because cephalopods need a **hobby.**
Knitting, crochet, and hand-spinning	can be used to reduce their **stress.**
If left untreated, the **stress**	leads to **health problems.**
High blood pressure in squid, for example,	is exacerbated by a lack of fiber-arts opportunities.

Table 9.12

Similarly, passive constructions can be used to move old information into the topic position and new information into the comment position. This can be done when the author wants to create a topic-comment chain, as described in Chapter 8 and illustrated in Table 9.12.

The English language has enormous flexibility in sentence construction, and part of the fun of writing is tinkering with sentences to create the particular effect you want. The suggestions in this chapter are not meant as absolute rules to be applied in every case. Rather, they are meant to introduce the concepts of readability and imageability and to show how those qualities are affected by sentence structure and word choice. These suggestions give writers a place to start when a sentence seems mediocre but it's not clear how to improve it. Still, if you write a sentence that sounds perfect to your ear, even if it violates some or all of these suggestions, I hope that you will keep and enjoy it, suggestions be damned. Your writing belongs to you.

10

WORDS

Words are fun. One of the simplest pleasures in editing an almost-finished document is trimming unnecessary words and finding better alternatives for words that aren't quite right. Words can typically be changed without affecting much else in the sentence, paragraph, or document, which means that you can rethink word choices without having to rethink the whole argument. This makes for a pleasant, low-stress kind of revision.

In academic and scientific writing, words are not just chosen because they sound good or create a mood. When a writer is trying to teach the reader something (as is often the case in writing about research), words serve as important placeholders for new concepts (Carey, 2009; Sarnecka, 2016).

For example, when little children learn to count, they don't initially understand what the number words refer to, or how the counting system works. At first, they just learn a string of words (e.g., "one, two, three, four, five . . ."). Each of the words stands for a number, but the child doesn't know that. And the order of the words is not arbitrary—the list must be recited in the same order each time, or the counting won't produce a valid result. (In other words, if you try to count a group of objects by saying "three, one, six, four, two," and you conclude that there are two objects in the group, you will be incorrect.) The point is that children initially learn the words and their order as placeholders—the child knows that they mean something, but isn't sure what they mean.

The same thing happens when we learn other scientific concepts. For example, humans naturally have the intuition that the earth we live on is a flat horizontal plane. But as children, we are told by adults that the earth is actually round. This idea is so different from our intuitions that it's difficult to make sense of. Children wonder: If it's like a ball with people living all over it, why don't the people on the bottom of the ball fall off? Words like "gravity" become placeholders for new, partially formed and poorly understood concepts about the earth and its shape (Vosniadou & Brewer, 1992). Over time, by continuing to have conversations that include those placeholder words, we (or at least most of us) are able to fill them in with more elaborated concepts. In this sense, words are not just labels for information we already hold. They are an important part of the process by which we learn new, and especially counterintuitive, information.

Choose simple and specific words

As an academic writer, you know a lot more about your subject area than most of your readers. Sometimes you have to introduce technical terms, which are meaningful to experts and function as placeholders for nonexperts at first. At the same time, you can make your writing as easy to process as possible by conveying all nontechnical information in the clearest, simplest terms possible.

CHOOSE SHORT, COMMONLY USED WORDS

When we read, even silently, we use our verbal working memory to hold the words in our minds for processing. But our working memory can only hold as much as we can say in about two seconds. So the length of each word (i.e., how long it takes to pronounce) really matters. The shorter each word is, the more words you can hold in mind (Baddeley, Thomson & Buchanan, 1975). And the more of the sentence you can hold in mind, the easier it is to interpret the sentence's meaning.

Keeping words and sentences short is one way to make things easier for readers. Flesch-Kincaid Readability Tests (discussed in Chapter 9) are calculated from just the number of words per sentence and the number of syllables per word. To make your writing as readable as possible, choose short words over long ones.

A similar principle holds for word frequency. The more often we hear a word, the more easily we can retrieve its meaning from memory. So the meanings of common words are easier to retrieve than the meanings of rare ones. Thanks to the internet, you can now look up the frequency of any English word, but I'm not suggesting you do that when you write. First, doing that would be a pain in the neck. Second, what matters is actually not the frequency of the word in the 14-billion-word corpus of internet English; it's the frequency with which your readers encounter the word. So use the word that is most common in your research community. Table 10.1 shows some examples of fancy (long and rare) words and possible plain (short and common) replacements.

Fancy word	Plain word
adjacent	next
advantageous	helpful
aggregate	total
alleviate	ease
allocate	give
alternatively	or
ameliorate	fix
anticipate	expect
apparent	clear
ascertain	learn
attempt	try
beneficial	helpful
component	part
conceal	hide
concerning	on
consequently	so
contains	has
currently	now
discontinue	stop
emphasize	stress
encounter	meet
equitable	fair
demonstrate	show
evident	clear
exclusively	only
exhibit	show

Fancy word	Plain word
facilitate	help
fearfulness	fear
frequently	often
however	but
inception	start
initial	first
monitor	watch
necessitate	need
nevertheless	still
notify	tell
numerous	many
objective	aim
obtain	get
option	choice
perform	do
permit	let
portion	part
possess	have, own
provide	give
purchase	buy
remain	stay
require	need
selection	choice
subsequent	next
subsequently	then
sufficient	enough

Table 10.1

CHOOSE CONCRETE/IMAGEABLE AND SPECIFIC WORDS

Abstract words refer to things that cannot be directly sensed, like qualities or ideas. Imageable words are those for which it is easy to create a mental image; concrete words refer to sensory experiences more broadly—they can involve not only vision, but other senses as well. As mentioned in Chapter 9, the more concrete or imageable a word is, the faster and more accurately it is processed. There are databases of word concreteness (e.g., Brysbaert, Warriner & Kuperman, 2014) just as there are databases of word frequencies.

Concreteness and imageability are helpful to communication. Making things concrete and imageable is often difficult in academic writing, because we write about abstractions (theories, claims, evidence, conclusions, etc.) We can't avoid all abstraction, but we can swap in concrete words for abstract ones whenever possible, and we can support abstract statements with concrete examples, as discussed in Chapter 9.

Abstract (refers to an idea or quality)	Concrete (refers to something you can see, hear, touch, taste, or smell)
The infants **enjoyed** the puppet show.	The infants **smiled, laughed,** and **reached for** the puppets.
Group A **scored higher** than Group B.	Participants in Group A **recalled an average of 20% more words** than those in Group B.
Improved Meyer lemon trees **do better** than previous hybrids.	Improved Meyer lemon trees **grow faster, produce more fruit, and resist pests better** than previous hybrids.
Srinavasan and Schultheiss (2019) **questioned the evidence** presented by Lee and Vandekerckhove (2016).	Srinavasan and Schultheiss (2019) **pointed out that undergraduates** in the Lee and Vandekerckhove (2016) study **were tested at the end of finals week and were likely sleep deprived.**

Table 10.2

Living thing	Artifacts	Experiences
Eukaryote	Mass-produced goods	Memorable experiences
Animal	Electronics	Pleasant memorable experiences
Mammal	Consumer electronics	Holidays
Quadruped	Computers	Family holidays
Dog	Laptops	Family holidays on the Salmon River
Herding dog	Macbook Air laptops	Our family holiday on the Salmon River
German shepherd	This Macbook Air laptop that I'm working on right now	The final dinner at the end of our family holiday on the Salmon River in 2013
Athena (my dog)		

Table 10.3

Just as concrete words are usually better than abstract ones, so are specific words usually better than general ones. Note that general and specific are not absolute categories, but a continuum. Table 10.3 shows sets of words, ordered from general to specific.

Your communication will be as clear as possible if you choose the most specific word that captures the category you want to refer to. For example, once you've established that the stimuli in your experiment were puppets and the participants were children, you don't have to keep writing sentences like "Each participant saw one of two stimulus items." Readers will follow your argument more easily if you write, "Each child saw one of two puppets." Table 10.4 gives additional examples.

General (refers to a broad class or category)	Specific (refers to a narrower class or category, or even to a specific individual or situation)
Participants	Survey respondents, preschoolers, undergraduates, nursing mothers, chimpanzees, etc.
Stimuli	Puppets, pictures, sounds, word lists, etc.
Demographics	Age, gender, years of education, sexual orientation, disability status, racial/ethnic identity, political affiliation, household income, etc.
A survey	A survey of 4,550 Amazon Turk respondents

Table 10.4

AVOID OR EXPLAIN AMBIGUOUS WORDS

If you know that different groups of readers use a word in different ways, you should either avoid that word or explain what you mean by it. Words like "theory," "bias," and "significance" mean different things to scientists and nonscientists (Wellcome Trust, 2018), and some words are even used differently from one field of science to another. For example, in my work on children's number-concept development, I interact with people who study the brain and also with people who study education. In brain research, the term "number sense" (e.g., Dehaene, 2011) refers to an ancient perceptual system that humans share with other animals. In education research, "number sense" (e.g., Jordan, Kaplan & Locuniak, 2006) means not only innate number perception, but also skills we learn in childhood, like counting and simple arithmetic. This situation is obviously ripe for confusion, and I try to avoid the term "number sense" when I write. But when I have to use it, I define it.

Be kind to your readers

Clear communication is an act of generosity toward the reader. When you try to bridge the gap between your understanding and the reader's, you are shouldering as much of the joint burden of communication as you can. Most academic writing could be better in this regard. Not because academic writers are ungenerous—on the contrary, most researchers are eager to share what they have learned. The problem is the curse of knowledge: Many writers are either unaware of it or don't know how to overcome it. Below are some suggestions for overcoming it at the word level.

USE TECHNICAL TERMS CAREFULLY

Imagine that you are an avid chess player, but you are on vacation without any internet. The only way you can play chess is over the phone. On the first day of your vacation, you call your best friend Annie, also an avid chess player, and challenge her to a game. Naturally, you both describe your moves using standard algebraic notation. Your game with Annie sounds like this:

> YOU: d4
> ANNIE: Nf6
> YOU: c4
> ANNIE: e5

On the second day of your vacation, you call another friend: Bridgette. Bridgette also loves to play chess, but she learned way back in the 1960s using descriptive notation, and she has never changed. Descriptive notation is clumsier than algebraic notation—it takes longer to describe the moves, and occasionally the same description can refer to two different possible moves. But this is the system that Bridgette uses, and you want to play with her, so you use it too. Your game with Bridgette starts with the same four moves, but now they sound like this:

YOU: Pawn to Queen 4.
BRIDGETTE: Knight to King Bishop 3.
YOU: Pawn to Queen Bishop 4.
BRIDGETTE: Pawn to King 4.

On the third day of your vacation, you call your friend Cassidy, who knows how to play chess but has never played seriously and doesn't know any notational system. Describing your moves to Cassidy is much more work than describing them to Annie or Bridgette. But you want to play chess, so you make the effort. The first four moves of your game with Cassidy are the same as in the previous two games, but they take much longer to describe:

YOU: OK, first move . . . The pawn in front of my queen
            moves up two.
CASSIDY: OK, then the knight on my left moves up and
            toward the center.
YOU: OK got it. Now the pawn in front of the bishop near
            my queen moves up two.
CASSIDY: OK. The pawn in front of my king moves up two.

On the fourth day of your vacation, you call Daria, who has no knowledge of chess at all. She has been asking you to teach her for a long time, and you decide to do it now. Playing chess with Daria is a slow, difficult process full of misunderstandings and corrections. The same first four moves now sound like this:

YOU: OK so for my first move, I am taking the pawn that's in front of the queen, and moving it forward two spaces.

DARIA: Wait, I thought a pawn could only move one space.

YOU: Usually that's true, but on the first move it can go two spaces. Only on the first move.

DARIA: Oh, OK. And knights can jump over other pieces, right?

YOU: Right, they're the only piece that can do that.

DARIA: OK, then I'd like to move my knight, the one on my left, up two spaces. So it will jump over the pawn and land in front of it.

YOU: Remember, it also has to move one square to the right or left. It can't just move two spaces forward; it has to make an "L" shape.

DARIA: Oh, yes. OK. Then I guess it will move . . . one space toward the center? So it's in front of the pawn that's in front of the bishop. The bishop next to the king. Can it move there?

YOU: Yep, that's fine. Now I'm taking the pawn that's in front of the bishop—the bishop next to my queen— and moving that pawn forward two spaces.

DARIA: Wait, you said you could only do that on the first move. This is your second move.

YOU: Not the *player's* first move, the *pawn's* first move. Each pawn can move two spaces, but only the first time *it moves*.

DARIA: Oh, OK! So can I move the pawn that's in front of my king two spaces?

YOU: Yes.

DARIA: OK, I'll do that.

All of these conversations described the same four moves. But the conversation with Annie took only four words, whereas the conversation with Daria took 248. In each case, the less your opponent knew about chess, the more effort you had to make—and the more words you had to use—to communicate the same information. Technical terms used by experts are like standard notation in chess. They are elegant and precise, but novices don't know them and they take time to learn.

This is why communicating clearly about your research to non-experts is difficult. Explaining things in ordinary language takes up a lot more space on the page and doesn't convey the meaning as precisely as the technical terms do. But to bridge the gap between the reader's knowledge and your own, you have to use language they understand.

USE ACRONYMS CAREFULLY

An acronym is an abbreviation made from the first letters of two or more words. For example, POTUS for "president of the United States" is an acronym. So are "PhD," "FBI," and "ATM." (Actually, those last three are initialisms, because we actually say the letters, rather than pronouncing them as words. But the word "acronym" is commonly used for both types of abbreviation.) Some acronyms become so common that after a while, people treat them as words. This happened with "radar" (from Radio Detection And Ranging), "scuba" (Self-Contained Underwater Breathing Apparatus), and "laser" (Light Amplification by Stimulated Emission of Radiation).

Common acronyms like the ones above are no problem, and you should use them freely. But for acronyms that your readers may not know, I have three rules to suggest. (1) Don't make up your own acronyms. (2) Don't ask your readers learn an acronym unless you need to use it a lot. (3) Define an acronym the first time you use it.

First, avoid making up new acronyms unless it's absolutely necessary. Even if you've been thinking about the pros and cons of import tariffs on small mammal grooming accessories for the past three years, and everyone in your lab calls them ITSMGAs, is it really necessary to make your readers learn that? No. Instead, introduce the concept, explain what it means, and then subsequently refer to it by a word people can interpret, such as "tariffs." Your work is probably hard enough for people to understand, without you adding to the problem by inventing new acronyms.

Second, don't make your readers learn any acronym (even one used by experts beyond your lab) unless you need to use it a lot— let's say at least five times. The reason for this, again, is that learning an acronym creates work for the reader. It's not worth the effort unless the acronym will appear frequently in the document.

Third, if you do decide to introduce an acronym, define it the first time it appears unless it's truly common knowledge (e.g., USA, RSVP, etc.). Of course, many acronyms that ordinary people don't know might be common knowledge in your discipline. For example, at the conferences I attend, no one needs to say that fMRI stands for *functional magnetic resonance imaging*, because everyone present knows it.

If the curse of knowledge makes it hard to guess which acronyms will be a problem for your readers, follow these general rules: For work aimed at a public audience, only use acronyms that would appear without a definition in a national newspaper like the *New York Times* or the *Washington Post*. For work aimed at a disciplinary audience, just take your best guess and ask your penguin huddle for help.

DEZOMBIFY THE NOMINALIZATIONS

Just as English has a lot of prefixes that can make words negative, we also have a lot of suffixes that can make things into nouns. The technical word for noun is "nominal," and the verb for making something into a noun is "nominalize." The new noun that you make by adding one of these suffixes to a word is called a "nominalization."

Some nominalizations are really helpful. For example, the suffix -ER turns a verb into a noun meaning the person who does that action; the suffix -EE turns a verb into a noun meaning the person who receives the action. So we can talk about "advisers" and their "advisees," "employers" and their "employees," "interviewers" and "interviewees," and so on. It's much quicker to say, "The interviewee was nervous, but the interviewer was kind" than to say, 'The person being interviewed was nervous, but the person performing the interview was kind."

Nominalizations are often useful in academic writing. When we make a verb or an adjective into a noun, we can zoom out and talk about the action itself (in the case of a verb) or the quality itself (in the case of an adjective). For example, the word "discriminability" is a nominalization meaning "ease of being discriminated." It packs a lot of meaning into a few syllables. But in many cases, nominalizations add a layer of abstraction without adding meaning. The two sentences below have the same meaning, but the second sentence is shorter and clearer.

Emily had the **responsibility** of **supervision** over 10 research assistants.

Emily was **responsible** for **supervising** 10 research assistants.

From a reader's perspective, nominalizations are usually harder to process than the verb or adjective they came from: They are longer, less common, and more abstract. Helen Sword, author of *Stylish Academic Writing* (2012) calls them "zombie nouns" because they "cannibalize active verbs, suck the lifeblood from adjectives and substitute abstract entities for human beings."

Like passive-voice constructions, nominalizations make it easier to hide the actor in a sentence. For example, when Republicans were preparing for their 2012 national convention in Tampa and the city was being threatened by Tropical Storm Isaac, Governor Rick Scott told reporters, "There's not an anticipation that there will be a cancellation" (Alvarez, 2012). Scott could have avoided the nominalizations by saying, "We don't anticipate canceling," but that would have forced him to say who was doing the anticipating and canceling.

You can often make writing clearer by turning nominalizations back into the verbs and adjectives they came from. This is an act of kindness for your readers as well as for the poor nominalizations, who probably don't want to be zombies. (Does anyone?)

Not all nominalizations can or should be eliminated; some are useful. For example, the word "writing" is a nominalization used throughout this book. The word "nominalization" itself is a nominalization, and I just used it twice in the same sentence! Sometimes nominalizations can't be eliminated because it would change the meaning of the sentence, as in this pair.

I gave him a strong **reference**.

I referred him strongly.

With fewer nominalizations, your writing will be easier to read, and people will read it faster. That's usually a good thing, but at

Nominalizations throughout	Just one nominalization, at the end
Our **delight** at the **invitation** from our friends in England did not prevent our **avoidance** of the **booking** of the **visit**. Our **uncertainty** about our work schedules and the kids' summer schedules, and the **possibility** of a **visit** by family, all caused **delays**. But eventually the **wait** had to end: It was time to make a **decision**.	We were delighted when our friends invited us to visit them in England, but we avoided booking the trip for a long time. First we didn't know our work schedules, then we didn't know the kids' summer schedules, then for a while it looked like family might be coming to stay with us. But eventually we knew we couldn't wait any longer: It was time to make a **decision**.

Table 10.5

times you may deliberately choose to use a nominalization to slow things down. For example, if you want readers to stop and take in an important point, you might use a nominalization to break the rhythm a bit, and make the nominalized word seem weightier or more formal, as in Table 10.5.

However you choose to use nominalizations, you can't use them if you can't see them. It's worth learning to recognize the suffixes that are used to form nominalizations, so that when you revise your writing, you can make conscious decisions about which nominalizations are useful and necessary. Tables 10.6 and 10.7 list examples of suffixes commonly used to form nominalizations.

BUST THE CLUSTERS

English lets us use nouns as though they were adjectives, to modify other nouns. When two nouns appear together and the first one modifies the second one (e.g., "bus stop"), it's called a noun compound. "Discriminability" is a nominalization; "discriminability ratio" is a noun compound. Like nominalizations, noun compounds

Suffix	Nominalization	Verb
-ANCE	acceptance	accept
-ENCE	admittance	admit
	adherence	adhere
	attendance	attend
	governance	govern
	preference	prefer
	reference	refer
-MENT	advancement	advance
	argument	argue
	assessment	assess
	commitment	commit
	displacement	displace
	enhancement	enhance
	enjoyment	enjoy
	excitement	excite
	replacement	replace
-TION	activation	activate
-SION	cancellation	cancel
	conclusion	conclude
	contamination	contaminate
	conversion	convert
	demonstration	demonstrate
	deviation	deviate
	participation	participate
	relation	relate

Table 10.6

Suffix	Nominalization	Adjective
-ENCE	independence	independent
	invariance	invariant
	permanence	permanent
	residence	resident
	salience	salient
	significance	significant
-ITY	ability	able
-TY	certainty	certain
	rarity	rare
	solidity	solid
	uncertainty	uncertain
	universality	universal
-NESS	happiness	happy
	illness	ill
	lateness	late
	openness	open
	steadiness	steady
	wellness	well
-Y	adequacy	adequate
-CY	ascendancy	ascendant
	difficulty	difficult
	latency	latent
	legitimacy	legitimate
	normalcy	normal
	truancy	truant

Table 10.7

can be an efficient way to pack a lot of information into a few syllables. But because they are just a couple of nouns stuck together, they don't offer many grammatical clues to help readers figure out their meaning.

Take "bus stop," for example. We know from real-world experience that a bus stop is a place designated for a bus to stop and let passengers on and off. But if you didn't know that, you could imagine several other meanings. A bus stop could refer to an object that is placed behind the wheels of a bus to stop it from rolling downhill—like a doorstop, but for a bus. Or it could refer to one instance of the bus stopping, as in "the fugitive slipped away during an unscheduled bus stop." Or it could refer to the police stopping a bus for a traffic violation—like a traffic stop, but with a bus.

A noun compound can be formed from just two nouns, but the fun doesn't stop there. English lets you throw as many nouns onto the pile as you want. And if you have some spare adjectives lying around, go ahead and throw them on, too. English is very flexible that way. This flexibility can give rise to monster noun phrases, where a head noun is modified by three or four (or more) nouns and adjectives. These phrases are called "noun stacks," "noun strings," or "noun clusters."

Noun clusters are useful in the same ways and for the same reasons as nominalizations: They pack a ton of information into a small space. That's why the people who write newspaper headlines love them. But the meanings of noun clusters are often ambiguous. If a simple compound like "bus stop" has many possible meanings, imagine how many a longer cluster has. Table 10.8 lists some real-life examples.

Learn to notice noun compounds and clusters and ask whether their meaning is clear. If not, break them up. Start by moving the head noun from the end of the cluster to the beginning. Then rearrange words, replace nominalizations, add prepositional phrases,

Examples of noun clusters
online real time cloud data landscape view (Johnston, 2014)
underground mine worker safety protection procedures development (plainlanguage.gov)
failed password security question answer attempts limit (Pope, 2011)
Ben Douglas Bafta race row hairdresser James Brown "sorry" (BBC News, 2011)
Slough sausage choke baby death woman jailed (BBC News, 2010)

Table 10.8

and add hyphens to clarify what modifies what. On the whole, this will increase your word count (so it may not always be possible), but it will make things easier for your reader.

Omit needless words

One of the simplest and most satisfying tasks in revision is getting rid of words you don't need.

By the time you have a full-length draft of whatever you are writing, it probably resembles the shelf of coffee mugs in a kitchen cabinet. The good mugs are there, but so are many that no one uses: chipped mugs; cracked mugs; a mug shaped like a coiled rattlesnake that somebody brought back from Arizona; a mug with a broken handle, which was repaired with superglue, but which will probably break again as soon as it's filled with hot coffee. Each mug seemed fine when it was purchased, but after a few years many of them just take up space and make it harder to reach the mugs that people actually use.

Drafts get cluttered too, which is just fine, because creativity makes things grow in all directions. To omit needless words is to prune the writing back in order to show off its lovely shape.

LEARN TO SPOT NEEDLESS WORDS

Most people find speaking easier than writing, and some writers overcome the difficulty of drafting by writing things down they way they would explain them out loud, or even by dictating a first rough draft into a phone or computer. When we speak, we use extra words because being redundant is helpful in spoken language, where listeners must process language as fast as it is spoken. Readers, however, see a whole sentence at once and often don't need the extra linguistic scaffolding to get their bearings, so written language can be more elegant and less cluttered than speech.

Strunk and White, authors of the classic *The Elements of Style* (2008), offer this famous advice:

> Omit needless words. Vigorous writing is concise.
> A sentence should contain no unnecessary words, a
> paragraph no unnecessary sentences, for the same
> reason that a drawing should have no unnecessary
> lines and a machine no unnecessary parts.

To name just a couple of examples, sentences beginning with "There is . . ." or "There are . . . " can often be restated without those words. Similarly, it is often possible to omit opening phrases such as "Research has shown that . . . " and "These results suggest . . ."

The examples could go on forever, but the answer in each case is the same: Read your draft line by line, think about the meaning

Needless words at the beginning	Needless words omitted
There is one variable that mediates [X], and that variable is [Y].	The only variable that mediates [X] is [Y].
There are many who disagree.	Many disagree.
Much recent research suggests that [X] (followed by citations).	[X] (followed by citations).
These results suggest that [X].	[X].

Table 10.9

you want to convey with each sentence, and delete every word that dilutes or distracts from that meaning. With practice, you will learn to recognize words and phrases that can be shortened or omitted, and you might even enjoy this pruning process.

ELIMINATE REDUNDANCIES

Redundancies are a special kind of needless word. These are words or phrases that duplicate content that is already present in the sentence, without adding anything new. Here are six types of redundancy to look for and delete.

Acronyms with one of the words spelled out

This is not so much a redundancy as an objective error. For example, ATM stands for "automated teller machine," so "ATM machine" means "automated teller machine machine." Other examples include "fMRI imaging," "GOP party," "GRE exam," "HIV virus," "ISBN number," "LCD display," "PIN number," "SAT test," "RAM memory," "UPC code," and so on. Avoiding this mistake is easy—when you use an acronym, just take a moment to remember what the letters stand for.

Pairs of synonyms

Another common type of redundancy is the pair (or trio) of synonyms joined by a conjunction. For example, "basic and fundamental" is a redundancy because both words mean the same thing. Either word is sufficient to convey the meaning, so you can just pick one. Some more examples: *each and every; first and foremost; full and complete; hope and desire; inadvertent and unconscious; pick and choose; surprising and unexpected; true and accurate; various and sundry; way, shape, or form.*

A special note for legal writers: Legal terms such as "aid and abet" and "null and void" are terms of art. These are redundancies that shouldn't be edited out because they are the standard, accepted terminology. (Because of the history of the common law, many of these are Latinate/Anglo-Saxon doubles.) So if you're writing in a legal setting, leave those in.

Phrases that can be replaced by a single word

If you can replace a whole phrase with just one word, you should probably do it. The process is not automatic—each substitution works in some contexts but not others. For example, consider substituting the word "some" for the phrase "a number of." It works for this pair of sentences:

* There are **a number of** things I'd like to discuss.
* There are **some** things I'd like to discuss.

But not for this pair:

* Participants' data were excluded for **a number of** reasons.
* Participants' data were excluded for **some** reasons.

Because each substitution only works in some contexts, the best you can do is learn to recognize phrases that might be replaceable and decide on a case-by-case basis. Table 10.10 shows some phrases that can often be replaced by single words.

Redundant adverbs

One common type of clutter is the pairing of a verb with a redundant adverb. For example, "surround" means "encircle completely." So "completely surround" means "completely encircle completely." As always, there are exceptions. For example, I think the use of "completely surrounded" is justified in the paragraph that follows, because it contrasts with an earlier example of someone being *incompletely* surrounded.

Phrase	Single-word equivalent
a number of	some
add an additional	add
adversely impact on	hurt
afford an opportunity to	let
as of yet	yet
ask the question	ask
at a later time	later
at an earlier time	earlier
at the present time	now
by means of	using
concerning the matter of	about
despite the fact that	although
during the course of	during
for a period of	for
for the purpose of	to
for the reason that	because

Table 10.10 (continued on next page)

Phrase	Single-word equivalent	Phrase	Single-word equivalent
in a confused state of mind	confused	make an attempt; make an effort	try
in a situation where	if	make a request for	request
in addition	also	off of	off
in between	between	on the basis of	based on
in excess of	over	on the part of	by
in order that	so	outside of	outside
in the case of	when	owing to the fact that	because
in the event that	if	provided that	if
in the majority of instances	usually	subsequent to	after
in the near future	soon	subsequently	then
is able to; is capable of; is in a position to	can	the reason for; the reason why	why
is applicable	applies	the way in which	how
it is possible that	may	whether or not	whether
it is probable that	probably	with the exception of	except

Table 10.10 (continued)

The movie *A Bridge Too Far* describes what happened to the British 1st Parachute Division when, with their backs to the Rhine river, they got **surrounded** by the Germans. The British managed to evacuate about 2,000 of their paratroopers across the river under cover of darkness. At the battle of Stalingrad, by contrast, the German 6th Army was **completely surrounded** by the Soviets, and none of them managed to escape.

Table 10.11 lists examples of verb-adverb combinations that are often redundant.

Redundant adjectives

Watch out for redundant adjective-noun pairs such as "added bonus" and "advance warning." The same caveat given in other cases also applies here: The same adjective-noun pair may be redundant in one context and not in another. For example, the phrase "current incumbent" is redundant in the first sentence below, but not in the second.

* Polls show the challenger ahead of the current incumbent by seven to ten points.
* In the 1984 gubernatorial race, the incumbent suffered a humiliating defeat. The **current incumbent** doesn't want that to happen in 2020.

Table 10.12 provides examples of adjective-noun pairs that are often redundant.

Redundant verb-adverb combinations			
(completely) surround	connect (up)	join (together)	reconstruct (anew)
(entirely) eliminate	cooperate (together)	lift (up)	recur (again)
(first) conceive	descend (down)	meet (together)	refer (back)
(mutually) interdependent	drop (down)	meld (together)	reflect (back)
(now) pending	dwindle (down)	merge (together)	repeat (again)
(originally) created	eliminate (altogether)	mix (together)	reply (back)
(still) persists	empty (out)	open (up)	retreat (back)
(still) remains	enclosed (herein)	orbit (around)	revert (back)
add (up)	eradicate (completely)	penetrate (into)	rise (up)
ascend (up)	extradite (back)	plan (ahead)	separate (apart)
assemble (together)	first (discover)	plunge (down)	skip (over)
blend (together)	gather (together)	previously listed (above)	splice (together)
collaborate (together)	heat (up)	proceed (ahead)	start (off)
combine (together)	hoist (up)	protest (against)	start (out)
commute (back and forth)	integrate (together)	raise (up)	vacillate (back and forth)

Table 10.11

Redundant adjective-noun pairs			
(actual) fact	(empty) hole	(natural) instinct	(regular) routine
(added) bonus	(empty) space	(new) construction	(safe) haven
(advance) planning	(end) result	(new) innovation	slow (speed)
(affirmative) yes	(final) conclusion	(new) invention	small (size)
(basic) fundamentals	(foreign) import	(old or overused) cliché	(small) speck
(basic) necessities	(free) gift	(old) custom	(sum) total
(brief) moment	(future) plans	(old) proverb	(temper) tantrum
(careful) scrutiny	(general) public	(open) trench	(terrible) tragedy
(close) proximity	(harmful) injuries	(passing) fad	(true) facts
(closed) fist	(hidden) ambush	(past) experience	(unexpected) emergency
(component) parts	(joint) collaboration	(past) history	(unexpected) surprise
crisis (situation)	(knowledgeable) expert	(past) records	(unintentional) mistake
(current) incumbent	(major) breakthrough	(personal) friend	(universal) panacea
(current) status quo	(major) feat	(personal) opinion	(usual) custom
(desirable) benefits	(mental) telepathy	(polar) opposites	undergraduate (student)
emergency (situation)	(mutual) cooperation	(present) incumbent	weather (conditions)

Table 10.12

Redundant prepositional phrases

Like adverbs and adjectives, prepositional phrases are often redundant with the expressions they modify. Table 10.13 gives examples where a prepositional phrase duplicates the meaning in a verb; Table 10.14 gives examples with nonverbs.

QUESTION THE QUALIFIERS

Whereas redundancies don't add any meaning, qualifiers do add a little bit. The question is whether they add enough to justify the space they occupy, and whether the sentence or paragraph would be stronger without them.

If your draft is a shelf of coffee mugs, qualifiers are the chipped ones, the weird ones, the ones with the uncomfortable handles. They're not exactly useless, but a lot of them should probably go. The two main types of qualifier to watch for are intensifiers and hedges.

Intensifiers

An adverb or adjective used to strengthen the meaning of another expression is called an intensifier. Table 10.15 lists some common ones. The surprising thing about intensifiers is that they backfire. As Williams and Bizup (2017, p. 131) note, "When most readers read a sentence that begins with something like 'obviously, undoubtedly, it is clear that, there is no question that,' and so on, they reflexively think the opposite." When an author uses too many intensifiers, the writing takes on a desperate quality, as if the author expects not to be believed. If you invite a colleague for lunch at 12:30 and she says, "I can't—I have a meeting at 1:00," you believe her. But if she says, "I seriously can't—I definitely have a real meeting at exactly 1:00,"

Redundant verb–prepositional phrase combinations			
classify (into groups)	fill (to capacity)	look ahead (to the future)	reelect (for another term)
compete (with each other)	grow (in size)	look back (in retrospect)	scrutinize (in detail)
depreciate (in value)	indict (on a charge)	meet (with each other)	spell out (in detail)
discover (for the first time)	integrate (with each other)	plan (in advance)	surround (on all sides)
evolve (over time)	introduce (for the first time)	postpone (until later)	warn (in advance)

Table 10.13

Redundant nonverb–prepositional phrase combinations			
autobiography (of his/her own life)	few (in number)	large (in size)	soft (to the touch)
biography (of his/her life)	first (of all)	mutual respect (for each other)	sole (of the foot)
brief (in duration)	green (in color)	nostalgia (for the past)	tall (in stature)
cacophony (of sound)	honest (in character)	off (of)	ten (in number)
consensus (of opinion)	incredible (to believe)	outside (of)	unusual (in nature)
equal (to one another)	interdependent (on each other)	period (of time)	visible (to the eye)

Table 10.14

Type	Intensifiers	Examples
ADVERBS	absolutely, basically, certainly, clearly, completely, definitely, exceptionally, extremely, fully, highly, indeed, literally, naturally, obviously, particularly, pretty, quite, rather, really, remarkably, truly, undoubtedly, unusually, utterly, very	**Clearly,** the failed replications **naturally** make us question whether we can **really** be **completely** confident about the original findings.
Adverbs used with comparatives (e.g., better, worse, higher, lower, more X, less X)	a lot, far, much, quite a lot, way	Modern sprinters run **much** faster than their ancient counterparts.
Adverbs used with superlatives (e.g., best, worst, highest, lowest, most X, least X)	absolutely, by far, easily,	This is **easily** the best-written manuscript I've reviewed all year, **by far**.
Adverbs used with negatives	absolutely, at all, in the least, whatsoever	I **absolutely** don't believe that today's for-profit publishing model benefits science **at all**.
ADJECTIVES	absolute, actual, basic, central, complete, crucial, essential, fundamental, important, incredible, key, major, perfect, principal, real, total, true, utter	The **incredible** thing about registered reports is that the principal authors can get **crucial** feedback from **real** reviewers on the **actual** introduction and method sections before data are collected.

Table 10.15

you probably think, *Why doesn't she want to have lunch with me?* Somehow, the more intensifiers a statement has, the less sincere it sounds.

Hedges

The other kind of qualifier to watch for is the hedge. Hedges are the opposite of intensifiers: They express the author's hesitation, caution, or uncertainty. Table 10.16 gives examples of three common hedge types.

This is a hedged statement:

> In certain respects, these data may appear to some observers to be less than fully consistent with the hypothesis that planting gingerbread cookies around lemon trees may in some cases seem to have a tendency to somewhat increase fruit yields.

Type	Hedges
Adverb	allegedly, almost, apparently, arguably, comparatively, conceivably, fairly, in a certain sense, in certain respects, in part, in some respects, in some ways, nearly, often, partially, perhaps, possibly, predominantly, presumably, probably, rather, relatively, seemingly, so to speak, sometimes, somewhat, sort of, to a certain degree, to a certain extent, usually, virtually
Quantifier	a certain number of, many, most, some
Verb	appear, appear to be, be sure, believe, can, could, doubt, indicate, look like, may, might, seem, suggest, tend, think

Table 10.16

This is the same statement without hedges:

> These data are inconsistent with the hypothesis that planting gingerbread cookies around lemon trees increases fruit yields.

Although all hedges express uncertainty, not all expressions of uncertainty are hedges. Researchers make a lot of statements: Some are broad; others are narrow; sometimes we are very certain; other times less so. Our writing expresses those nuances. A simple way to think about is this: If the author is hiding behind it, it's a hedge. When authors draw weak conclusions because the data don't warrant strong conclusions, that's responsible scholarship. When authors draw weak conclusions because they fear the criticism they would get for saying what they really think, that's hedging. Criticism is painful, so it's no wonder that new researchers in particular tend to go into a defensive crouch. Instead of writing:

> Based on these findings, I believe [X]

they write something that sounds like:

> The evidence presented here might, under certain circumstances, be interpreted by some people to mean [X], although other people might not interpret it that way, which is fine, and I'm not saying I interpret it that way, although I'm also not saying I don't . . .

Authors also hedge by putting single or double quotes around words that they feel self-conscious about—a practice that seems to say, *I'm using this word, but if you don't like the word, don't yell at me! I didn't really mean it!*

The problem with defensive hedging is that it makes your writing unclear. It's true that if no one can figure out what you are saying, you won't get much criticism. But you won't have many readers either, and your work won't have any impact. By the same token, it's true that as soon as you say something clear, someone will argue with you. But that's what academics do—we argue. Everyone is trying to publish, and lots of academics are actively looking for statements to argue with, just so they have something to write about. Don't take it personally.

That brings us to the last piece of advice in this book: When you write, imagine a friendly, open-minded reader. Don't write for the person who criticized your work during a recent poster session, or the reviewer who recommended rejection for your last manuscript. If you do, your writing will be defensive and guarded. Plus, writing like that is no fun. It requires you to spend hours having imaginary arguments and feeling unhappy.

Imagine instead a reader who is well-educated, but not an expert in your research—a reader who is thoughtful, genuinely interested in learning, and receptive to what you have to say. Imagine, in short, the people in your writing workshop. If you practice a feedback forum as part of your meetings, it becomes even easier to imagine those people as your readers. In this way, your penguin huddle can support you not only during meetings, but every time you sit down to write.

EPILOGUE

The overarching message of this book is that you can be a productive academic writer and also enjoy your life. The key is to have a sustainable writing practice, honed by instruction and supported by community. For that, a writing workshop like the one we've developed over the past 10 years at UC-Irvine can make all the difference.

For many academics today, writing is not the pleasant creative activity that it could be. Each of us is surrounded by other academic writers, but our groups (our cohorts, departments, labs, etc.) do not function as real communities of practice around the central problem that we all face. Most of us want to write more and write better, and we all want to work hard enough to be successful without sacrificing our physical and mental health. Yet early-career academics in particular often feel isolated and discouraged. When a group of people is facing a common set of problems and each of them feels alone, that is a failure of community.

Responding to this problem, our writing workshop has become a community of practice for both academic writing and well-being. We are also a community of instruction, in which an experienced researcher (me) passes along knowledge about writing in general, and academic writing in particular, to the next generation of researchers.

If you feel skeptical about whether these practices would work for you, I respect that. Skepticism is an excellent quality in a researcher. At the time of this writing, we are beginning to run the first randomized controlled trials of the writing workshop, which should yield some quantifiable data about whether the workshop is as effective as it seems. Until then, the only evidence I can offer is my own experience: Over dozens of iterations of the workshop, we have tried many practices, discarding some and keeping others. The ones in this book are the ones we kept because we liked them, and because they worked for us. I encourage you to experiment and find the ones that work for you.

I hope that each person who reads this book will find something in it to help transform an existing community, such as a lab or a seminar or just a group of friends, into a real community of practice around writing and well-being. These communities can change the culture of academia.

The cold, harsh academic environment that my generation accepted as inevitable was not really fit for human habitation. It was also wasteful, because it prevented people from performing as well as they could, and it drove many talented and highly trained people out of research altogether. It's time to change the way we do things. Let's transform this environment into one that truly supports the production of science and scholarship, by supporting the humans who produce it.

Remember, it's hard to be a lone penguin. *But you are not alone, Penguin!* You are surrounded by others who are facing the very same challenges as you. Why not huddle with them and face those challenges together?

REFERENCES

Abele, A. E., & Wiese, B. S. (2008). The nomological network of self-management strategies and career success. *Journal of Occupational and Organizational Psychology, 81*(4), 733–749. https://doi.org/10.1348/09631 7907X256726

Alhola, P., & Polo-Kantola, P. (2007). Sleep deprivation: Impact on cognitive performance. *Neuropsychiatric Disease and Treatment, 3*(5), 553–567.

Alvarez, L. (2012, August 23). Republicans in Tampa Prepare for Tropical Storm Isaac. *The New York Times*. Retrieved from https://www.nytimes.com/2012/08/24/us/politics/republicans-in-tampa-prepare-for-tropical-storm-isaac.html

Anderson, H., & Daniels, M. (2016, April). The largest analysis of film dialogue by gender, ever. Retrieved June 22, 2019, from The Pudding website: https://pudding.cool/2017/03/film-dialogue/index.html

Baddeley, A. D., Thomson, N., & Buchanan, M. (1975). Word length and the structure of short-term memory. *Journal of Verbal Learning and Verbal Behavior, 14*, 575–589.

Bafta race row stylist apologises. (2011, May 30). *BBC News*. Retrieved from https://www.bbc.com/news/uk-england-london-13594607

Bansak, K., Hainmueller, J., & Hangartner, D. (2016). How economic, humanitarian, and religious concerns shape European attitudes toward asylum seekers. *Science, 354*(6309), 217–222. https://doi.org/10.1126/science.aag2147

Barnes, D. E., Yaffe, K., Satariano, W. A., & Tager, I. B. (2003). A longitudinal study of cardiorespiratory fitness and cognitive function in healthy older adults. *Journal of the American Geriatrics Society, 51*(4), 459–465. https://doi.org/10.1046/j.1532-5415.2003.51153.x

Becker, H. S. (2007). *Writing for Social Scientists: How to Start and Finish Your Thesis, Book or Article* (2nd ed.). Chicago, IL: University of Chicago Press

Belcher, W. L. (2019). *Writing Your Journal Article in Twelve Weeks* (2nd ed.). Chicago, IL: University of Chicago Press.

Berchtold, N. C., Castello, N., & Cotman, C. W. (2010). Exercise and time-dependent benefits to learning and memory. *Neuroscience, 167*(3), 588–597. https://doi.org/10.1016/j.neuroscience.2010.02.050

Berndt, R. S., Haendiges, A. N., Burton, M. W., & Mitchum, C. C. (2002). Grammatical class and imageability in aphasic word production: Their effects are independent. *Journal of Neurolinguistics, 15*(3), 353–371. https://doi.org/10.1016/S0911-6044(01)00030-6

Blumenthal, J. A., Babyak, M. A., Doraiswamy, P. M., Watkins, L., Hoffman, B. M., Barbour, K. A., . . . Sherwood, A. (2007). Exercise and pharmacotherapy in the treatment of major depressive disorder. *Psychosomatic Medicine, 69*(7), 587–596. https://doi.org/10.1097/PSY.0b013e318148c19a

Boice, R. (1983). Contingency management in writing and the appearance of creative ideas: Implications for the treatment of writing blocks. *Behaviour Research and Therapy, 21*(5), 537–543. https://doi.org/10.1016/0005-7967(83)90045-1

Boice, R. (1990). *Professors as Writers: A Self-Help Guide to Productive Writing*. Stillwater, OK: New Forums Press.

Booth, W. C., Colomb, G. G., Williams, J. M., Bizup, J., & Fitzgerald, W. T. (2016). *The Craft of Research* (4th ed.). Chicago, IL: University of Chicago Press

Bouquet, J. (2018, October 14). May I have a word . . . about toolkits, real and metaphorical. *The Guardian*. Retrieved from https://www.theguardian.com/theobserver/commentisfree/2018/oct/14/may-i-have-a-word-about-toolkit

Bowcott, O., & Watt, H. (2017, April 12). Melania Trump accepts *Daily Mail* damages and apology in libel case. *The Guardian*. Retrieved from https://www.theguardian.com/us-news/2017/apr/12/melania-trump-accepts-damages-and-apology-from-daily-mail

Brown, G. (1983). Prosodic structure and the given/new distinction. In A. Cutler & D. R. Ladd (Eds.), *Prosody: Models and Measurements* (pp. 67–77). Berlin, Germany: Springer. https://doi.org/10.1007/978-3-642-69103-4_6

Brysbaert, M., Warriner, A. B., & Kuperman, V. (2014). Concreteness ratings for 40 thousand generally known English word lemmas. *Behavior Research Methods, 46*(3), 904–911. https://doi.org/10.3758/s13428-013-0403-5

Budde, H., Voelcker-Rehage, C., Pietraßyk-Kendziorra, S., Ribeiro, P., & Tidow, G. (2008). Acute coordinative exercise improves attentional performance in adolescents. *Neuroscience Letters, 441*(2), 219–223. https://doi.org/10.1016/j.neulet.2008.06.024

Buranyi, S. (2017, June 27). Is the staggeringly profitable business of scientific publishing bad for science? *The Guardian.* Retrieved from https://www.theguardian.com/science/2017/jun/27/profitable-business-scientific-publishing-bad-for-science

Cameron, J. (2019). Morning pages. Retrieved June 20, 2019, from Julia Cameron Live website: https://juliacameronlive.com/basic-tools/morning-pages/

Carey, S. (2009). *The Origin of Concepts.* New York, NY: Oxford University Press.

Cayley, R. (2011, February 9). Reverse outlines. Retrieved June 21, 2019, from Explorations of Style website: https://explorationsofstyle.com/2011/02/09/reverse-outlines/

Cayley, R. (2015, April 9). The evolution of signposting. Retrieved April 5, 2019, from Explorations of Style website: https://explorationsofstyle.com/2015/04/09/the-evolution-of-signposting/

Clance, P. R., & Imes, S. A. (1978). The imposter phenomenon in high achieving women: Dynamics and therapeutic intervention. *Psychotherapy: Theory, Research & Practice, 15*(3), 241–247. https://doi.org/10.1037/h0086006

Coltheart, V., Laxon, V. J., & Keating, C. (1988). Effects of word imageability and age of acquisition on children's reading. *British Journal of Psychology, 79*(1), 1–12. https://doi.org/10.1111/j.2044-8295.1988.tb02270.x

Cowell, A. (2018, October 5). 50 years later, troubles still cast "huge shadow" over Northern Ireland. *The New York Times.* Retrieved from https://www.nytimes.com/2018/10/04/world/europe/northern-ireland-troubles.html

Curry, S. (2012). Sick of impact factors. Retrieved August 26, 2018, from Reciprocal Space website: http://occamstypewriter.org/scurry/2012/08/13/sick-of-impact-factors/

Davis, G. (2005). Doctors without orders. *American Scientist, 93*(3), S1.

Dehaene, S. (2011). *The Number Sense: How the Mind Creates Mathematics, Revised and Updated Edition.* New York, NY: Oxford University Press.

Dimsdale, J. E., & Young, M. D. (2006). *University of California Office of the President Student Mental Health Committee Final Report.* Oakland, CA: University of California Office of the President.

Dr. Psyphago. (2013, January 16). Scientists conclude: "No further research is needed." Retrieved April 11, 2019, from Collectively Unconscious website: https://collectivelyunconscious.wordpress.com/2013/01/16/scientists-conclude-no-further-research-is-needed/

Drucker, P. F. (1954). *The Practice of Management.* New York: Harper & Row.

Ehrmann, M. (1948). *The Poems of Max Ehrmann* (B. Ehrmann, Ed.). Retrieved from www.desiderata.com

Epley, N., & Schroeder, J. (2014). Mistakenly seeking solitude. *Journal of Experimental Psychology: General, 143*(5), 1980–1999.

Evans, T. M., Bira, L., Gastelum, J. B., Weiss, L. T., & Vanderford, N. L. (2018). Evidence for a mental health crisis in graduate education. *Nature Biotechnology, 36*, 282–284. https://doi.org/10.1038/nbt.4089

Farr, J. N., Jenkins, J. J., & Paterson, D. G. (1951). Simplification of Flesch reading ease formula. *Journal of Applied Psychology, 35*(5), 333–337. https://doi.org/10.1037/h0062427

Feldman, D. B., & Silvia, P. J. (2010). *Public Speaking for Psychologists: A Lighthearted Guide to Research Presentations, Job Talks, and Other Opportunities to Embarrass Yourself.* Washington, DC: American Psychological Association.

Flood, M., & Ivanovich, D. (2004, February 20). Defiant Skilling pleads not guilty / Former Enron CEO faces 35 felonies related to firm's collapse. *SFGate.* Retrieved from https://www.sfgate.com/business/article/Defiant-Skilling-pleads-not-guilty-Former-Enron-2821777.php

garson. (2014, May 9). What is important is seldom urgent and what is urgent is seldom important. Retrieved June 20, 2019, from Quote Investigator website: https://quoteinvestigator.com/2014/05/09/urgent/

garson. (2017, November 18). Plans are worthless, but planning is everything. Retrieved June 20, 2019, from Quote Investigator website: https://quoteinvestigator.com/2017/11/18/planning/

Gernsbacher, M. A. (2013). *Improving Scholarly Communication: An Online Course.* Retrieved from https://osf.io/z9dh7/

Gilmore, R. O., & Adolph, K. E. (2017). Video can make behavioural science more reproducible. *Nature Human Behaviour, 1*, 0128. https://doi.org/10.1038/s41562-017-0128

Gourmet Girl. (2013, June 30). Sunday brunch . . . eggs, bacon & easy cheddar black pepper biscuits. Retrieved June 22, 2019, from Gourmet Girl Cooks website: https://www.gourmetgirlcooks.com/2013/06/sunday-bruncheggs-bacon-easy-cheddar.html

Graff, G., & Birkenstein, C. (2018). *They Say/I Say: The Moves That Matter in Academic Writing* (4th ed.). New York, NY: W. W. Norton & Company

Graves, L. (2019). *Scientific Poster Design: How to Keep Your Poster from Resembling an "Abstract Painting."* Retrieved from http://hsp.berkeley.edu/sites/default/files/ScientificPosters.pdf

Guarino, C. M., & Borden, V. M. H. (2017). Faculty service loads and gender: Are women taking care of the Academic Family? *Research in Higher Education, 58*(6), 672–694. https://doi.org/10.1007/s11162-017-9454-2

Halliday, M. a. K. (1967). Notes on transitivity and theme in English Part I. *Journal of Linguistics, 3*(1), 37–81. https://doi.org/10.1017/S0022226700012949

Hand, E. (2016, April 15). No pressure: NSF test finds eliminating deadlines halves number of grant proposals. Retrieved June 13, 2018, from Science | AAAS website: http://www.sciencemag.org/news/2016/04/no-pressure-nsf-test-finds-eliminating-deadlines-halves-number-grant-proposals

Hanson, R. (2009). *Buddha's Brain: The Practical Neuroscience of Happiness, Love, and Wisdom.* Oakland, CA: New Harbinger Publications.

Heath, C., & Heath, D. (2007). *Made to Stick: Why Some Ideas Survive and Others Die.* New York, NY: Penguin Random House.

Hess, G., Tosney, K., & Liegel, L. (2013). Creating effective poster presentations. Retrieved June 22, 2019, from https://go.ncsu.edu/posters

Hirshkowitz, M., Whiton, K., Albert, S. M., Alessi, C., Bruni, O., DonCarlos, L., … Hillard, P. J. A. (2015). National Sleep Foundation's sleep time duration recommendations: Methodology and results summary. *Sleep Health: Journal of the National Sleep Foundation, 1*(1), 40–43. https://doi.org/10.1016/j.sleh.2014.12.010

Hoffman, P., Jones, R. W., & Lambon Ralph, M. A. (2013). Be concrete to be comprehended: Consistent imageability effects in semantic dementia for

nouns, verbs, synonyms and associates. *Cortex*, *49*(5), 1206–1218. https:
//doi.org/10.1016/j.cortex.2012.05.007

Hogenboom, M. (2015, November 7). In the frigid Antarctic winter, emperor
penguins get too hot. Retrieved April 1, 2019, from http://www.bbc
.com/earth/story/20151107-how-penguins-avoid-overheating

Hughes, D. J., & Bell, H. (1993). On strategy (1871) / Über strategie (1871).
In *Moltke on the Art of War: Selected Writings* (p. 92). Novato, CA: Presidio
Press.

Jayakody, K., Gunadasa, S., & Hosker, C. (2014). Exercise for anxiety disor-
ders: Systematic review. *Br J Sports Med*, *48*(3), 187–196. https://doi.org
/10.1136/bjsports-2012-091287

Jessen, F., Heun, R., Erb, M., Granath, D.-O., Klose, U., Papassotiropoulos,
A., & Grodd, W. (2000). The concreteness effect: Evidence for dual cod-
ing and context availability. *Brain and Language*, *74*(1), 103–112. https://
doi.org/10.1006/brln.2000.2340

Johnston, M. R. (2014, July 15). What a (noun) cluster. Retrieved December
15, 2018, from Content Rules, Inc. website: http://contentrules.com/
noun-cluster/

Jordan, N. C., Kaplan, D., Nabors Oláh, L., & Locuniak, M. N. (2006). Number sense growth in kindergarten: A longitudinal investigation of children at risk for mathematics difficulties. *Child Development*, *77*(1), 153–175.
https://doi.org/10.1111/j.1467-8624.2006.00862.x

Junger, S. (2015, June). How PTSD became a problem far beyond the battle-
field. *Vanity Fair*. Retrieved from https://www.vanityfair.com/news/2015
/05/ptsd-war-home-sebastian-junger

Kawachi, I., & Berkman, L. F. (2001). Social ties and mental health. *Journal of
Urban Health*, *78*(3), 458–467. https://doi.org/10.1093/jurban/78.3.458

Killgore, W. D. S. (2010). Effects of sleep deprivation on cognition. *Progress in Brain Research*, *185*, 105–129. https://doi.org/10.1016/
B978-0-444-53702-7.00007-5

Kim, S. M., Wagner, J., & Dawsey, J. (2018, September 28). Kavanaugh vote:
Senate Republican leaders agree to new FBI background investigation
of Kavanaugh. *Washington Post*. Retrieved from https://www.washington
post.com/powerpost/senate-committee-prepares-to-vote-on-
kavanaugh-nomination-as-key-senators-remain-silent/2018/09/28
/0b143292-c305-11e8-b338-a3289f6cb742_story.html

Kincaid, J., Fishburne, R., Rogers, R., & Chissom, B. (1975). Derivation of new readability formulas (Automated Readability Index, Fog Count And Flesch Reading Ease Formula) For Navy Enlisted Personnel. *Institute for Simulation and Training*. Retrieved from https://stars.library.ucf.edu/istlibrary/56

Kramer, A. F., Hahn, S., Cohen, N. J., Banich, M. T., McAuley, E., Harrison, C. R., . . . Colcombe, A. (1999). Ageing, fitness and neurocognitive function. *Nature*, *400*(6743), 418. https://doi.org/10.1038/22682

Levecque, K., Anseel, F., De Beuckelaer, A., Van der Heyden, J., & Gisle, L. (2017). Work organization and mental health problems in PhD students. *Research Policy*, *46*(4), 868–879. https://doi.org/10.1016/j.respol.2017.02.008

Liberman, M. (2004, January 21). I challenge anyone to refute that this negative is not unnecessary. Retrieved June 23, 2019, from Language Log website: http://itre.cis.upenn.edu/~myl/languagelog/archives/000371.html

Liberman, M. (2009, April 4). Misunderestimation. Retrieved June 23, 2019, from Language Log website: https://languagelog.ldc.upenn.edu/nll/?p=1292

Lin, N., Ye, X., & Ensel, W. M. (1999). Social support and depressed mood: A structural analysis. *Journal of Health and Social Behavior*, *40*(4), 344–359.

Locke, E. A., Shaw, K. N., Saari, L. M., & Latham, G. P. (1981). Goal setting and task performance: 1969–1980. *Psychological Bulletin*, *90*(1), 125–152.

Lynne, S. (2018, August 20). Group organization protects from the cold: Emperor penguin. Retrieved September 12, 2019, from AskNature website: https://asknature.org/strategy/group-organization-protects-from-the-cold/

Maestre, F. T. (2019). Ten simple rules towards healthier research labs. *PLOS Computational Biology*, *15*(4), e1006914. https://doi.org/10.1371/journal.pcbi.1006914

Malecki. (2012, November 1). Researcher degrees of freedom. Retrieved June 22, 2019, from Statistical Modeling, Causal Inference, and Social Science website: https://statmodeling.stat.columbia.edu/2012/11/01/researcher-degrees-of-freedom/

Martinez, M. E. (2010). *Learning and Cognition: The Design of the Mind* (1st ed.). New York: Pearson.

McCarthy, M. (1991). *Discourse Analysis for Language Teachers*. Cambridge, UK: Cambridge University Press.

McDonough, C., Song, L., Hirsh-Pasek, K., Golinkoff, R. M., & Lannon, R. (2011). An image is worth a thousand words: Why nouns tend to dominate verbs in early word learning. *Developmental Science, 14*(2), 181–189. https://doi.org/10.1111/j.1467-7687.2010.00968.x

Miller, G. A. (1956). The magical number seven, plus or minus two: Some limits on our capacity for processing information. *Psychological Review, 63*(2), 81–97. https://doi.org/10.1037/h0043158

Morrison, M. (2019). *How to Create a Better Research Poster in Less Time (Including Templates)*. Retrieved from https://www.youtube.com/watch?v=1Rw-JbhkCA58

Ng, T. W. H., Eby, L. T., Sorensen, K. L., & Feldman, D. C. (2005). Predictors of Objective and Subjective Career Success: A Meta-Analysis. *Personnel Psychology, 58*(2), 367–408. https://doi.org/10.1111/j.1744-6570.2005.00515.x

Pain, E. (2018, March 6). Graduate students need more mental health support, study highlights. *Science.* Retrieved from https://www.sciencemag.org/careers/2018/03/graduate-students-need-more-mental-health-support-new-study-highlights

Paivio, A. (2013). *Imagery and Verbal Processes*. New York, NY: Psychology Press https://doi.org/10.4324/9781315798868

Paivio, A., Yuille, J. C., & Madigan, S. A. (1968). Concreteness, imagery, and meaningfulness values for 925 nouns. *Journal of Experimental Psychology, 76*(1, Pt.2), 1–25. https://doi.org/10.1037/h0025327

Palmer, S. D., MacGregor, L. J., & Havelka, J. (2013). Concreteness effects in single-meaning, multi-meaning and newly acquired words. *Brain Research, 1538*, 135–150. https://doi.org/10.1016/j.brainres.2013.09.015

Penedo, F. J., & Dahn, J. R. (2005). Exercise and well-being: A review of mental and physical health benefits associated with physical activity. *Current Opinion in Psychiatry, 18*(2), 189.

Pier, E. L., Brauer, M., Filut, A., Kaatz, A., Raclaw, J., Nathan, M. J., ... Carnes, M. (2018). Low agreement among reviewers evaluating the same NIH grant applications. *Proceedings of the National Academy of Sciences*, 201714379. https://doi.org/10.1073/pnas.1714379115

plainlanguage.gov. (n.d.). Avoid noun strings. Retrieved June 23, 2019, from plainlanguage.gov website: https://www.plainlanguage.gov/guidelines/words/avoid-noun-strings/

Pope, M. (2011, August 4). Fun (or not) with noun stacks. Retrieved June 23, 2019, from Mike's web log website: http://mikepope.com/blog /DisplayBlog.aspx?permalink=2292

Purrington, C. (2019). Designing conference posters. Retrieved June 22, 2019, from Colin Purrington website: https://colinpurrington.com/tips /poster-design

Radloff, L. S. (1977). The CES-D scale: A self-report depression scale for research in the general population. *Applied Psychological Measurement*, *1*(3), 385–401.

Richardson, J. T. (1975). Concreteness and imageability. *The Quarterly Journal of Experimental Psychology*, *27*(2), 235–249.

Robbins, N. B. (2013). *Creating More Effective Graphs*. Myrtle Beach, SC: Chart House.

Rockey, S. (2013, July 23). Individual development plans for NIH-supported trainees. Retrieved June 20, 2019, from NIH Extramural Nexus website: https://nexus.od.nih.gov/all/2013/07/23/individual-development-plans-for-nih-supported-trainees/

Rougier, N. P., Droettboom, M., & Bourne, P. E. (2014). Ten simple rules for better figures. *PLOS Computational Biology*, *10*(9), e1003833. https://doi .org/10.1371/journal.pcbi.1003833

Rutherford, T. (2019, March 2). Reflections on applying for an NSF CAREER grant. Retrieved June 22, 2019, from Dr. Rutherford's Lab website: https: //rutherfordlab.wordpress.com/nsf-career-app-reflections/

Sandstrom, G. M., & Dunn, E. W. (2014). Social interactions and well-being: The surprising power of weak ties. *Personality and Social Psychology Bulletin*, *40*(7), 910–922. https://doi.org/10.1177/0146167214529799

Sarnecka, B. W. (2015). *Learning to Represent Exact Numbers*. Retrieved from https://escholarship.org/uc/item/6tq9j73k

Sarnecka, B. W. (2016). How numbers are like the earth (and unlike faces, loitering or knitting). In D. Barner & A. S. Baron (Eds.), *Core Knowledge and Conceptual Change*. New York, NY: Oxford University Press.

Sarnecka, B. W. (2018, August 20). Parasites in peril [*Psychology Today*]. Retrieved June 22, 2019, from Thinking, Writing, Science website: https://www.psychologytoday.com/blog/thinking-writing-science /201808/parasites-in-peril

Sausage baby death woman jailed. (2010, June 4). *BBC News*. Retrieved from https://www.bbc.com/news/10241928

Scan promises early cancer detection. (2001, October 8). *BBC News*. Retrieved from http://news.bbc.co.uk/2/hi/health/1581979.stm

Scardamalia, M., & Bereiter, C. (1987). Knowledge telling and knowledge transforming in written composition. In *Cambridge Monographs and Texts in Applied Psycholinguistics: Vol. 2. Advances in Applied Psycholinguistics Vol 2: Reading, Writing and Language Learning* (p. 142). Cambridge, UK: Cambridge University Press.

Scardamalia, M., & Bereiter, C. (1991). Literate expertise. In *Toward a General Theory of Expertise: Prospects and Limits*. Cambridge, UK: Cambridge University Press.

Schimel, J. (2012). *Writing Science: How to Write Papers That Get Cited and Proposals That Get Funded*. Oxford University Press.

Schuman, R. (2014, May 11). Adjuncts! Local non-mom cut her grading WAY down with this weird old trick. Retrieved February 20, 2019, from PAN KISSES KAFKA website: https://pankisseskafka.com/2014/05/11/adjuncts-one-area-non-mom-cut-her-grading-way-down-with-this-weird-old-trick/

SCMP News. (2018, October 13). Thousands march in Berlin to protest against anti-racism https://buff.ly/2QOZ00C [Tweet]. Retrieved June 23, 2019, from @SCMPNews website: https://twitter.com/SCMPNews/status/1051256209163075584?ref_src=twsrc%5Etfw

secundem_artem. (2012, November 3). Academic jokes. Retrieved June 22, 2019, from The Chronicle of Higher Education website: https://www.chronicle.com/forums/index.php?topic=47823.0

Segal, S. J. (1971). *Imagery: Current Cognitive Approaches*. Cambridge, MA: Academic Press. https://www.sciencedirect.com/book/9780126354508/imagery

Social Sciences Feminist Network Research Interest Group. (2017). The burden of invisible work in academia: Social inequalities and time use in five university departments. *Humboldt Journal of Social Relations*, *39*, 228–245. Retrieved from JSTOR.

Strain, E., & Herdman, C. M. (1999). Imageability effects in word naming: An individual differences analysis. *Canadian Journal of Experimental Psychology / Revue Canadienne de Psychologie Expérimentale*, *53*(4), 347–359. https://doi.org/10.1037/h0087322

Strunk, W., & White, E. B. (2008). *The Elements of Style: 50th Anniversary Edition*. New York: Longman.

Sword, H. (2012). *Stylish Academic Writing*. Cambridge, MA: Harvard University Press.

Thomas, K. (2014, May 8). We don't want anyone to know, say depressed academics. *The Guardian*. Retrieved from http://www.theguardian.com/higher-education-network/blog/2014/may/08/academics-mental-health-suffering-silence-guardian-survey

UC Berkeley Graduate Assembly. (2014). *Graduate Student Happiness & Well-Being Report*. Retrieved from http://ga.berkeley.edu/wp-content/uploads/2015/04/wellbeingreport_2014.pdf

Van Boxtel, M. P. J., Paas, F. G. W. C., Houx, P. J., Adam, J. J., Teeken, J. C., & Jolles, J. (1997). Aerobic capacity and cognitive performance in a cross-sectional aging study. *Medicine & Science in Sports & Exercise, 29*(10), 1357–1365. https://doi.org/10.1097/00005768-199710000-00013

von Fintel, K. (2004, January 21). No head injury is too trivial to ignore. Retrieved June 23, 2019, from Semantics, etc. website: https://www.kaivonfintel.org/no-head-injury/

Vosniadou, S., & Brewer, W. F. (1992). Mental models of the earth: A study of conceptual change in childhood. *Cognitive Psychology, 24*(4), 535–585. https://doi.org/10.1016/0010-0285(92)90018-W

Wellcome Trust. (2018, August 28). When you talk about science, are you sure the words you are using don't mean something different to others? Here are five examples of scientific lingo to use with caution pic.twitter.com/kV24VmqtGA [Tweet]. Retrieved December 20, 2018, from @wellcometrust website: https://twitter.com/wellcometrust/status/1034445250066931713

Wenger, E. (1998). *Communities of Practice: Learning, Meaning, and Identity*. Cambridge, UK: Cambridge University Press.

Wenger, E. (2011). *Communities of Practice: A Brief Introduction*. Retrieved from https://scholarsbank.uoregon.edu/xmlui/handle/1794/11736

Williams, J. M. (1990). *Style: Toward Clarity and Grace*. Chicago, IL: University of Chicago Press

Williams, J. M., & Bizup, J. (2017). *Style: Lessons in Clarity and Grace* (12th ed.). New York, NY: Pearson

Williams, R. (2014). *Non-Designer's Design Book* (4th ed.). San Francisco, CA: Peachpit Press.

Williamson, A. M., & Feyer, A.-M. (2000). Moderate sleep deprivation produces impairments in cognitive and motor performance equivalent to legally prescribed levels of alcohol intoxication. *Occupational and Environmental Medicine, 57*(10), 649–655. https://doi.org/10.1136/oem.57.10.649

Wolchover, N. (2016). What no new particles means for physics. *Quanta Magazine*. Retrieved from https://www.quantamagazine.org/what-no-new-particles-means-for-physics-20160809/

Wood, A. M., Froh, J. J., & Geraghty, A. W. A. (2010). Gratitude and well-being: A review and theoretical integration. *Clinical Psychology Review, 30*(7), 890–905. https://doi.org/10.1016/j.cpr.2010.03.005

Yaffe, K., Barnes, D., Nevitt, M., Lui, L. Y., & Covinsky, K. (2001). A prospective study of physical activity and cognitive decline in elderly women: Women who walk. *Archives of Internal Medicine, 161*(14), 1703–1708.

Zhu, M., Yang, Y., Hsee, C. K., Johar, G., & Lee, L. (2018). The mere urgency effect. *Journal of Consumer Research, 45*(3), 673–690. https://doi.org/10.1093/jcr/ucy008

CREDITS

Figure 7.3	Image by Pexels from Pixabay
Figure 7.4	Image by Michal Jarmoluk from Pixabay
Figure 7.7	Images by Trock (2018) freshstitches.com
Figure 7.8	Image by Gerd Altmann from Pixabay
Figure 7.9	Image by Pete Linforth from Pixabay
Figure 7.10	Image by OpenClipArt-Vectors from Pixabay
Figure 7.11	Image by Clker-Free-Vector-Images from Pixabay
Figure 7.18	Venn (1866), Illustration by Dirk-Jan Hoek
Figure 7.26	Image by Anja Kiefer from Pixabay
Figure 7.27	Image by Meli1670 from Pixabay
Figure 7.28	Image by Christine Trewer from Pixabay

INDEX

Page numbers in *italics* indicate figures and tables.

Abstracts, 157–158
Academic environment. *See also* Research;
    Service; Teaching; Tenure-track jobs
    deadlines in, 64
    flexibility in, 45
    imposter syndrome and, 32
    isolation in, 72
time management and, 50–51
    well-being in, 11, 13, 23, 325
    work/life balance in, 13–14
Academic writing. *See also* Writing practice
    audience and, *105*, 106
    communities of instruction and, 5, 8–9
    communities of practice and, 5–8
    curse of knowledge and, 104, 108–110,
        250, 252
    expectations for, 62
    graduate students and, 2–3, 8
    incomprehensible, 103–104, 107–108
    inspiration and, 80–81
    instruction in, 2–3
    ninja writing and, 7, 79–80
    nominalizations in, 303–305, *305*
    productivity and, 82–83

reviewing and, 35–36
    revising for readers in, 103–110
    technical terminology and, 104–109
Accessibility, 230
Accountabilibuddies arrangements, 23
Accountability groups, 17
Acronyms, 301–302, 311–312
Active voice, 287, *287*, 288
Advisors, 46–47, 67–68
Age Quod Agis (do what you are doing), 30
Angelou, Maya, *224–225*
Anseel, F., 5
Anxiety, 3–5, 12–13, 71–72
Applied research, 207
Arxiv, 167
Assigned readings, 18
Authors, 112
Awards, 180

Becker, H. S., 18
Belcher, W. L., 18
Bereiter, C., 97
Berlin, Irving, 28
BibTeX, 115, 169

Binge writing, 9, 22, 74

BioAriv, 167

Birkenstein, C., 18

Bizup, J., 18, 318

Boise, R., 81

Booth, W. C., 18

Brauer, M., 181

Carnes, M., 181

Cayley, R., 261

Center for Epidemiologic Studies
    Depression Scale, 3

ClinicalTrials.gov, 143

Colomb, G. G., 18

Comment-topic chains. *See* Topic-
    comment chains

Communities of instruction, 5, 8–9, 325

Communities of practice, 5–8, 12, 44,
    325–326

Comparatives, 258, *260*

Concreteness, 283–286, 295, *295*

Cowell, A., 247

The Craft of Research (Booth et al.), 18

Creating More Effective Graphs (Robbins), 18

Curry, S., 167

Curse of knowledge
    academic writing and, 104, 250, 252
    acronyms and, 302
    in conversation, 251–252
    revision and, 104, 108–109
    talks and, 204, 206
    technical terminology and, 108–109

Data
    existing datasets, 144–145
    graphs and, 150–151, *151*, *152*, 153
    modeling new, 145
    new statistical methods for, 145

Deadlines, 64–65

Defense Advanced Research Projects
    Agency (DARPA), 187

Depression, 3–5, 71–73

Desiderata (Ehrmann), 37

Discussions, 18

Discussion section, 166, 168–169

Dissertations, 139–140, 176

Drafts
    argument structure in, 98–99
    feedback and, 98
    literature reviews and, 130–132
    signposting in, 261–262
    suspending judgment, 101–102
    topic-sentence outlines and, 97–99

Egap.org, 143

Ehrmann, M., 37

Eisenhower, Dwight D., 48, 66

The Elements of Style (Strunk & White), 310

Elevator pitch
    elaboration in, 198
    examples of, *199*–202
    graduate students and, 197–198, 202
    headlines in, 198

Empathy, 30

Empirical journal articles, 125–126, 140

Equal-odds rule, 82–83

Evans, D., 3

Exercise, 71–72

Feedback, 14, 19–20

Feedback forums, 19–21

Feldman, D. B., 231

Fellowships, 177–178

Figures
    clarity of information in, 153–154,
        154, 155
    describing research methods, 148–149
    design for reading formats, 153
    plotting data, 146–147, *147*, 148, *148*
    in presentations, 149–150, 228,
        228–230
    results section and, 164

Filut, A., 181
Fitzgerald, W. T., 18
Flesch-Kincaid Readability Tests, 270, 293
Free-writing, 21, 100

Gelman, Susan, 2
Gernsbacher, M. A., 237
Goals
    individual development plans and, 58, 67
    planning and, 66–67
    shared writing logs and, 24
    writing accountability groups and, 14, 16, 39
Google Docs, 19, 115
Google Drive, 19
Grading, 52
Graduate students. *See also* Postdocs
    academic writing and, 2–3, 8
    advisors and, 46–47, 67–68
    anxiety and, 3–5, 12–13
    depression and, 3–5, 73
    dissertation proposals and, 176
    expectations for, 61–62
    important tasks and, 48
    individual development plans and, 57–60
    literature reviews and, 114–115
    research and, 46–48
    thinking like a founder, 46–48
    uncertainty and, 60–61
    writing workshops and, 17, 26
Graff, G., 18
Grants, 179
Graphs
    avoiding misleading readers in, 151
    clarity of information in, 153–154, 154, 155–156
    design for reading formats, 153

errors in, 153
making data stand out in, 150–151
principles for, 150–151, 153
quantitative data and, 151, 151–152
Gratitude, 28

Heath, C., 18
Heath, D., 18
Hebbian learning, 27
Hedges, 321, 321, 322–323
Hsee, C. K., 50
Human sentence processing, 265

Imageability
    active *vs.* passive voice and, 287, 287, 288, 288, 289, 289
    concrete subjects and, 283–285, 285, 286
    memory and, 283–284
    mental images and, 283
    sentences and, 265–266
    words and, 295
Important tasks, 48–50, 56
Imposter syndrome, 3, 32
IMRaD structure
    audience and, 140–141
    discussion section in, 166, 168–169
    empirical studies and, 140
    example of, 141
    introductions and, 158–162
    literature reviews and, 160
    method sections in, 162–164
    papers presenting multiple experiments, 144
    papers with existing datasets, 144–145
    in place of dissertations, 139
    results section in, 164–165
    scientific articles and, 67, 139, 141
Individual development plans (IDP)
    adapting, 60

example of, *59*
graduate students and, 57–60
long-term goals and, 58
postdocs and, 57
research and, 57
setting goals and, 67
structure of, 58–60
success and, 56–57
tenure-track jobs and, 58
writing workshops and, 57
Inspiration, 80–81
Institute for Education Sciences (IES), 187
Institutional Review Board (IRB), 175
Intensifiers, 318, *320*, 321
Interactions, 72–73
Introduction, method, results and
    discussion structure. *See* IMRaD
    structure
Introductions
    big question in, 160
    forks and, 161–162, *163*
    literature reviews and, 160
    little questions in, 161
    opening sentences, 159
    registered reports, 158–159, 169
    scientific articles and, 158–162
Introductory literature reviews, 111–113
IRB. *See* Institutional Review Board (IRB)

JASP, 171
Johar, G., 50
Journal articles
    free servers for, 167
    impact factors, 167
    IMRaD structure in, 140
    pre-acceptance and, 142
    preregistering, 142–143
    publication bias and, 142
    reading empirical, 125–126
    reading strategically, 121–125
    registered reports and, 141–143

skimming, 123–124
Journaling, 21

Kaatz, A., 181
Kapwing, 230
Keywords, 158
Kindness, 29
Knowledge, 77–78, 97, 104. *See also* Curse
    of knowledge

Language
    accessibility in, 230
    concreteness and, 283–284
    imageability and, 283–284
    sentences and, 265, 289
    spoken, 266–267, 269–270, 310
    verbal working memory and, 269–270
    written, 267, 270, 310
Language Log (blog), 280
LaTeX, 115
Lauffer, A., 123
Lee, L., 50
Liberman, M., 280
Literature reviews
    author reviews, 112
    introductory, 111–113
    length of, 113
    mind maps and, 119, *120*
    new researchers and, 113
    note-taking system, 129
    reading lists and, 115–118
    reading strategically, 121–128
    scientific article introductions and, 160
    senior researchers and, 112
    skimming, 123–124
    stand-alone, 111–112
    student, 112, 114–119
    tasks for, 115
Literature review writing
    concluding sentences in paragraphs,
        135–136

introductory/concluding paragraphs in, 137
paragraph transitions, 134–135
rough drafts in, 130–132
topic-sentence outlines in, 132–134
Lynne, S., 11

Made to Stick (Heath & Heath), 18
Martinez, M., 82
Meetings, 14
Mental health, 3–5, 12–13, 34
Mere urgency effect, 48–50
"The Mere Urgency Effect" (Zhu et al.), 50
Meta-material, 157–158
Method sections, 162–164
Miller, G. A., 270
Mindfulness, 30
Mind maps, 119, *120*
Misnegation, 280, *281*
Moltke, H. von, 65
Morrison, M., 203
Morrison-style posters, 203, *205*
Multiple experiments, 143, *143*, 144
Multiple negations, 280

Nathan, M. J., 181
National Institutes of Health (NIH), 57, 178, 181, 187, 192
National Science Foundation (NSF), 64, 186–187
National Science Foundation Graduate Research Fellowship Program (NSF GRFP), 178, 186
Near-peer mentoring, 17
Negative words, *282*
Ninja writing, 7, 78–80
Nominalizations, 303–305, *305*, *306–307*
The Non-Designer's Design Book (Williams), 18
Nonfiction books, 127–128

Note-taking systems, 129
Noun clusters, 308–309, *309*
Noun compounds, 305, 308

Office hours, 52
Open Science Framework (OSF), 143

Paragraphs
clarity in, 235, 250–252
comparatives in, 258, *260*
concluding sentences in, 135–136
consistent wording in, 253–257
hamburger, 236, *236*, 237–238
introductory/concluding, 137
managing information flow in, 245, *245*, *246*
old/new information in, 246–247
pronouns in, 258, *259*
revising and, 239–244
serial, 239
signposting in, 258, 260–261, *261*, 262–263
topic chains in, 247–248, *248*, 249, *250*
topic-comment chains in, 248–249, *249*, *250*
transitions in, 134–135, 238
Passive voice, 287, *287*, *288*, *289*
Pearl, Lisa, 89, 231
PhD students. *See* Graduate students
Phonological working memory, 269
Pier, E. L., 181
Planning your time. *See also* Term plans; Individual development plans (IDP)
academic environment and, 50–51
deadlines in, 64–65
exercise and, 71–72
graduate students and, 46–48
important tasks and, 48–50
interactions and, 72–73
office hours and, 52
plans *vs.* wishes in, 60–61

play and, 70–71
prioritizing tasks and, 73–74
service and, 53–55
setting goals and, 66–67
sleep and, 69–70
streamlining teaching, 52
teaching and, 52
term plans and, 62–65, 67–68
uncertainty and, 60–61
urgent tasks and, 48–50, 55–56, 74
weekly plans and, 68
well-being and, 45
writing and, 45–46, 49–50, 55–56,
    74–75
Play, 70–71
Positivity
    Age Quod Agis (do what you are doing),
        30
    empathy and, 30
    gratitude and, 28
    kindness and, 29
    practice for, 28
    savoring and, 29
    self-efficacy and, 34–35
    thinking habits and, 27–28
Postdocs, 3, 17, 57, 61–62
Postdoctoral fellowships, 178
Posters
    disciplinary level and, 205
    information clarity in, 202–203
    Morrison-style, 203, *205*
    presenting, 203–204
    traditional, *204*
Predoctoral fellowships, 178
Preregistrations, 142–143
Presentations
    accessibility in, 230
    curse of knowledge and, 204
    disciplinary level and, 205
    elevator pitch, 197–198, *199*–201, 202,
        202

exceptions to read-aloud rule, 227–228
figures in, 148–150, 228, *228–229*,
    230, *230*
focusing material in, 215
keeping attention in, 216–217,
    218–222, 223, *223*
lists in, 213–215
making points in, 210–211
participation in, 212
posters, 202–204, *205*
practicing, 230–231
question-and-answer practice, 232–234
relevance in, 212–213
revealing data in tables, 225, *225*–227
revealing quotations in, 223, *224–225*
subfield level, 206
talks, 204–206, 228
technology and, 232
telling a story in, 206–207, *209*,
    210–213
text in, 216, *216*, 217, *217*
time management and, 232
timing, 231
video in, 228, 230
Pritchard, D., 208
Pronouns, 258, *259*
Proposals
    awards and, 180
    blurbs in, 185–186
    budget justification in, 193
    dissemination plan in, 193–194
    dissertations and, 176
    explaining unfair advantage in,
        189–192
    facilities in, 193
    fellowships and, 177–178
    following instructions for, 195
    funding, 177–182, 185
    grants and, 179
    IRB, 175
    literature review summary in, 188–189

method sections in, 192

planned research approval and, 175–176

presenting plan in, 192–193

problems motivating research in, 187–188

proofreading, 195

research for, 182–183, *183*, 184, *184*

review of, 194

submitting, 195–196

timeline in, 193

writing, 185–187

PsyArxiv, 167

Publication bias, 142

Qualifiers, 318, 321

Quantitative research, 146–147, *147*, 148, *148*, 150

Raclaw, J., 181

Readability

avoiding multiple negations, 280–281

longer sentences and, 271–272

long structures and, 275, 280

sentences and, 265–266

shortening sentences for, 270–271

subject-verb closeness, 273, 275

writing sentences for, 272

Readers

academic writing and, 103–105, *105*, 106–110

hedging and, 323

revising for, 103–110

Reading, 121–128

Reading lists, 115–118

Redundancies

acronyms, 311–312

adjective-noun pairs, 315, *317*

adverbs, 313

phrases, 312–313, *313–314*

prepositional phrases, 318, *319*

synonym pairs, 312

verb-adverb, 315, *316*

References, 169

Registered reports

advantages of, 167

feedback on, 176

forks and, 162

introductions in, 158–159, 169

method details in, 163–164

post-hoc analyses in, 168

preregistering, 143

publication bias and, 141–142

results section in, 165

reviewing and, 142

unexpected findings in, 168

Rejection

celebrating reviewers, 35–36

celebrating those who succeed, 37–38

celebrating yourself, 34–35

reframing, 31–32, 34–37

shared collection of, 32, *33*

taking comments seriously, 36–37

Research

applied, 207

finding a story in, 207–208, 210

finding time for, 49

graduate students and, 46–48

human participants and, 175

individual development plans and, 57

literature reviews in, 111–115

skepticism in, 326

telling a story in, *209*

translational, 207

writing and, 1–2, 104

Research methods, 146, 148–149

Research presentations. *See* Presentations

ResearchRegistry.com, 143

Results section, 164–165

Reverse outlines, 97–101

Review articles, 111–112, 116–117. *See also* Literature reviews

Reviewers, 35–37

Revise and resubmit decisions, 171–174

Revision

curse of knowledge and, 104, 108–109

readers and, 103–110

scientific articles and, 171–174

signposting in, 262–263

technical terminology and, 104–109

words and, 291

RIDIE, 143

RMarkdown, 115

Robbins, N. B., 18

Roosevelt, Teddy, 38

Rutherford, T., 186

San Francisco Declaration on Research
Assessment (DORA), 167

Savoring, 29

Scardamalia, M., 97

Schimel, J., 18, 168

Scientific articles. *See also* Registered
reports

discussion section in, 166, 168–169

drafting IMRaD, 156–165

existing datasets in, 144–145

figures in, 146–150

graphs in, 150–151, 153–156

IMRaD structure in, 67, 139–141, 144

introductions in, 158–161

meta-material in, 157–158

method sections in, 162–164

new empirical data/new statistical
models in, 145

papers presenting multiple
experiments, 143, *143*, 144

quantitative data, 146–148

references in, 169

results section in, 164

revise and resubmit decisions, 171–174

sharing data, 171

supplemental materials in, 170–171

unexpected findings in, 168

Scott, Rick, 304

Sentences

abstractions and, 286

active *vs.* passive voice in, 287, *287*,
288, *288*, 289, *289*

imageability in, 265–266, 283–284

longer, 271–272

misnegation in, 280, *281*

negative words, *282*

readability in, 265–266, 270–272,
276–279

shortening, 270–271

spoken language and, 267, *267–268*,
269, *269*, 270, *273–274*

writing imageable, 284–285, *285*,
286–289

writing readable, 272–273, 275,
280–281

written language and, 267, 270

Service, 50, 53–55

Shared writing logs, 16–17, 21–25. *See also*
Writing logs

Signposting, 258, 260–261, *261*, 262–263

Silvia, P. J., 231

Simonton, Dean, 82

Sleep, 69–70

Social accountability

shared writing logs and, 22

urgent tasks and, 48–49

writing groups and, 14, 16–17

writing time and, 49–50

Social huddling, 12

SocialScienceRegistry.org, 143

Speaking, 92

Spoken language

communication and, 266

utterances in, 267, *267–268*, 269, *269*,
273–274, 275

verbal working memory and, 269–270,
275

SPSS, 171

Stand-alone literature review, 111–112

Strategic reading
empirical journal articles and, 125–126
literature reviews and, 121–124
nonfiction books and, 127–128
steps for, 124–125

Strunk, W., 310

Student literature review
examination of, 114
learning through, 112, 114–115
mind maps and, 119, *120*
platforms for organizing, 115–116
reading list length and, 118
reading lists and, 115
works cited in, 116–117

Style (Williams), 18

Stylish Academic Writing (Sword), 304

Supplementary materials, 170–171

Sword, H., 304

Talks, 204–206, 228

Teaching, 48, 50, 52, 84, 92, 104

Technical terminology
academic writing and, 104–109
audience and, 105–106
defining, 107
feedback for, 109–110
words and, 298–301

Tenure-track jobs, 53–55, 58

Term plans
deadlines and, 64–65
discussions with advisors on, 67–68
example of, *63*
flexibility in, 65
priorities in, 63
structure of, 62–*63*
writing workshops and, 65

They Say, I Say (Graff & Birkenstein), 18

Thinking, 82, 99–100

Thinking habits

development of, 27–28
graduate students and, 46–48
positivity and, 28–31
reframing rejection, 31–32

Time management. *See* Planning your time

Titles, 157

To-do lists, 73–74

Topic chains, 247–248, *248*, 249, *250*

Topic-comment chains, 248–249, *249*, *250*, 289

Topic-sentence outlines, 97–101, 103, 132–134

Translational research, 207

Uncertainty, 60–61

Urgent tasks, 48–50, 55–56, 74

Verbal working memory, 269–270, 283

Video, 149, 170, 228, 230

Weekly plans, 68

Well-being, 6–7, 11, 13, 23, 45, 325

White, E. B., 310

White Christmas, 28

Williams, J. M., 18, 318

Williams, R., 18

Wolchover, N., 271, 275

Word frequency, 293

Words
ambiguous, 297
commonly used, 293, *294*
concrete/imageable, 295, *295*
eliminating redundant, 311–313, *313–314*, 315, *316–317*, 318, *319*
hedges, 321, *321*, 322–323
intensifiers, 318, *320*, 321
nominalizations, 303–305, *305*, *306–307*
noun clusters, 308–309, *309*
noun compounds, 305, 308

omitting needless, 309–311, *311*
as placeholders, 291–292
qualifiers, 318, 321
readers and, 298, 301
revision and, 291
simple and specific, 292
specific, 296, *296, 297*
technical terminology and, 298–301
use of acronyms, 301–302
Work/life balance, 13–14
Write-on-site groups, 14–16, 39
Writing. *See also* Academic writing
deciding what counts as, 83–85
enhanced thinking and, 40–41
expertise in, 96–97
finding time for, 45–46, 49–50, 55–56,
74–75
imposter syndrome and, 3
as knowledge telling, 97
as knowledge transforming, 97
meditative qualities of, 41
novices and, 96–97
research and, 1–2, 104
social accountability and, 49–50
as thinking, 82, 99–100
Writing accountability groups, 14, 16–17,
39
Writing buddies, 15
Writing classes, 14
Writing for Social Scientists (Becker), 18
Writing habit, 21–22, 24, 26
Writing logs, 16–17, 23–24, 26. *See also*
Shared writing logs
Writing practice. *See also* Writing process
alternating little rewards for, 89–90
cultivating, 77–78
daily time amounts, 85–86
deciding what counts, 83–85
delaying, 92–94
drafting with kindness, 87–89
drafts and, 101

expertise and, 96–97
inspiration and, 80–81
lowering quality, 90–91
lowering quantity, 88–89
negative self-talk and, 95–96
ninja writing and, 78–80
not "real" writing and, 91–92
productivity and, 82–83
questioning beliefs on, 78–83
scheduling quiet time with friends,
94–95
speaking and, 92
Writing process
cultivating, 101–102
drafts and, 97–99, 102
revising for readers in, 103–110
structure and, 103
suspending judgment, 101–102
topic-sentence outlines in, 97–101, 103
Writing Science (Schimel), 18
Writing workshop
adapting, 39
assigned readings in, 18
as community of practice, 12, 41–42,
44, 325–326
discussions in, 18
effectiveness of, 326
feedback forums in, 19–21
feedback in, 14, 19–20
free-writing and, 100
inclusiveness in, 42–43
individual development plans and, 57
near-peer mentoring in, 17
peer-based practices, 39
reverse outlines in, 99–101
size of, 39–40
social support in, 49, 72
structuring meetings in, 14
term plans and, 65
thriving together in, 43–44
well-being and, 6–7, 23

write-on-site groups, 14–16

writing accountability groups, 14,
    16–17

writing accountability groups and, 49

writing classes in, 14

writing habits and, 22–23

Writing Your Journal Article in Twelve Weeks
    (Belcher), 18

Written language, 267, 270, 310

Yang, Y., 50

Zhu, M., 50

Zombie nouns, 304

Zotero, 115, 129, 169

ABOUT THE AUTHOR

Barbara W. Sarnecka is a professor of cognitive sciences at the University of California, Irvine. She is the creator of the Graduate Writing Workshop seminar, and she currently studies how doctoral writing groups can be used to support writing productivity, skill development, and well-being in PhD students. Other research in Sarnecka's lab focuses on conceptual change and cognitive development from infancy through adulthood. This includes studies of numerical cognition in early childhood, social cognition in infancy through childhood, exploratory play and decision-making in middle childhood, conceptual change in science education, and adult moral cognition and reasoning.

Printed in the USA
CPSIA information can be obtained
at www.ICGtesting.com
LVHW022352070923
757598LV00029B/668